PARENTS' GUIDE TO
HIKING & CAMPING

Look for these other Trailside® Series Guides:

Bicycling: Touring and Mountain Bike Basics
Canoeing: A Trailside Guide
Cross-Country Skiing: A Complete Guide
Fly Fishing: A Trailside Guide
Hiking & Backpacking: A Complete Guide
Kayaking: Whitewater and Touring Basics
Rock Climbing: A Trailside Guide
Winter Adventure: A Complete Guide to Winter Sports

Trailside: Make Your Own Adventure is a registered trademark of New Media, Inc.

Copyright © 1997 by New Media, Incorporated
All rights reserved
Printed in Hong Kong

First Edition

The text of this book is composed in Bodoni Book with the display set in Triplex
Page composition by Christensen Design
Color separations and prepress by Bergman Graphics, Incorporated
Manufacturing by South China Printing Co. Ltd.
Illustrations by Ron Hildebrand

Book design by Bill Harvey

Library of Congress Cataloging-in-Publication Data

Cary, Alice.
Parents' guide to hiking & camping: a trailside guide / by Alice Cary.
p.   cm. — (A Trailside series guide)
Includes bibliographical references and index.

ISBN 0-393-31652-1

1. Outdoor recreation for children — Handbooks, manuals, etc.
2. Family recreation — Handbooks, manuals, etc.
I. Title. II. Series.
GV191.63.C37   1997   796.5—dc21   96-40320 CIP

W. W. Norton & Company, Inc., 500 Fifth Avenue, New York, N. Y. 10110
http://www.wwnorton.com
W. W. Norton & Company Ltd., 10 Coptic Street, London WC1A 1PU

1 2 3 4 5 6 7 8 9 0

PARENTS' GUIDE TO HIKING & CAMPING

A TRAILSIDE GUIDE
BY
ALICE CARY

A TRAILSIDE SERIES GUIDE

W. W. NORTON & COMPANY

NEW YORK   LONDON

CONTENTS

PART V: A FINAL WORD

For Jim and Will and
all the adventures ahead

BIG BOOTS,
LITTLE BOOTS

Christopher Robin was sitting outside his door, putting on his Big Boots. As soon as he saw the Big Boots, Pooh knew that an Adventure was going to happen, and he brushed the honey off his nose with the back of his paw, and spruced himself up as well as he could, so as to look Ready for Anything.

A. A. Milne, *Winnie-the-Pooh*

As soon as I learned I was pregnant, I knew an Adventure was going to happen, but, unlike Ready-for-Anything Pooh, I did a bit of fretting. For many years my husband and I had hiked and backpacked all the time — obsessively, some felt obliged to inform us. In fact, about a week before we heard our good news, we'd finally managed to climb Mount Washington on George Washington's birthday. The New Hampshire peak is 6,288 feet high, small as summits go, but famed for producing some of the fiercest weather in the world. Two years in a row wind and snow had forced us back, but that third year, we finally made it. Little did I realize I was carrying much more than a backpack and an ice ax to the summit.

As soon as we began to spread the news of our baby-to-be, certain friends seemed to take particular delight in saying, "Well, *you're* not going to be running up mountains anymore." All too often, when young children are involved, people focus on reasons *not* to do something. One of the most popular (and respected) child-rearing books adds fuel to the fire, advising: "Even if you're an experienced camper, camping out with a small child can be grueling."

Nonsense. As long as you have the right attitude and information, children of any age are ready to be part of your outdoor adventures. Today our son Will — now nearly three — is always ready to go. The minute he hears the word "outside," he runs to the door, stands by his sneakers, and looks — well — Ready for Anything. So far those "Anythings" have included hiking, camping, biking, canoeing, and cross-country skiing. Happily, Will is hardly alone. Plenty of parents start their kids out right from the start — I know of bicycling enthusiasts who carried their newborn sons home from the hospital in a bike trailer!

Certainly there are challenges. During a camping trip when Will was nearly two, for example, we hiked with a friend to a waterfall. As we approached, I began to regret coming on the trip as I envisioned Will teetering near the edge, then falling and being swept away. Instead, however, all of us were able to enjoy the glorious spot — water rushing over rocks, sun shining, no one else there. Will sat on my lap as we picnicked, then held our hands as we explored the rocky ledges.

What's more, soon we struck gold, finding what our friend dubbed the "Babysitting Hole." Perfectly carved out of the stone and just a few feet from the water's edge, this pothole formed a natural "playpen" for our inquisitive toddler. We plunked Will in, and there — safe, sound, and overjoyed — he tossed pebbles while we relaxed by his side. He cried when it was time to leave. The incident serves as my personal reminder that more often than not children and nature seem made for each other.

Unfortunately, as more and more people flock to the Great Outdoors, and doing so becomes almost fashionable, it's easy to lose sight of the basics. Whether you prefer hiking, biking, canoeing, camping, or simply strolling close to home, remember, you don't need fancy gear, dramatic destinations, or expensive guides. What you do need are energy and excitement — two things children possess in abundance. Young explorers seem to understand that adventures are a state of mind, not so much *what* you do as *how*.

How then, exactly?

Think of this book as providing

Ben Wiltsie, age 4, running from waves along the Monterey coast, California. The earlier you expose your children to the outdoors, the more strongly they will take to it.

the blocks you'll need to build your own family's adventures. The focus is on child-related aspects of each activity. For example, you'll learn how to select a personal flotation device for your child, but not for yourself; you'll learn which type of insect repellents are safe and effective for children; you'll learn how to plan outings geared to children's abilities. (Suggestions are geared to the 14-year-old and younger crowd, since older teenagers usually want to be on their own, and adult

guidebooks usually suit their needs as well as yours.)

This is not meant to serve as an all-purpose, how-to guide; for more generalized discussions, consult the corresponding *Trailside* guide or other books listed in Sources & Resources at the back of this book.

My goal is to share trail secrets that work for Will, Jim, and me. Because interests and abilities vary greatly from family to family and from child to child, there aren't always

Ben Wiltsie, five years later, swims in Bowman Lake, Glacier National Park, Montana.

"right" answers. With that in mind, I've also sought advice from a variety of experts across the country, as well as trail-tested tips from other parents. Look for the following features:

⊃ AGES AND STAGES: brief descriptions of interests and abilities you can expect from children at different ages.

❓ AGE-OLD QUESTIONS: specific problems and solutions.

❖ BEST-BET READING: to help you wade through the jungle of nature-related books on the market, lists of the cream of the crop, including starred ratings (✳) for books that shouldn't be missed.

✐ RECOMMENDATIONS: outdoor products, gear, games, and activities designed specifically for children.

♥ PARENT-TO-PARENT: parents across the country share their experiences, what works and what doesn't.

GEAR TALK: advice on exactly what your child needs and how to use it effectively and efficiently.

MIND YOUR MANNERS: how to teach children safe, thoughtful conduct that respects people and the environment.

TECHNIQUE TIPS: ways to make outings more enjoyable, to avoid trouble, and to turn unavoidable adversity into cheer.

What rewards will you and your family reap from outdoor adventures? Most important, fun. After that the answers are as endless as the number of trails waiting to be explored.

Best of all, you're embarking on a lifelong quest. Kids outgrow almost everything left and right — clothes, toys, hobbies, foods, even friends. Outdoor adventures are one thing families can share for the rest of

In today's complicated world, there is much to be said for returning to basics: a tent, a lantern, two sleeping bags, and a book to share.

their lives, whether it's tomorrow or 30 years from now, when the kids are carrying *their* children on their backs.

START A TRADITION

Instead of the Mother's Day/ Father's Day brunch routine, make the holidays occasions for family outings. The honoree of the day can choose the destination, or the rest of the family may want to plan a surprise, complete with picnic. Keep track through the years with a special photo album.

Practicing gymnastics, Eureka Dunes, California. Wide open spaces not only bring out, but also amply accommodate a child's exuberant energy.

Each year brings new interests and abilities: The baby in the backpack is soon walking, the girl on training wheels whizzes away, last year's passenger learns to paddle. Should you ever feel frustrated by a certain stage, remind yourself that your child's boots get bigger each year, and before you know it, they'll have left you behind. Savor each moment; you may find yourself yearning for an age you thought would never end.

No matter how old your children are, now is the time to start your adventures. So grab your Big Boots and go.

ADVENTURE
AT YOUR
DOORSTEP

"We can pretend we are Arctic explorers," said Lucy.
"This is going to be exciting enough without any pretending," said
Peter, as he began leading the way forward into the forest.

C. S. Lewis, *The Lion, the Witch, and the Wardrobe*

When I was a kid, I had a pith helmet, my own safari hat. My oldest brother bought it during a Boy Scout trip he took to Philmont, New Mexico. I wore it everywhere, whether tromping through the woods or playing in the basement. I don't know what became of that hat, but I wish I had it now, for my son, Will. To me, the helmet symbolized adventure. Now, if that hat were perched on Will's head, I would have a magical double vision: the memories of my own childhood "safaris," and those waiting for Will, the ones he'll share with his father and me. Someday Will could pass the hat on to his children, and, with it, our thirst for excitement.

Hat or no hat, however, adventures await.

ATTITUDE, NOT ALTITUDE

To get started, you don't need a towering peak or a roaring river; you need the right attitude. I'm trying to teach Will to shout "Cowabunga!" — remember Snoopy's battle cry as he races into the surf? Will is generally ready for anything, but he also has a cautious nature, often hesitating at the outset of anything new. As a mother, I'm grateful for his mindful ways, but I also want him to learn to charge into the unknown like Snoopy on his surfboard — within reason, of course.

Such bravado is one of the many life lessons that can be gleaned from family outings: Whether our children are canoeing a swift river, tackling a school project, or wading through office obstacles once they become adults, we hope they will face each new challenge with curiosity and gusto.

As adults we tend to charge ahead, intent on the getting there rather than the going, trying to bring children up to adult speed instead of learning to go at a child's pace. Walking with a child forces us to look longer and closer at things we might otherwise miss. The change in perspective can transform a familiar spot into a strikingly different landscape.

Too often adults get caught up with numbers — how far, how high, how quickly, and on and on. The heart of a family adventure, however, is often a singular moment that may be difficult to measure but impos-

sible to forget: a child splashing in an icy mountain stream; a proud paddler going solo for the first time; your family, safe and sound, enjoying being together in a campfire's embracing glow.

When Will was nearly two, he toddled along one particular trail, squealing with joy at every root and rock he encountered. *Never* have I had such an enthusiastic hiking partner. Now, instead of worrying about being held back, I think about how boring a child would be who charged ahead, noticing nothing, muttering, "I've got to do 10 miles today; I've got to do 10 miles."

And, as Jim likes to remind me, "The mountains aren't going anywhere." They'll be waiting when — and if — Will is ready to climb them.

CLOSE-TO-HOME ACTION

Ideally, family adventures should be part of our daily routines, not reserved for weekend or summer binges. Practically speaking, however, many families are so hard-pressed for time that they hardly have a chance to squeeze in a meal together, much less one more activity. So before you pull out your appointment book and frantically search for an opening, relax. Remember, when kids are young, small doses of new experiences go a long way.

Adventure Reading

An ideal time to start is at bedtime,

Mollie and Summer Wuerthner with a giant eucalyptus tree at Fort Ross State Park, California. Begin close to home, exploring local wonders large and small.

because armchair explorations are the easiest to arrange. It's a snap to outfit your child with an "expedition library" of fact, fiction, and fun from your local library or bookstore. There's a wealth of exciting classics, activity books, junior field guides, and adventure sagas, with more being published all the time. What better way to generate enthusiasm, and encourage reading at the same time? Throughout these pages, and in Sources & Resources, I'll recommend "Best-Bet Reading" selections that will help pump up the entire family's adrenaline.

Your Neighborhood

For starters, head for the yard or a park, throw a blanket over a clothes-line tied between two trees, and, presto, you've established base camp.

In his book *Sharing Nature with Children*, naturalist and teacher Joseph Cornell recommends taking "micro-hikes," in which each person positions a three- to five-foot-long string somewhere of interest, then explores inch by inch on his or her belly, examining small wonders. Another exciting outing is a short night hike — in the dark your own yard may feel as unfamiliar as a lunar landscape.

Most of us travel the same routes day after day; as a result, uncharted territory is right at our doorsteps. There's probably a wood lot, a park, or a street you haven't explored, or your child may have some special places to show you. A month or two ago Katie, my first-grade friend, pulled Will and me behind some for-sythia in her backyard. She likes to play school there, and, indeed, the bushes are so tall they form an outdoor room, offering a whole new window on a yard I visit many times each week. In her school, Katie taught me a valuable lesson about perspective.

Neighborhood trips are perfect occasions for spontaneity, since little if any preparation or gear is necessary. One of our hiking pals told me that as a child, her father used to pile the kids in the car and let them decide where to go. Turn left, they'd instruct, and he'd turn left, and on and on, until they ended up heaven knows where. You could try this on foot, on bikes, or in a boat — while taking care not to get lost.

Adventure is as much about new ways of seeing as it is about seeing new places. Perhaps you and your family already have a few favorite stomping grounds. On your next visit suggest that everyone look more closely, spot something they've never noticed. Make a game of it and wait until the end of your outing to compare notes.

Think of your first jaunts as training sessions for upcoming outings. We usually finish dinner at 7:00 or 7:30, which, on summer evenings, leaves enough time for a 30-minute walk. The duration is inconsequential; what's important is that Jim and I set aside the cares of the day and focus entirely on Will and his wan-

START A FAMILY OUTING CLUB

✐ Joanna "Jai" Biscegli has always been an active mom — when her daughter, Kateri, was eight months old, she put her in a baby jogger and ran the Boston Marathon. Not surprisingly, after her second daughter, Brielle, was born, Biscegli began looking for an alternative to traditional, sedate outings like story time, play groups, and mall cruising.

Finding none, in the spring of 1995 she started the Vermont Family Outing Club. Word quickly spread through her press releases, and soon 30 or more parents and children, ranging from 6 months to 6 years old, joined her and the girls for 2-mile round-trip hikes, a picnic, and sometimes a stop at a playground.

With Kateri walking most of the way and Brielle in a backpack, Biscegli busily tries to keep track of the group. "I keep my eyes open all the time," she says. She also carries a first-aid kit and keeps her first-aid training up-to-date.

While she enjoys biking, skiing, and roller-blading, Biscegli

derings. Last year I hovered whenever the terrain got steep, now he scrambles up himself.

At some point you'll be ready to cap off your meanderings with a backyard sleep-out. Make it easy and fun. If you want to keep things low-key, don't even schedule the night ahead of time. Private schools have "headmaster's holidays" — on an especially beautiful morning, someone blows a whistle to announce that classes are canceled for the day. Blow your own whistle (or set up the tent) when everyone's in a good mood, schedules seem manageable, and the weather is fine. You don't have to fuss — better to go ahead with a simple celebration than to aim

Lure reluctant hikers with promises of swimming holes. For a child, a hike without a destination is akin to doing errands with Mom: not a big draw.

says, "Hiking is the easiest way to get families together with young children. It seems like the most practical sport to use as the basis for our adventures."

Participants meet at the same time and place on the first and third Thursday of every month, rain or shine. They sign a liability release, receive handouts (club information, and, for instance, an article about avoiding bug bites), and hear the details of the day's trip. Then they travel to the trailhead.

The Vermont Family Outing Club scrapbook is filling quickly.

To offset the expenses of phone calls, handouts, and map purchases, Biscegli charges each family $1 per outing, or a $10 annual membership fee. Members, in turn, receive a quarterly newsletter.

While there are plenty of outing groups for adults and school clubs for teenagers, few seem to exist for parents and young children. Check to see if there's one in your area; if not, start organizing. Certainly this is an idea whose time has come.

for elaborate plans too complex to set into motion. Don't have a tent yet? Just grab that clothesline and a blanket or bedspread.

FARTHER AFIELD

You won't have to go far to find a place your family can explore for an hour or two, a spot for a "mini-trip" that can be scheduled amid the obligatory soccer games, birthday parties, laundry, and errands. Such an outing will require a bit more planning than a neighborhood expedition — you may want to pack a snack or picnic, for instance — but preparations can still be minimal.

The easiest way to enlarge your territory is to ask friends for recommendations — or invitations, especially if you're trying a spot for the

ENTICING RELUCTANT EXPLORERS

In many families, enthusiasm for family trips and outings is a given. If you don't happen to be so lucky, here are some suggestions:

I'm itching to get out there, but my kids aren't quite so gung-ho.
Give the kids plenty of input in your plans. It's important that they not simply be told, "We're now going on a 10-day bike trip," or "We're now going canoeing." Also, consider your children's interests and strengths. If they're unusually active, for instance, boating may not be a good choice.

My daughter and I are raring to go camping, but my husband hates the outdoors. We'd really like to include him.
Compromise — plan a trip that includes an activity your husband will enjoy, perhaps a sightseeing excursion or a meal in a restaurant. If your husband agrees to come along, however, make him promise to smile and not complain. Otherwise, the trip won't be fun for anyone.

My wife thinks our baby is too young to be out on the trail. I say, the earlier, the better. How can I convince her?
Her worries may be eased by talking to another family that's taken their baby out. (I confess I was uneasy about taking Will canoeing until being reassured by Jerelyn and Alex Wilson.) Be sure you've addressed all of your wife's safety concerns, and made backup plans in case the baby seems unhappy. Perhaps then your wife will have enough confidence to give your proposal a try.

first time. Make similar inquiries at the nearest outfitter.

Involve older kids in the search. Check a map of your area for parks and trails; scan newspapers for outing opportunities; query public librarians about outing books, magazines, maps, clubs, and associations.

You may be surprised by what you find. Jim and I have lived in central Massachusetts for about 10 years now, and we thought we were familiar with most of the nearby parks and paths. However, a friend recently told us about a park we've never heard of, just 20 minutes away — a good example of how the quest for family recreation constantly broadens everyone's horizons.

DAY TRIPS

Anchors aweigh; you're off! Or, as my father used to announce at the start of many of our trips, his voice filled with mock solemnity, "Commence!"

The stakes get higher when you decide to devote all or part of a day to an outing. Just like Christmas, the occasion can be the best of times, or, after considerable anticipation and excitement, the fun can suddenly fizzle and turn to discord. If the key to real estate is location, location, location, then the key to family trips is plan, plan, plan — and, just as important, be flexible, be flexible, be flexible. Always remember that at times you will need to change or even forgo all of your planning.

Children born with an urge to climb find adventure at every turn — sometimes to their parents' dismay.

Start Small

To avoid a flop, start with small outings you know your child (and you) can handle, then build from there. The secret to success is always the same: Don't bite off more than your kids can chew. Take it easy; make it fun.

One of our local hiking favorites is the 1,832-foot Mount Watatic. With an elevation gain of only 650 feet, it's a perfect mountain for beginning

READY FOR ACTION

hikers of any age. Will can already manage part of it himself, and in a year or two he'll be ready to walk the 2.3-mile loop on his own. The rocky summit offers rewards for all ages: a fire tower, an abandoned ski lift, plenty of rock scrambling, and, on clear days, views of the Boston skyline, about 50 miles away. In the spring and fall, migrating hawks soar overhead, and there's plenty of blueberry picking in summer.

With young children, you can return to the same mountain over and over — just as they enjoy reading the same picture books time and time again. For them, each climb brings different rewards, while familiar sights increase their sense of ease and confidence. There are endless variations: Go in a different season, bring a new friend along, try a new trail.

After Will masters Watatic, we'll take him to Mount Monadnock, about an hour away in New Hampshire.

This 3,165-foot peak is practically everybody's favorite in these parts; reportedly, it vies with Mount Fuji for the title of most-climbed mountain in the world.

If your area doesn't happen to have its own equivalents of Watatic or Monadnock, you may be wise to choose a trail, not a goal. If you're bent on a steep climb to a summit, be sure you're not setting your family up for failure, even if you *do* accomplish your goal. While some kids thrive on goal setting and find such carrots helpful, others may find an arduous challenge frustrating, and everyone may end up exhausted and barely speaking. A successful outing is one in which everyone comes home happy, ready to return another day.

If only there were some magic formula for predicting stamina based on a child's age, shape, and temperament. Of course there isn't, and even the most obvious advice, don't be overly ambitious, is frustratingly nonspecific. A rule of thumb: Most families average about a mile an hour on fairly level terrain. After an outing or two you'll have a more precise idea of how fast, how far, and how long your family travels.

Trail Bait

In addition to choosing distance and elevation carefully, think about what you'll encounter along the way. Your idea of an outdoor escape may be a backwoods, get-away-from-it-all retreat, but that may be the last thing in the world your kids will enjoy. Don't beat around the bush: *Ask your kids what they'd like to see, what kinds of areas they'd like to explore.* You might want to ask older kids to design an imaginary map of their dream hike or camping trip.

Make sure your destination offers something for everyone — a swimming hole, perhaps, or boulders for climbing, even an ice cream stand. (When hiking among adults and feeling weary, we sometimes joke about the Coke machine or hamburger joint waiting at the top of the mountain. Use this gag with extreme caution with kids: They're likely to believe you and then be terribly disappointed.)

Waterfalls never fail to enthrall kids, to say nothing of most adults. Learn about such attractions close to home and set out on a sunny morning carrying a pack loaded with lunch and towels.

Just as a fisherman always has plenty of bait on hand, learn to scrutinize trail descriptions and topographical maps for features that will lure the kids. Take along your own bait, too: Stash a few surprises in

Is your family's snail-like pace driving you bonkers? Does the trip feel more like frustration than fun? Sounds like you need an adults-only getaway. Several times a year my husband and I take turns scheduling hiking, backpacking, or cross-country skiing trips with our friends. It's rejuvenating to bag some peaks for a change and put in some heavy-duty days. By the time evening rolls around, however, I'm usually feeling a tad homesick — and ready to plan our next family outing.

your pack — Snickers bars, a small puzzle or activity, a squirt gun or two. If your child likes to draw, slip in paper and crayons. Young geographers will enjoy reading trail descriptions aloud and charting your party's progress on a map.

Brush up on some trail songs; think back to favorites from your camping or scouting days. Simple games like "20 Questions" or "I Spy" can also be fun while resting or moving. Here are two more games adapted for family explorers:

● "How Many Mountains?" (or Lakes? Or Ponds?) Decide on a category such as mountains, then try to name as many as possible. If your children are too young or don't know enough names to keep the game going, ask them to make up their own fun names. Mount Hot Fudge Sundae, for example, or Ticklenaked Pond (there actually *is* a pond by that name in Vermont). Add some order

by making lists in alphabetical order.

● "How Long Till We Get There?" You come to a crossroads or trailhead and know you've got 2.3 more miles to go. Appoint someone timekeeper, then have everyone guess how long you'll take to get there. This game can seriously motivate a child who's bent on winning a bet!

For more "trail bait" suggestions, see individual chapters in Part III: Hit the Trail!, as well as the nature and activity chapters.

The ABCs of Pacing

You've done everything right: You've picked the right trail and you're loaded with diversions. But before you take the first step, face the fact that at some point your child is likely to complain. Don't feel defeated; remember, kids gripe at home, too. Here are three ways to help keep grumbling to a minimum.

● Be ready to ADJUST your plans. Be responsive to both trail conditions and your family's mood. Once on the trail, the skies may open up or bugs may buzz. Should you encounter a thunderstorm or genuine downpour, there's no shame in turning back. The best explorers don't fool around; they know when to call it a day. As for those bugs, get out the spray or vow to come back when they're less vicious. Whatever the problem, remember to ask yourself two all-important questions: Are we still having fun? If not, if we tough it out longer, is a payoff likely?

For the most part, trail conditions are out of your control. Thankfully, your family isn't — although they may be just as unpredictable. One week the kids may literally run or pedal their little legs off; the next week they may balk at much easier terrain. What gives?

We all have our bad days. One father of a six-year-old told me that in the middle of an outing he realized his usually enthusiastic son would rather be home playing Power Rangers that day.

Whether you're on a day trip or a longer outing, breaks are key to happiness (and endurance) on the trail. Watch for signals of flagging energy and stop, either to snack, admire the view, or even take a nap.

"Kids can't always communicate their needs," he told me. "They don't wake up in the morning and say, 'You know, I've had a stressful week — I'd rather just putz around the house today.' " So they shortened their trip and headed home to those Power Rangers.

Adjusting plans doesn't always mean calling it quits — that's the alternative of last resort. Maybe the kids are perfectly happy to play in a creek or watch a caterpillar. Go with the flow; let them. You may hike for three hours and the one thing they remember is that cater-pillar.

❷ Take plenty of BREAKS. Kids need breaks for mental as well as physical reasons. Your child may be hungry, thirsty, hot, cold, or just plain bored or frustrated. Tend to their needs with a snack, swim, game, or other diversion. That six-year-old's father schedules a 15-minute break every hour. Similarly, you may want to stick to a regular schedule, or you may prefer to stop on an as-needed basis. Regardless, don't wait until disaster strikes, because by then it's too late.

❸ CHEER them on; don't chastise. You know the routine: As always, build up your children's egos. "Boy, this heat is a killer," you might say. "I'm feeling it too. But I bet we can make it to the top of that hill, then we'll rest." If the kids are lagging behind, suggest that *they* take the lead. A simple change in position can sometimes work wonders on anyone's psyche. When you finish your journey, be sure to congratulate everyone on a job well done.

BACK AT HOME

You've explored the neighborhood, enjoyed some local trips, taken a dayhike or two, and perhaps camped out in the backyard. That's it for basic training; now you're on your way to becoming a bona fide family of adventurers.

The best way to keep the momentum going is to plan more trips, take on new challenges. In the meantime, keep the kids busy on the home front.

Create a Family Adventure Calendar

✎ One way to set the mood is to start a family calendar. Make a list of activities to try and places to go, then schedule a few dates, even if it's nothing more than a few half-hour trips. Later, after you return, jot down a memory or two, turning your calendar into a logbook. The kids may enjoy being recordkeepers and decorating the calendar with drawings and stickers.

Any calendar will do, but an outdoor theme works best. The Sierra Club publishes a calendar for kids, complete with over 100 stickers — including some for hikes, camping trips, and park visits; Little, Brown has a "Make Your Own Calendar," also with stickers, in which young artists can paint, draw, or paste their own scenes.

Start a Reading Club

✏ So many extraordinary nature and adventure books are available that you can easily formalize your family's literary pursuits with a reading club. The public libraries here in Massachusetts developed a "Reading Is Natural" summer program emphasizing nature themes, which could easily be adapted for home use. Young readers kept logs of the books they read, with a goal of reading seven books, or 700 pages. Preschoolers tried to listen to 20 books. From time to time participants were rewarded with small prizes — wildlife pencils and pens, a magnifying insect viewer. Your child's "reward" could come in the form of a family outing.

Plan a Family In-ing

✏ You don't even have to leave the living room to enjoy a night of family adventure. Instead of stepping out, light the fire, pop some popcorn, and enjoy an in-ing. Read a story out loud or watch an adventure movie:

Adventures of the Wilderness Family, 1975. In this variation on *Swiss Family Robinson*, a Los Angeles family finds excitement after moving to the Rocky Mountains and building a cabin.
Breaking Away, 1979. Good for older kids, this story focuses on four col-

lege friends in Indiana, one of whom is determined to enter a bicycle race.
The Enchanted Forest, 1945. A hermit teaches a boy to love the woods.
Gentle Giant, 1967. This feature film about a boy and his bear, starring Dennis Weaver, Vera Miles, and Clint Howard, launched the *Gentle Ben* TV series.
My Side of the Mountain, 1969. An excellent film based on Jean George's wonderful book about a boy who decides to spend a year alone in a forest.
Swiss Family Robinson, 1960. The Disney classic.
Third Man on the Mountain, 1959. A Disney story about a Swiss boy determined to climb the Matterhorn (here called the Citadel).

Advice from Peter Whittaker

✏ If anyone can lay claim to coming from an outdoorsy family, it's Peter

BRING AN EXTRA PAIR OF HELPING HANDS

"My rule of thumb for camping," says Jerelyn Wilson, "is one more adult than the number of children. That allows the adults some flexibility so one isn't always left behind to baby-sit. The adults can take turns pairing off in different ways."

Wilson has been accompanying her husband, Alex, on research trips for his *Quiet Water Canoe Guides* (Appalachian Mountain Club Books) for nine years now, ever since their two daughters were infants.

"I'm always on the lookout for single women who don't have children," she says. "And single men can be helpful too."

Long-time hiker Debbie Bockus seconds Wilson's advice. "Whenever anyone offers to go with you," she says, "take them up on it! It's so wonderful to have someone else take your kids for a few miles when you are exhausted and they can't seem to get going either. It's amazing what a different point of view can do to get kids going again."

Whittaker, host of the television show, *Trailside: Make Your Own Adventure.*

In 1963 his uncle, Jim Whittaker, became the first American to climb Mount Everest. His father, Lou, has led numerous expeditions to the Himalayas, including the three highest peaks in the world: Everest, K2, and Kangchenjunga. The Whittaker family has owned and operated one of the largest guide services in the United States, Ranier Mountaineering, Inc., since 1967.

So it's no great surprise that Peter started breaking records early on: At age 12 he became one of the youngest people ever to climb Mount Rainier, and by age 16 he was a mountain guide. In the years since, he's returned to the summit more than 175 times. Now he and his wife live at the base of the mountain, running Summits Adventure Travel, an international company specializing in mountaineering, trekking, and skiing.

Although he has no children, Peter has strong opinions about introducing kids to the wilderness.

"It's important for parents to realize that some children just don't like to hike, just as some adults don't like it," he says. "The neat thing about my father was that we were encouraged. I think every parent needs to open up that door and see if it's something the kid wants to do."

What's a parent to do when push comes to shove?

Peter advises parents to nudge, not push.

His cautionary tone originates from all-too-vivid memories of that first ascent of Rainier.

"It was probably one of the worst experiences of my life," he recalls. "It was a terrible day, cold and snowy. I don't know why, but I was in long johns and jeans. They got wet and froze solid. One thousand feet below the summit we took an old route and came to a dead end at a crevasse. We had to turn around and go back. I was literally in tears and thinking: This is not fun."

Yes, he admits, there was no doubt pressure from his family of famous climbers. "May-be that was the reason I was doing it more than the fact that I really wanted to," he says. "These are gray areas parents need to be aware of."

However, Peter's final words on his family's influence are positive: "I can't thank my father and mother enough for having the patience to teach me wilderness skills.

Mollie and Summer Wuerthner swimming at Follensby Clear Pond, Adirondack State Park, New York. Such moments make carrying a toddler in a backpack worth every step.

I was very, very lucky, and it was something I wanted to do."

As a guide, he's seen many families over the years. What's the most common mistake parents make?

"Too much ambition," he says. "I see that on Rainier all the time."

FINDING OUT ABOUT THINGS OUTDOORS, by Eliot Humberstone (*Usborne Explainers*, ages 7–9). Lots of illustrations accompany brief discussions on subjects from rain to rivers, seasons, the sun.

THE GATES OF THE WIND, by Kathryn Lasky, illustrated by Janet Stevens (*Harcourt Brace*, ages 4–8). Old Gamma Lee has a real nose for adventure, so she packs up everything she owns and heads to "the steepest part of the highest mountain." Gamma Lee has gusto!

OUT OF SIGHT! OUT OF MIND!, by Claude LaPointe (*Harcourt*, all ages). Three kids stay inside, sure nothing ever happens in the boring outdoors. The illustrations in this clever, mostly wordless tale show how much they're missing.

✳ TOM BROWN'S FIELD GUIDE TO THE FOR-GOTTEN WILDERNESS, by Tom Brown (*Berkley Books*, grades 5– adult). Fascinating wildlife discussions to help you chart your own course through city, suburbs, and country.

✳ THE WILD INSIDE: SIERRA CLUB'S GUIDE TO THE GREAT INDOORS, by Linda Allison (*Sierra Club Books*, ages 8–12). Put on your safari hat and try out this treasure chest of imagi-native activities, from stalking spiders and flies to finding the "River Through Your House."

✳ THE ZABAJABA JUNGLE, by William Steig (*Sunburst Books*, ages 4–7). Young Leonard encounters all kinds of amazing animals in this picture-book journey by a master sto-ryteller and artist.

FAMILY ADVENTURE GEAR

I left New York in May. I had a penknife, a ball of cord, an ax, and $40, which I had saved from selling magazine subscriptions. I also had some flint and steel which I had bought at a Chinese store in the city. The man in the store had showed me how to use it. He had also given me a little purse to put it in, and some tinder to catch the sparks.

Jean Craighead George, *My Side of the Mountain*

For adults, gear is an investment. Buy a backpack or a pair of boots and you can count on using them for years, until they're battered and frayed.

Not so with kids. Just about the time their boots and packs begin to feel comfortable and worn in, they've outgrown them.

So how do you figure out how much equipment your kids really need?

When you're a newcomer to anything — say, hiking, biking, or parenting, for that matter — everything has a way of looking potentially vital. That was certainly the case when Will was born. Whenever I perused those baby catalogs that started appearing in our mailbox, I saw so many things I was sure would make our family life not only safe but blissful.

Certainly some items were life-savers, such as Will's baby swing and his front pack carrier. Others, such as a sling carrier, were frills we hardly used. And there were many more items we never ordered — pads to cover table corners, doorknob protectors, electric bottle warmers — that we lived happily without.

Before you get gung-ho about kids' gear, concentrate on some essential principles:

● Children need to be protected from the elements just as adults do,

sometimes more. For instance, they are more quickly affected by hypothermia, dehydration, and heat exhaustion. Everyone in your family should have what they need to be safe and comfortable.

● Buy *your* stuff first. Consider the safety spiel airlines give before takeoff: Adults need to administer their own oxygen before seeing to their children's needs. Similarly, before buying gear for your children, you need a good working knowledge of the types of things you yourself need — boots, jackets, sleeping bags, and so on. That way you'll be more adept at improvising on items your child is likely to quickly outgrow. (Since an in-depth discussion of adult gear is beyond the scope of this book, consult a more general guidebook, such as Karen Berger's *Hiking & Backpacking: A Complete*

WHERE TO BUY KIDS' CLOTHING

✎ Start with outdoor outfitters and catalogs like Campmor and L. L. Bean.

RailRiders makes children's shorts and pants out of Supplex, while Columbia manufactures shorts and a lightweight jacket from "Perfecta Cloth," texturized nylon.

Campmor has polypropylene

underwear for children, as well as PVC-coated rain suits. Children's fleece and pile jackets are widely available — they're popular for general schoolwear as well as on the trail.

For hats with neck flaps, look for Cherry Tree and Flap Happy hats. Outdoor Products offers nylon gaiters for children, while Wigwam makes rag-wool socks and Thermax liners. Polartec produces fleece socks for children.

Guide, in the *Trailside* series. Gear guides are also helpful; *Backpacker Magazine*, for instance, publishes an annual buyer's guide each spring.)

● You can buy what your child needs without going broke. You already have what you need for day trips. You can gradually add the rest as your outings become more extensive.

Toddler Nick Wiltsie, ready for anything and dressed for the part. Recommends parent Ray Dahl: "Buy clothing large so kids can wear it as long as possible. Rolled sleeves and cuffs are part of the game."

Once you're ready to shop, find an outfitter you can trust. Look for stores where children's gear is readily apparent, not shoved in a corner or available by special order only. Good stores have ramps to walk up and down when trying on boots, tents pitched and ready for inspection, clerks who don't look aghast when you bring in the kids.

Ideally, your outfitter is also a parent, someone who understands that your child may refuse to wear certain items, someone who has lugged a child in a carrier, someone who knows what the parents of a five-year-old need for a backpacking trip.

FOOTWEAR

The comfort of your child's feet can make or break a trip, and a good pair of boots will increase surefootedness. Whatever your child puts on his feet should be comfortable and allow plenty of room for socks with good padding and bulk.

Options

Your child may long for real hiking boots — a sign that he is tough and trail-ready — not to mention trendy. But while kids need supportive footwear, the expense of boots poses a dilemma for some parents, especially

THE TURTLE TRIP

On one of our first backpacking trips we couldn't afford rain gear so everyone wore trash bags. The kids looked like huge turtles walking down the trail! They were so small we couldn't see their heads — all we saw were big green round things with little legs sticking out.

Debbie Bockus — Hubbardston, Massachusetts

those whose wallets are still stinging from money shelled out for designer sneakers.

One approach is to take those sneakers on the trail, and to postpone the purchase of hiking boots as a rite of passage, something to be awarded at a certain time.

Age eight is a good transition time for many kids — at this stage they're often ready to begin taking longer, more rugged trips, or carrying heavier loads. Thus, real boots become a measure of experience and distinction, a sign that a child has successfully completed a certain number of trips or miles.

At any rate, a good pair of high-top sneakers is a better choice than a cheaply made boot, and the most practical solution for young children. Good high-tops provide traction and arch support along with the ankle support of a boot; all that's lacking is the shock absorption of a boot's heavy sole. However, kids don't weigh as much as adults and aren't likely to be shouldering overly heavy loads, so shock absorption isn't so crucial. Traction is, so double-check the treads of any sneakers to be used on the trail.

Once you decide your child is ready for hiking boots, don't fret. A quality pair doesn't cost much more than brand-name sneakers. Thus, hiking boots are practical as long as your child wears them to school and during other activities, as well as on the trail.

Whatever you do, however, avoid "pseudo"-boots with crepe rubber soles, which provide poor traction. If you're going to buy boots, buy real ones.

Sport sandals are all the rage these days, but, to my mind, a bad choice for hiking. In addition to providing inadequate support, they offer no protection from briars and other

GEAR TALK

RUBBER BOOTS

Rubber rain boots are great in-camp shoes for kids. They're easy to get on and off, and save tennis shoes or other footwear from rain, puddles, or morning dew.

hazards like poison ivy, into which kids are prone to wander. They're okay as spares, though, especially as camp shoes.

Boot Buying

Once you decide your child is ready for boots, be prepared to spend time, not to mention dollars, to ensure a good fit. Manufacturers of kids' boots include Merrell, Raichle, Ridge Outdoor, Tecnica, and Vasque, with prices ranging from $40 to $75.

Take along the socks your child will wear with the new purchase. Think about how difficult it can be to find a pair that fits *you* well, then factor in the difficulty your child may have in communicating how boots feel. Also, remember that your child may be loath to admit that the sharp-looking pair he's fallen in love with is actually a foot-killer . . . or at least not mention the misery until several miles out on the trail.

To ensure good fit, ask:
● Before lacing: Is there just enough room to squeeze your finger between the heel and the back of the boot?
● After lacing: Can you still wiggle your toes?
● Does your heel stay in place, without

Sport sandals make great camp shoes and are ideal for fording streams. Best of all, kids think they're cool.

♥

PARENT-TO-PARENT

CLIP THOSE TOENAILS

Before hikes, make sure your child's toe-nails aren't too long. Long toenails can dig into boots or shoes, causing sore toes. And while you're at it, check your own nails.

sliding up and down?

If each answer is yes, you've probably found a fit. Before buying, find out whether the boots can be returned if problems develop. Some stores and manufacturers accept returns for a considerable period.

Your proud new boot owner is likely to want to break in his boots on a trail. Don't let him. Explain that new boots have to be "trail-ready" — broken in like a wild horse. First, they should be worn inside for an hour or two, then, if all is well, sent outside for some "advance trail training."

Once you do hit the trail, try short hikes first, since new boots may cause blisters.

Extra Sneakers

Bring them. Along with extra socks. The first pair is likely to get muddy or wet. As we discovered with Will, even toddlers who spend most of their time being

A SUPER SYNTHETIC

We dress our 4½-year-old in Supplex pants for two reasons: They dry very fast, and dried mud brushes off easily. Mom and Dad wear them for the same reasons.

Rob Kleine — Phoenix, Arizona

carried will need spares. Throw in a pair of water shoes — not for hiking, but for stream crossings and play, and for camp shoes in warm weather. They don't weigh or cost much.

Socks

Cotton tube socks are popular, but they're unsuitable for hiking. Cotton absorbs moisture and causes blisters. Instead, buy socks made of synthetics or wool, depending on the weather. Also equip your children with a pair of thin, synthetic, wicking liners to wear underneath as added protection against blisters.

KIDS' CLOTHING

No doubt your kids already have well-worn play clothes, jackets, and coats. These may be okay for your yard and the playground, but they can spell disaster on a mountain.

On the trail, it's essential to avoid the universal kids' outfit: cotton jeans and cotton T-shirts. In the wild, they're sometimes called dead-men's clothes, because when cotton gets wet, you'd be better off naked. They soak up rain and sweat, steal warmth

from your body, and take longer to dry than wool or synthetics.

As with any piece of clothing, comfort, fit, and style are important. However, your children's outdoor clothes are much more than fashion statements — their primary job is to provide protection and shelter. In short, they're survival tools.

There's no need to panic: On short summer outings, your child probably won't need special clothes. On short hikes with Will he sometimes wears cotton. But read on to know when other clothes are needed, and how they should be worn.

Layering

To properly outfit children, parents need to:

● Find clothes made of the right fabrics and materials.

● Have the right layers on hand. This means playing it safe and carrying extra layers, even when the weather is balmy.

In short, kids need the same kinds of layers that adults do: an underlayer, an insulation layer, and an outer layer offering protection from wind and rain.

Your child doesn't need separate wardrobes for playground and trail. Start with small outings in which everyone can use clothing already on hand. As you venture farther afield, you can gradually add new, more effective layers. These new layers will also be effective close to home. A good layering system, for example, is more comfortable and often warmer than a bulky snowsuit.

FIRST LAYER On warm days, dress your child in a pair of shorts and a shirt.

On cool days, a pair of pants and long-sleeve shirt.

On cold days, start with an underlayer of long underwear. Simple as that.

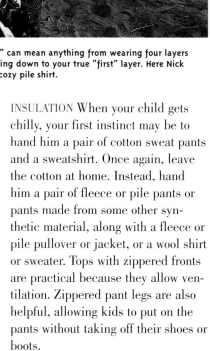

The catch word "layering" can mean anything from wearing four layers against the cold to stripping down to your true "first" layer. Here Nick Wiltsie is about to don a cozy pile shirt.

Whatever the temperature, remember to choose synthetics, not cotton, since synthetics dry faster when wet from sweat, rain, or a fall in a puddle or creek and, even when wet, provide warmth. Look for materials that wick away moisture, such as Capilene, Thermax, Coolmax, or polypropylene. Even with synthetics, though, with kids, it's good to have an extra set.

Note that two-piece long underwear is more practical than a one-piece union suit. It's easier to go to the bathroom with two pieces, and on some days your child may need only the top or bottom, but not both pieces. They also make great pajamas at home or on the trail.

INSULATION When your child gets chilly, your first instinct may be to hand him a pair of cotton sweat pants and a sweatshirt. Once again, leave the cotton at home. Instead, hand him a pair of fleece or pile pants or pants made from some other synthetic material, along with a fleece or pile pullover or jacket, or a wool shirt or sweater. Tops with zippered fronts are practical because they allow ventilation. Zippered pant legs are also helpful, allowing kids to put on the pants without taking off their shoes or boots.

OUTER SHELL Don't venture far without this layer, even if the weather is warm, because hypothermia can

George Wuerthner and daughter Summer at Willamette Pass, Willamette National Forest, Oregon. Bundling infants and toddlers against the cold is vital because they are not exercising as much as you are.

However, the material isn't particularly durable, so be prepared for tears and snags. Look for bargains at outfitters and discount department stores.

During winter, a ski jacket with a hood may also be needed. Avoid down jackets, which, like cotton, are practically useless when wet.

In an emergency, use a trash bag as a makeshift raincoat.

HATS, MITTENS, AND SCARVES

Humans young and old have built-in thermostats: their heads, hands, and feet. They're the first areas to get cold. Take a quick reading of your child's hands to tell whether all is well, or whether he needs to put on or take off a layer.

Hats are a necessity in summer as well as winter. In warm weather, they protect against sunburn and bug bites. The best ones have broad brims and neck flaps. In winter a wool or pile hat offers vital cold-weather protection, since the body loses heat through the head most quickly. For more protection, add a scarf, neck warmer, or balaclava.

Mittens are warmer than gloves. In extreme conditions, use a layering system specifically for hands: thin polypro gloves, wool mittens, and an outer-shell mitten.

In cold weather, use wool socks, sometimes two pairs.

Layer, layer, layer — from the tips of your child's toes and fingertips to face, ears, and head. Don't forget that layering is a year-round activity. Above treeline, for example, your

strike any time of year, and affects children more quickly than adults (see Chapter 12).

While you'll want to invest in Gore-Tex or Gore-Tex-like pants and jacket for yourself, such a purchase may be too costly for a growing child. The alternatives? We've all sweltered underneath thick slickers that don't breathe, so forget these. PVC-coated nylon jackets and pants are probably the best compromise in terms of affordability, breathability, and rain protection. The pants are also useful on dewy and wet summer mornings.

family may need warm hats, gloves, and thermal underwear, even in July.

How to Layer

All too often I see families trudging up a trail in long pants and heavy shirts, sweat rolling down their faces. If only they had worn shorts, they'd be having a lot more fun.

The mistake is easy to make. When I was new to hiking, I often felt chilly at the outset of each hike, and dressed accordingly. Five minutes

later I'd have to stop and shed layers as both the trail and my body temperature rose. Eventually I learned that it was best to start off a bit chilly.

The bottom line: Try to dress

DRESSING BABIES AND TODDLERS

It's no secret that babies and toddlers need the most protection of all. They get cold and hot more quickly (see Chapter 12), especially since they're apt to be sitting in a child carrier, not exerting themselves, while you work up a sweat.

Babies need the same layers as anyone else, but they may need more, and they may need them sooner. One-piece, footed pajamas and outfits are a useful inner layer, but not cotton. Also, since babies get wet from the inside as well as the outside, change diapers regularly. Leakage can contribute to hypothermia on a cold day; diaper rash is the warm-weather worry.

In addition to protection from

the sun, babies are especially vulnerable to bug bites. You may find mosquito netting helpful. When your infant rides in a child carrier, you'll have a hard time seeing the bugs feast; ask someone else to be on lookout and swat patrol.

On cold days, protect the hands and feet with baby-sized mittens and socks, then layer with larger socks — even your own. Put the first layer or two on hands and feet before adding the outer shell layer, so that socks and mittens stay tucked underneath. Fleece or pile baby bags are a good bet.

A quiet child isn't always a content or sleeping child — babies may be too hot or too cold to complain. Regularly feel hands, cheeks, and the back of the neck to gauge temperature.

THE ALL-ESSENTIAL BANDANNA

On overnight trips, bring more than one bandanna and up to five per child. We once made a list of their uses and it took up an entire page in our camp journal. Here are some favorites:

• For warmth around the neck or entire head.

• As a parachute toy (when used with string, another essential item).

• To put around a teepee made of sticks.

Jerelyn Wilson — Brattleboro, Vermont

your child for "just right," which means not only the average temperature but the average exertion of the day, and then bring layers for all extremes.

Don't count on children to let you know when they're hot or cold: they may not speak up until they're already very chilly, for instance. Check periodically and be ready with dry clothes or appropriate layers.

Also, be familiar with the possible temperature extremes in any destination you explore. On a summer jaunt on nearby Mount Watatic, for instance, I know we can get by with minimal layering. On Mount Washington, however, we'd never venture out without layers to protect us from freezing temperatures, even on a summer day.

Overnight Clothes

If conserving space and weight is important, a set of polyester long underwear or a shirt and pile sweat pants are more versatile choices than pajamas.

However, your child may insist on wearing pajamas. Try to oblige if possible. After all, taking along a bit of extra clothing is a small price to pay for happiness, comfort, and security at bedtime.

You've got it made, though, if your child is used to wearing long underwear as pajamas at home.

One note of caution: Don't let your children sleep in food-stained clothes, which may attract animals.

Sunglasses

Trailside TV host Peter Whittaker bristles at the number of children with no eye protection that he sees on Mount Rainier.

"It's a hot day, it's 80 degrees, and the snow is bright white," he says. "You've got parents with sunglasses on and little kids without them. You can really fry a child's eyes."

All too often, kids' sunglasses are regarded as toys or cute accessories, but they offer much-needed protection. Protect your child's eyes now, and you may help prevent cataracts later.

Although sunglasses usually aren't necessary in the woods, watch out for glare from water, sun, and snow, especially at high altitudes, where the sun's rays are more intense.

Attach a band to help prevent them from "disappearing," especially with babies. Baby Optics, Scott, Solar Sense, and Vuarnet make quality sunglasses for infants and children.

After-Outing Clothes

If you travel more than an hour or so away from home, it's nice to have a clean, dry set of clothes waiting in the car after an outing.

CHILD CARRIERS

I've always preferred to carry Will in a backpack instead of a stroller, both on the trail and in the mall. Whether we're gazing at birch trees or snatching up bargains, we're much more mobile; I have both hands free, and he has a much better view. We don't leave home without it.

Years ago I wouldn't have believed I'd be able to handle the load. I was raised in the South, where my parents taught me that young ladies, among other things, never lift heavy things. I didn't shed that mindset until I started training for my first backpacking trip, when I borrowed my friend's child carrier and toddler for a weekly workout.

When Will came along we first used a front carrier for outings. Will seemed happy, but Jim and I agreed that it strained our backs and necks. We also briefly tried a sling-like affair that saddled Will across our hips. It was okay, but in hindsight I wish we hadn't spent the money.

On the day Will turned four months old we put him in a backpack, and — hallelujah! — all of us were much happier. At first we used an inexpensive hand-me-down, but in a few months it was obviously unsafe. The around-the-waist restraint was insufficient to protect him, and when he stretched or craned his neck, he appeared ready to topple over. Such

WHEN IS YOUR BABY READY FOR A CHILD CARRIER?

A baby needs sufficient neck strength to withstand the bouncing and jouncing that occur in a backpack-style child carrier. Ask your physician to determine when your child is ready. On average, the moment comes at about five or six months, when a child has sufficient head control to sit with minimal propping.

If you wait too long to introduce a child carrier, you may decide the burden is too heavy, and your child may balk. Once you start using one, do so at least once a week to accustom both of you to the ride.

Never leave infants unattended in their child carriers, and place carriers on the ground, not on picnic tables, from which they could topple.

carrier. Going without one is the equivalent of putting your child in a car without a car seat — if you fall, he or she will have little or no protection. Even if you never set foot in the woods, once your child's weight and activity level increase, he or she can easily throw you off balance, or even fall out, making bargain backpacks unsafe. A good, durable pack will last for many years, many miles, and several owners, so check with friends for hand-me-downs.

cheap models aren't much more than fabric mounted around an aluminum frame, and aren't suitable for anything more than neighborhood strolls for a month or two after your baby leaves the front carrier.

The minute you head to the woods, your family needs a real child

Expect to pay about $75 and up for a good, new carrier; the money is well worth it. Some of the most popular carriers are made by Tough Traveler, Kelty, and L. L. Bean, who offer a variety of well-made models. Some friends of ours used their Tough Traveler for each of their two children until they were five years old. They called the carrier one of the "all-time best" purchases they'd ever made. We ended up with a Kelty; it was on sale and we knew it was a good brand. During the first week or two it felt like too much pack for our little guy, but those days didn't last long.

Shop for a child carrier with these features:

● Restraining straps. One of *the* most important features in a child carrier. There should be at least two

---

GEAR TIPS FROM AN EXPERT

Ray Dahl of Kearns, Utah, is an avid outdoorsman and father of three. In addition to a full-time position at the University of Utah, he works part time at REI to help pay for equipment for him and his family.

What advice does he have for families in the market for outdoor equipment?

✎ I look at my kids as small adults. If I have a need for a piece of equipment, then it's likely that my children have the same need.

✎ I believe boots offer important protection and support at any age. It's possible to get small boots at most children's shoe stores. We have had great luck with Osh Kosh boots, which we use as daily footwear in the winter and anytime we are outside.

✎ Buy clothing large so kids can wear it as long as possible. Rolled sleeves and cuffs are part of the game.

✎ Look for used outdoor clothing. We have yet to actually wear out any of the outdoor clothing we have for our kids, so you're likely to find a bargain.

✎ You can make your own gear if you have a sewing machine and lots of patience. I get patterns from Rain Shed, and also got some from Marilyn Doan's *The Sierra Club Family Outdoors Guide* (Sierra Club Books), which includes instructions for making rain pants, a child's sleeping bag, and simple packs.

✎ For backpacking trips we use an REI Mountain Hut 4, a free-standing geodesic dome designed for four adults. For car camping we have a GeoDome-6 from REI. Next year I will probably buy a two-person tent for our two older children. Later I will put all three of the kids into my old three-person tent, and Laura and I will take the two-person tent. Okay, I admit to being a gear-head!

sets: one for over the shoulders and another around the waist. On the trail, keep an eye on the straps — kids sometimes wiggle free from the shoulder set.

- Plenty of padding for both you and your child. You'll want padded shoulder straps, a padded sternum strap, and a padded hip belt. Think of all the padding on a regular backpack, then consider that *this* load will be wiggling, squirming, even jumping.
- Easy adjustability. Jim is nine inches taller than I am, yet we tote Will in the same pack. Our Kelty adjusts so effortlessly that we usually don't remember to fiddle with the straps until after the pack — and Will — is on our backs.

- Ease of cleaning.
- A frame stand to support the backpack when it's on the ground. You'll learn how to put on and take off the pack when no one's around to help by resting the frame stand on a chair, the edge of a car seat, or any other raised surface. *Never* leave your child in the pack unattended, however, even for a second. Will once toppled over in a trailhead parking lot while one of us locked the car.
- A pouch for storing diapers, bottles, snacks, and other small items.
- Loops on which to tie small toys.

Some models offer rain/sun hood accessories and extra carrying pouches (Tough Traveler makes one large enough to carry a compact sleeping bag).

?

AGE-OLD QUESTIONS

BABY BEDS AND PARAPHERNALIA

When traveling with a baby, try not to take so much stuff that your outing turns into an expedition. You'll be surprised at how much you can leave home and still be happy.

I once heard a woman explain that she needed a tent big enough to accommodate her child's portable crib. Forget the crib; the tent *is* one big playpen.

If the weather is warm, babies don't even need sleeping bags. Unfold an adult, rectangular bag as an insulated sleeping pad, placing your baby on top, between you and your spouse. Put your baby in pajamas,

and wrap him in blankets.

Tempted to bring a baby swing? They may be lifesavers at home, but try a front carrier or backpack instead.

Lugging a high chair or baby seat? Use the car seat.

What about a bathtub? Skip it. Substitute a sponge bath, no bath at all, or use a cooler as a tub.

Can't leave home without it? Some things are necessities; others, mere conveniences. Weigh the distinctions carefully.

Check the carrier's load limit; typical limits range between 35 and 60 pounds. You may need a heavier capacity than you anticipate — or even think you have the strength to lift. However, even after children "graduate" from the pack, there will be times when their stamina wanes and you end up hauling them. A friend of mine was exuberant to find that the Tough Traveler Stallion has the capacity to carry her six-year-old son, who has cerebral palsy.

BACKPACKS FOR CHILDREN

The instant your child shows any interest in a pack, by all means indulge! The earlier everyone learns to help with the hauling, the better off your family will be.

This isn't just a matter of convenience, but one of safety: Any child carrying a pack should have food and water in case he or she gets separated from the family. Any pack within reason is fine. Durability isn't even a real issue, since most kids won't be carrying a heavy load.

Daypacks

Even toddlers can tote small daypacks or fanny packs containing a toy or snack. Don't push until they're ready, though — this should be fun, not a point of conflict.

Six months ago, Will wouldn't have anything to do with a backpack. Even the snazzy Sesame Street styles didn't interest him; he shied away as if I were offering a straitjacket. One day, however, at the beginning of summer, I showed him one in a toy store, and he had a sudden change of heart. We took it home, and he liked it so much he didn't want to take it off, even when it was time to get in his car seat (I managed to convince him that this would be unsafe as well uncomfortable).

Even when preschoolers are proud of their packs, they tend to tire of carrying them amazingly quickly. If you repeatedly find yourself lugging your youngster's pack, either leave it in the car or, after issuing fair warning, refuse to take it when your child hands it over.

Backpacks

Sometime after children start school — or even earlier — have them begin to carry small items besides their own toys and a snack and water, even if it's nothing more than suntan lotion or a box of bandages. Small flashlights are another lightweight, practical item that kids like to carry. Such loads will help make them aware that you're not their personal packhorse. Then start training them to be responsible for an item or two of their own — say, a lightweight jacket or extra socks. On backpacking trips, your school-age child can carry a sleeping bag, stuffed inside his pack or strapped to the outside.

As with kids' boots, make advancement to a "real" pack — one bought at an outdoors store as opposed to a toy store — a rite of passage, a sign that your child is ready for more than "baby hikes."

The appropriate age depends on your child's strength and enthusiasm, as well as the nature of your family trips. There's no sense buying special equipment if you don't hike more than two or three times a year. On the other hand, six- and seven-year-olds in outdoors-oriented families may put a real pack to good use.

Regardless of your child's age, always check packs at the trailhead to make sure they're not overloaded. Help avoid this possibility by buying relatively small packs at first. As the weight kids carry begins to add up, the pack's construction and comfort come more into play, so switch from a "kiddy pack" to a real pack with strong seams, well-made hip and shoulder belts, and, most of all, comfort.

Eagle Creek makes a nifty pack for kids called the Eaglet, which comes with a whistle and an outside mesh pocket and water bottle, all for $22, fitting preschoolers to preteens. Tough Traveler offers the Kiddy Pack for ages 1–5 and the Elementary for ages 5–9 (both under $25), and the Cayuga for ages 11 and up ($40).

BASIC CAMP GEAR

Your home-away-from-home should be comfortable and hassle-free. Like the proverbial child who's seen but not heard, camp gear should be waiting when you need it, not demanding your attention.

Sleeping Bags for Children

Sleeping bags are a childhood necessity, right up there with roller skates, balls, and bikes. They're practical as well, on camping trips, at home or at friends' houses, when company comes or for slumber parties. Kids love to use them anywhere, even on top of their beds.

More than likely, your child already has a sleeping bag. If not, buy one — regardless — even if you have no intention of ever taking your child camping.

Sleeping bags come in three basic styles: rectangular, modified mummy, and mummy. The mummy bags are the warmest and lightest, but also too confining for some. Let your child try out each style, and encourage him or her to stretch and turn over, determining which feels best.

Another comfort factor is the bag's temperature rating. Three-season bags are the most practical. Summer bags usually aren't warm enough, even for average conditions; conversely, you and your family may not have plans for winter excursions.

Camping and backpacking families have three options when selecting sleeping bags for kids:
① Use a folded-over adult bag, suggests *Trailside* TV host Peter Whittaker. This converts the bag to your

child's size, while adding some extra padding underneath. It's essential to fold the adult bag, Whittaker warns, because small bodies aren't big enough to heat up an entire adult-sized bag, and a child will sleep cold. Another trick is to stuff extra clothing into the bottom of the bag, thereby filling the extra airspace. You can also tie the unused end off, making for a neater package.

② Let your child use the sleeping bag he has. More than likely it's designed for home use, not the outdoors, and is made of lightweight cotton. On hot summer nights you can probably get by with such a bag. A word of caution, however: They're not warm enough for cold or even chilly nights, when your child will need another bag or extra layers to sleep in. Also, if these bags get wet

THE 10 COMMANDMENTS OF TENTING

① Practice setting up your tent and taking it down at home, before your trip.

② Seal the seams before you go, or you'll have a wet night if it rains. Your tent probably came with sealer, or you can get a tube at an outfitter. Follow the instructions provided.

③ Use a ground cloth under your tent as protection from rips and moisture. Tuck the edges of the cloth underneath the tent so that water doesn't collect and leak inside.

④ No cooking or open flames inside the tent — too dangerous.

⑤ Try to avoid eating inside the tent, since crumbs attract critters. In bear country, this is an absolute no-no. Don't store food in your tent. Either hang it or put it in a

car or animal-proof container. Explain to your children why they can't stash away even a tiny snack.

⑥ Take off boots or shoes before entering the tent to avoid messes and protect the fabric.

⑦ Use the rain fly, even if the night is clear. I once took the lazy way out, thinking rain was out of the question, and awoke feeling like a kayaker! A tarp will also increase your rainy-day room — it's handy over a picnic table.

⑧ Shake as much water, leaves, and dirt off the tent before packing up.

⑨ Store the tent in a stuff sack instead of folding it into a tidy package. Using the same creases over and over weakens a tent.

⑩ Clean and air your tent when you get home. If it's packed away with any moisture, damage is likely.

or even damp, your child (and, therefore, *you*) will be miserable.

③ Buy a child-sized sleeping bag made of synthetic materials, designed for outdoor use. Such a purchase is a worthwhile investment. These bags keep young campers warmer than an adult-sized bag; they're not overly expensive; and your child can usually get several seasons' use. Synthetic materials keep kids warmer and drier than the cotton in bags used for slumber parties. Also, since they weigh less than adult bags, they're efficient for backpacking.

REI makes several junior models, priced from $50 to $100. Tough Traveler makes a modular sleeping bag called the Growing Bear, with two extensions at the head and foot, designed to fit children from 3' to 4'10". It weighs 2 pounds, is rated to 30°F, and costs $130.

🎵

DID YOU KNOW
In 1868 John Muir fell in love with the mountains of Yosemite. He climbed as many peaks as possible — sometimes in his underwear, since clothes got in the way. He also carried little, eating cracker crumbs and sucking tea bags. *Trailside* does NOT recommend this approach.

Tough Traveler also makes the Baby Bear, 32 inches long and $95, for the youngest campers.

Additional manufacturers of junior bags include Caribou Mountaineering, Cascade Designs, EC-Camp, Jack Wolfskin, Kelty, L. L. Bean, Lafuma America, and Slumberjack.

PILLOWS Pillows are handy for camping as well as the car trip to the trailhead. When I was a kid, I never traveled without one.

Don't forget to bring a pillow of some sort for each camper, either a regular one from home, a small couch pillow, or — if you're backpacking — a cushion formed from folded clothing, such as a fleece jacket.

MATTRESS PADS Kids are less sensitive than adults to the bumps and aches of sleeping on the ground, but if they see Mom and Dad bedding down on air mattresses, they'll want their own cushioning. Appease them with an inexpensive piece of foam rubber or closed-cell foam, or let them use your padded camp chair for the night. Reserve a few luxuries for adults.

Tents
Kids love any and all tents. They're right up there with ice cream and hot dogs. Even a makeshift tent will do — a blanket over a card table, a sheet pulled over their head.

Since anything will satisfy your child, buy one that makes you, the adults, happy. If you already own one, you're probably set — unless it happens to be particularly small.

Such was the case with Jim and me. For many years we used a two-person backpacking tent so tiny that our friends often poked fun at us. We tend to be minimalists, however, and were quite satisfied. Until Will came along, that is — when he was about six months old we bought a mid-priced, three-person dome tent, which seems enormous in comparison.

Tents and children were made for one another, and some full-grown campers find that tents bring out the kid in them. Here a clean, well-lighted (and ventilated) tent makes the perfect napping spot.

Take your time when shopping; a good tent will see you through years of adventures. Styles have changed from the musty, green canvas tent my family had when I was a kid, and there are plenty of good, reasonably priced models out there.

Today's versions look more like lunar landing modules than tents, adorned with vestibules, vaulted ceilings, and geodesic designs. (Those vestibules, by the way, can make a cozy sleeping space for a child.) Metal poles and stakes have been replaced by shock-cord poles, hooks, Velcro, and quick-release buckles.

Look for pouches and mesh lofts. The more, the merrier — kids will enjoy having their own pouches in which to stash their toys and headlamps.

After giving a tent the initial once-over, concentrate on what you'll be doing rather than the tent itself. Go inside, stretch out, and envision your camping routine: Imagine yourselves getting dressed and undressed. Do you have enough headroom? Imagine the tent filled with gear, clothing, and kids. Imagine a rainy day (at this point you may opt for a separate tent for each person!). If you intend to backpack, imagine yourself *carrying* the tent all day.

Help narrow your options by answering the following questions:
● How many people will use this tent?
● How often? (Frequent users often invest more money than average.)
● Is weight a factor? Will you backpack or have to carry the tent any distance before setting it up?
● What types of weather and terrain will your tent be subjected to? What's the order of importance of, say, air circulation, bug protection, and rain and snow protection? In hot climates, for instance, you'll want mesh windows and ceilings that allow plenty of air circulation — just the opposite of what you need in rain and snow.
● Is setup easy? Setup is a *major* issue. The easier, the better.

Capacity and weight run the gamut from sleek backcountry solos to huge, heavy affairs with two or more "rooms." If you plan mostly car camping, go for the extra room. The other day I found myself looking somewhat lustfully at a tent airing in a friend's backyard. It was about 6 feet tall and could sleep five or six adults — a veritable dance hall! It was far too heavy for backpacking, but I was told it sets up easily in ten minutes.

Instead of sharing one large tent, at some point your kids may want their own tent, an option many parents cheer. Most two-children families can use a three-person dome tent when the kids are small, then add another two-person tent when they're older.

Whatever your needs and the size of your family, here's a rule of thumb: It's much easier to use backpacking tents for car camping than it is to lug car-camping models into the backcountry. If you foresee a real variety of trips over the years, you'll probably want to purchase both.

Some respected names to consider are L. L. Bean, Camel, EMS, Eureka, Kelty, REI, Sierra Designs, and North Face.

One last word: You probably don't need the latest, highest-priced tent, but don't get one dirt cheap, either. Ultra-bargains seldom are.

FAMILY-
FRIENDLY
FOOD

I hear the fire going. Daddy's cooking marshmallows!

Will, at breakfast during a New Hampshire camping trip
(his father was *not* cooking marshmallows)

The cardinal rule of outdoor cooking is simplicity. By the time you're all ready to eat, everyone is beat from the day's adventures, but also famished. You may also be gearing up for an evening campfire or other activities, so there's no reason to spend any more time than necessary cooking, unless you particularly enjoy it.

Just because a meal is easy doesn't mean it can't be fun. Some-times nothing more than a few words will do the trick: calling pasta "wormy spaghetti," as children's author Roald Dahl did in *The Twits*, or referring to hamburgers as "mudburgers," mentioned in *James and the Giant Peach*. If you want the exact recipes, take a look at *Roald Dahl's Revolting Recipes*, illustrated by Quentin Blake (Viking). Although it's not an outdoor cookbook, some of the recipes can be adapted for trail use, or prepared

FORGET LOW FAT

Because of today's low-fat eating habits, Ray and I had to adjust the ideas of boys and girls we took camping and backpacking. We had to explain that high-fat foods are great for keeping warm, and that complex carbohydrates are great for energy when you have to carry everything yourself.

Laura Dahl — Kearns, Utah

ahead of time and packed away as surprises. And remember, when dining al fresco, as often as possible, let the kids lend a hand.

GORP-GULPING AND OTHER SNACKS

One thing your kids are sure to love about outdoor activities are the frequent snacks. They're more than just fun, they're a necessity. As calories are burned, they need to be replaced.

This is no trail secret: Every parent knows the miracle-producing capabilities of food (as well as sleep). Hand out a snack and, in a minute or two, a crotchety, sluggish hiker becomes a nonstop ball of fire. The trick is to get the calories in *before* they're needed, and thus avoid the crotchety phase. Offer snacks regularly: Once an hour is a good rule of thumb; in hot weather or when climbing steep sections, every 30 minutes.

Where else to start but GORP,

the concoction stashed away in nearly every backpack? There are numerous variations on the basic theme of "Good Old Raisins and Peanuts," including nuts, chocolate chips, M&Ms, dried fruit, yogurt balls, granola, coconut, cereal, and peanut butter or butterscotch chips. Before an outing, have a GORP-making party to determine who can come up with the tastiest mixture.

Insist on a base of at least a few healthy items, or buy *all* of the items and let the kids choose from these. Round out the nutritional content with something besides sugar; aim for carbohydrates, protein, and vitamins, for instance. And remember that if your toddler will be a taster, avoid nuts and other items that could cause choking.

If you let your kids concoct their own sweet sensations (gummy bears

Dried fruits and chocolate bars are favorites of hikers. With kids along, you know which of the two you'll run out of first.

and licorice, anyone?), make it a rule that they also sample some of your GORP as well. They're not likely to complain; fresh air and exercise make kids less fussy about food.

Power Pills

Need a quick energy boost? Whether you're 9 or 90, forget about the much-touted energy bars, which taste like day-old cardboard. Instead, try an approach created by the Bockus family of Hubbardston, Massachusetts. They've logged thousands of miles together, thanks to a secret energy potion.

Years ago, when young Jen and Chris were lagging on a trail in New Hampshire's White Mountains, their uncle plucked some peanut M&Ms from a GORP bag and explained that these were special "power pills" that would make them hike better and faster than any of the adults.

The kids took off, and from that day power pills became a regular part of Bockus family outings. Jen and Chris are in college now, but their parents still rely on the secret formula. Their mother, Debbie, says: "I, for one, do not believe that power pills

work only for children!"

You can use your own secret ingredients for your family's power pills, but dispense them freely when the going gets tough.

Additional trail favorites that are good for low-energy moments are fruit, cheese sticks, cereal, cookies (Fig Newtons are one of our favorites, especially the raspberry ones), candy, muffins, fruit roll-ups, date or banana bread, even GORP-like brownies.

DID YOU KNOW

Call Hershey's customer relations at 800-468-1714 for a pamphlet called "S'more Fun with Hershey's Milk Chocolate." Inside are recipes featuring nuts, peanut butter, fruit, and more. You'll also find the instructions for "Indoor S'mores," which call for microwaving one graham cracker half, one candy bar half, and a marshmallow on high for 10 to 15 seconds, or until the marshmallow begins to puff. After heating, add the other cracker half.

Meredith and Nick Wiltsie enjoy corn-on-the-cob and barbecue. Camping out doesn't mean leaving family-friendly food behind.

banana bread from turning into crumb cake; but getting rid of packaging will usually save space in your backpack.

Some packaging, however, is perfect for the trail, such as individual-sized servings of applesauce, yogurt, or pudding. Think small — miniatures make great trail food for kids, including bite-size pretzels, crackers, bagels, rice cakes, and candy bars.

Hard to beat are destinations that provide their own rewards — such as blueberries and blackberries — but make sure you know *exactly* what you eat from the wild.

Some foods travel better than others; apples hold up better than bananas, for example. Packing helps too — a plastic tub can prevent your

CAMP MEALS

If you're worried about trail meals, don't. Cooking outside is easier than at home. What's more, most children become less finicky about food: They're hungry, eating outside is a novelty, and, somehow, most things taste great.

Menu options are unlimited if you're car camping, since you're likely to have access to grocery stores — even restaurants — and can keep food fresh in a cooler. You can easily have champagne and caviar, for instance, although the kids will go on strike. Even when you're backpacking, there's no reason to suffer. These days it's easy to whip up good meals using ingredients that can withstand trail travel without adding too much weight to your pack.

Find a Family Favorite

In the Cary family, "Coal River Special" has meant camping for several generations. My cousin Mike describes it best by saying: "It's just goulash." Slight variations have evolved, but the basic theme is hamburger, a can of tomato soup, a can of Franco-American spaghetti, green peppers, and onions. A far cry from gourmet, but we love it because of the memories it evokes.

STOVES

While campfires are the time-honored cooking method of campers everywhere, there's no denying that stoves are more efficient and easier on the environment; fires consume resources and lengthen meal preparation time. In some areas, fires aren't allowed — the area is too fragile, the risk of fire too great. And to be honest, camp stoves are easier on parents and kids too. Even where fires are allowed, it's much simpler to cook on a stove and save the campfire for pure evening enjoyment.

No camper should be without a stove. Styles vary from backpacker models to multi-burner units, while fuels include liquid gas, gas cartridges, and wood and other flammable materials. The pros, cons, and quirks of various models are the subject of heated debate among campers and backpackers. To find the right stove for your family, talk to friends and an outfitter, and consult gear guides, such as *Backpacker* magazine's annual spring guide. Basically, you need to decide whether you need a backpacking stove or a larger model.

continued on page 58

Safety and simplicity are key, especially with kids around. We use a Coleman two-burner stove for car camping, a terrific unit that's hard to beat. Depending on the size of your family and the nature of your adventures, you may need a stove with several burners, and perhaps more than one stove.

Car campers might also consider propane as a fuel source, although the fuel containers are too heavy for backpacking. In Sequoia National Park we tented next to a couple who cooked and heated with propane. Although it was a cold September night and their toddler was ill, they had all stayed warm thanks to their propane-powered heater.

For backcountry trips, we started out with a white-gas-fueled backpacking stove. It was a sturdy workhorse but occasionally finicky, and we eventually grew tired of having to prime the gas. We switched to a Gaz cartridge stove that uses a mixture of butane and propane. It's a snap to use: Just turn a knob and light a match. The new stove also has a lantern attachment, another plus for families. But if we plan to cook at a high altitude, where white gas is the most reliable fuel, we still drag out our old stove.

Whichever model you choose, *always test it and check fuel supplies before each trip.* You don't want to discover a problem in front of a group of expectant, hungry campers.

The dish originated in West Virginia with my late grandfather, who worked for the railroad. He began his career in the 1920s, when railroad crews cooked in cabooses on potbellied stoves and used whatever ingredients happened to be on hand. Back at home, when my grandmother would ask what my grandfather had had for dinner out on the tracks, he would simply reply, "Coal River Special," because that was the area where the crew had been traveling.

Such a no-fuss meal was a natural for the rest of the family's scouting and camping trips.

We're also developing new favorites of our own. One I've dubbed "Jim's Favorite" is easy for older children to prepare in camp or at home: Brown 1 pound of ground turkey; add chopped onion. Drain grease and add one 16-ounce can of baked beans and one-quarter cup of ketchup.

The Bockus family of Hubbardston, Massachusetts, swears by

"Mountain Mush," made from Lipton's chicken soup mix, a can of chicken, and a can of peas.

"I'm not sure if it's really delicious," Debbie Bockus says, "or only delicious after you've hiked 10 miles in the rain. Whatever the reason, we find it wonderful! It was one meal we always knew the kids would eat."

Give Coal River Special, Jim's Favorite, and Bockus Mountain Mush a try. Maybe they'll become part of your camp meal repertoire. If not, invent your own creations.

KEEPING PARENTS ENERGIZED

Kids are more exhausting than the trail. By all means, take lots of complex carbos to keep the parents' energy equal to the kids'!

Laura Dahl — Kearns, Utah

CREATIVE COOKING

Don't miss the opportunity to let older kids try their hand at various styles of outdoor cooking:

COAL COOKING If you're lucky, your campsite may have a grate. If not, use rocks, logs, or whatever's on hand to hold a pot or skillet securely over a fire. Keep the flame low and the coals hot; stir constantly. Coat the outside of the pot with soap or dishwashing detergent to help prevent permanent soot buildup.

FOIL COOKING Martha Stewart may prefer parchment, but real wilderness chefs use foil. You can cook a tremendous variety of dishes in the shiny stuff: meat, vegetables, stew, biscuits, and fruit. Kids will love assembling their own packets and tossing them in the embers. Use a heavy foil or double-wrap packets. Diced vegetables and meat will cook in 10 to 15 minutes; baked potatoes take 40 to 50 minutes. Carefully rotate the packet halfway through cooking. Don't wrap food too tightly — leave room for expansion; and watch out for steam when opening packets.

SPUD BUCKETS Potatoes can be cooked in so many ways; one method your kids will remember requires a large can. Fill the can halfway with damp dirt or sand. Bury potatoes in the bucket so they don't touch each other. Place the can upright in hot coals for 45 minutes or so. During cooking you may need to moisten the dirt or sand.

EGGXACTLY Use a knife to cut a hole in the small end of an egg. Put the egg in hot ashes, hole side up, and bake for 10 to 20 minutes.

A hot dog on a stick and a close friend around a campfire on Lake of the Woods, Ontario: what more could a kid ask for? Beaches are among the safest, most impact-free places to build campfires, particularly if you burn driftwood.

duff or pine cones. Older kids can help lay the fire (see Chapter 7).

Many campsites have fire rings — a wild kitchen just waiting for a cook. But if you decide to give your family a camp-fire meal and see no place to cook, do it the low-impact way: Dig a fire pit.

Choose a level spot away from trees. In a circle about 2 feet wide, clear away any debris, then dig several inches down to mineral soil, being careful to cut neat squares of

Campfire 101

Kids love to help get fires started — it's an easy way to keep them busy. One adult can supervise (closely) while the other works on food preparation. Even preschoolers can collect wood and tinder, such as pine needle

SUPREME CUISINE

While adult cooks rely on Julia Child and the *New York Times Cookbook*, camping kids shouldn't be without ✳ *Cooking on a Stick: Campfire Recipes for Kids* (Gibbs Smith). Linda White's book contains simple, creative recipes that require little cutting or cleanup. Each recipe has an enticing name, such as Cozy Caves, Snail on a Limb, Ranger's Apple Pie, and

Bird's Nest Breakfast.

There are also snack suggestions, such as Moose Lips and Deer Baubles — a necklace of cereal and dried fruit kids can nibble on the trail. Safety is stressed throughout; instructions are included for building a fire. Fran Lee's bright illustrations add a nice touch. Give your kids this book and let *them* plan your camping menus.

A marshmallow on a stick turns dark brown, first step in every young outdoorsmen's favorite dessert: S'mores!

sod. Later, after you douse the fire, cover the hole by replacing the sod, hiding all traces of your fire.

Cooking on a Stick

When I think of camp meals, the old Jiffy-Pop slogan comes to mind: "As much fun to cook as it is to eat!" (Jiffy-Pop popcorn, by the way, is an excellent choice for outdoor snacking.) Childhood isn't complete until you've roasted food on a stick. Start with hot dogs and marshmallows, the staples of campfire cookery. You can also cook vegetables and other meats as well; dream up your

text continued on page 64

MENU IDEAS

BREAKFAST How much energy you want to put into outdoor breakfasts depends to a large extent on the day's activities. Make sure you leave plenty of time to accomplish your goals.

EASY. Probably the most popular entree is oatmeal, either in instant, flavored packets or from make-your-own packets. Turn your cereal into a GORP-like affair with fanciful additions.

continued on page 62

FUN. We call them flippy-floppers — pancakes, of course. As with oatmeal, additions are called for, anything from berries to nuts. My own trail favorites are chocolate chips or M&Ms. Arrange them to form a face or another design. Excellent multi-grain mixes that require only the addition of water are ideal.

Kids also enjoy toasting their own bread over the fire, then adding such toppings as cinnamon and sugar, cocoa and sugar, or applesauce.

HEARTY. Home fries; corned beef hash, either from a can or make your own; omelets.

MORE IDEAS. Bagels, English muffins, granola bars, cereal (with fresh or powdered milk), French toast, refrigerator biscuits and buns, and, last but not least, a real kid-pleaser: Pop Tarts.

THE WINNER. If you want to get sleepyheads out of their sleeping bags in a hurry, promise pancakes with chocolate chips. Corned beef hash is a close runner-up.

L U N C H Unless you're stuck in camp on a rainy day, trail lunches are usually on-the-move meals. Kids are used to bag lunches, so the fare is nothing knew.

MOVABLE FEASTS. Crackers and cheese (string cheese keeps well), yogurt (it keeps a day or two without refrigeration, although "natural" brands without preservatives and liquids lose their body), summer sausage, small cans of tuna or other meats, ramen noodles, Pringles (cardboard can packaging prevents these chips from being crushed).

THE WINNER. PBJ is tough to beat. Consider more durable alternatives to bread such as bagels, English muffins, or pita bread.

D I N N E R Keep it simple, popular, and filling. And bring fresh vegetables.

HEALTHY AND HEARTY. Stir-fries are easy, especially for car campers. I also like to make meals ahead, at home, and reheat them in camp. Cornbread is a nice addition — I swear by Jiffy mix, even at home. Don't forget something fresh — celery, carrots, and cucumbers travel well, and a few herbs can breathe life into a meal. Potatoes are heavy but offer many possibilities; one of my favorites is potato soup.

EASY KID STUFF. Most kids give thumbs-up to macaroni and cheese; it's easy, cheap, lightweight — a hiking as well as a kid staple. If you don't mind MSG, serve up Hamburger Helper meals with fresh or dehydrated meat. Packaged soups are another easy starter for "trail casseroles"; rice, pasta, and Stovetop stuffing mixes are also good bases.

THE WINNER. Without a doubt, hamburgers and hot dogs cooked over a campfire. Kids will vote for macaroni and cheese as first runner-up.

DESSERTS Instant pudding is fun to prepare outdoors, as are other no-bake dessert mixes, such as cheesecake. Fruit cups are easy and healthy, using either fresh or canned fruit.

CREATIVE. Invent your own foil-wrapped goodies using chocolate chips or chocolate bars. Another scouting favorite is "Snow on the Mountain" — soda crackers topped with melted chocolate and coconut.

CAMPFIRE TREATS. Toast a taffy apple by roasting an apple over a fire until the apple's skin is ready to peel off, then roll the apple in brown sugar. Hold the apple over the fire once more, until the sugar caramelizes.

POPPING FRESH. Nothing beats popcorn, cooked either the old-fashioned way with oil and pop-corn or with good old Jiffy-Pop. Kids accustomed to microwave packets will think all this is some-thing new.

THE WINNER. S'mores. They're a camping must!

BEVERAGES It's essential to keep your kids hydrated since dehydration is a common and potentially dangerous outdoor hazard. Water is the best trail drink, but you'll also want to give your family nutrition and variety.

LIGHTWEIGHT. Tang is crowd-pleasing and handy, as are other powdered beverages, such as Kool-Aid. Gatorade is especially helpful on hot days, available in liquid and powdered forms.

MILK OPTIONS. Powdered formula is handy for infants. Car campers can keep fresh milk in a cooler. In the backcountry, powdered milk may or may not appeal to your family; it works best mixed with other things. Milk that doesn't need refrigeration is available in juice-box-style packaging.

WEIGHTY TREATS. For dayhikes, freeze a juice box the night before and treat your child to a trail slush. A can of soda can enliven a limp daytripper; I often carry a Coke as a summit reward.

HOT STUFF. Cocoa for the kids; tea or coffee bags for the folks. A favorite among long-distance hikers is hot Jell-O.

THE WINNER. Water. Don't leave home without it.

♥

MARSHMALLOW AND S'MORE STICKS

At the hardware store get 3- or 4-foot-long, 3/8- or 1/2-inch-wide dowels, along with a package of bamboo skewers. Cut the dowels in half and at the end of each, drill a 1/16-inch-wide hole 1 to 11/2 inches deep. Trim the skewers as needed to fit snugly into the hole, and voilà, S'more sticks par excellence!

Advantages: 1. The assembled stick is long enough to keep the kids out of the fire. 2. Theoretically, the sticky end can be thrown away at the end of the evening. In reality, the kids get the whole stick sticky. 3. The kids don't fight over the "good" sticks, or use poison oak or ivy sticks.

Charley Renn — Corvallis, Oregon

text continued from page 61

own "trail kebobs."

Sticks should be green (growing) wood, which doesn't burn as easily as dead wood. Gather them in your own yard so you don't destroy campsite vegetation. You can also make sticks out of wooden dowels and bamboo skewers.

While kids love cooking on a stick, it can turn into a parent's nightmare. Read everyone the riot act before handing out the sticks, watch the kids carefully, and confiscate any sticks used improperly. Hot dogs and marshmallows inevitably fall off, so once the feast is finished, have the kids pick up the scraps.

Freeze-Dried and Dehydrated

While there's nothing like a pot of chili warming over a campfire to make you and your kids feel like cowboys, when you decide you're ready for longer trips, especially if you're backpacking, you'll need to resort to some no-fuss, lightweight meals.

At first, on overnight trips, indulge. Go shorter distances so you can carry more food. You want your kids to think of backpacking meals as fun feasts, not C-rations. Work up to longer trips and the necessarily more limited menus.

Commercially prepared freeze-dried meals are as handy as they come. With many, just add boiling water and eat right out of the bag, no dishes needed. These pouches vary greatly in quality — some are gourmet, others cardboard. Such meals are equally convenient for car camping, at the end of a long day when no one feels like fussing. Keep a few on hand with standard food supplies.

If you like the convenience but not the cost of commercial packages, consider dehydrating your own food. You can dry a surprising range of food, such as fruits, vegetables, stew, and soup. Dehydrators cost about $80.

S'mores

S'mores are the pièce de résistance of the camping world — those gooey treats of chocolate and marshmallows sandwiched between graham cracker halves. It definitely seemed like a gourmet treat when I took my first bite as a Girl Scout.

The recipe: Break a graham cracker in two. Top one of these halves with half of a Hershey bar. Roast a marshmallow to perfection. Place it on top of the Hershey bar. Top the sandwich off with the remaining half of the graham cracker.

For a scouting variation on the traditional S'more theme, try Banana Boats. Peel back a long strip of banana peel, scoop out some banana and fill with marshmallows and chocolate chips. Replace the peel, wrap your "boat" in foil, and bake the banana in embers until all is melted, about 15 to 20 minutes.

KEEP THE WATER BOTTLES HANDY

In my experience with kids, they will drop from heat stroke before digging a water bottle out of a pack. A holder makes a big difference — to make one, all you need is 3 feet of twine.

With one end tie a slip knot around the bottle's neck; with the rest of the twine tie a bowline (the one where the rabbit comes out the hole) to position the bottle on the hiker's sternum. Put the loop around the hiker's neck and head down the trail. If your child complains about the cord cutting into his or her neck, point out that by drinking the water they will lighten the load.

Charley Renn — Corvallis, Oregon

INFANT FEEDING

Before setting out on the trail with your baby, double-check to make sure you have *all* the feeding equipment you need. Jim and I learned this lesson the hard way. During a dayhike when Will was about eight months old, we left the nipple for his bottle in the car. Luckily, we were only a few miles away when we missed it, but Will had already announced he was hungry, and those few miles were very long, *loud* miles.

Breastfeeding

Breastfed babies have the easiest of all appetites to satisfy outdoors. The only real issue is finding a comfortable spot for nursing. If you're car camping, a fold-up chair is much easier on your back than a picnic table, though the car is probably the best spot. At night, make sure your sleeping bag has plenty of room — mummy bags aren't designed for nursing mothers. When hiking or biking, a portable camp chair may feel like luxury living. When canoeing, wrestling with both mom's and baby's flotation devices during breastfeeding presents challenges — but no matter how awkward, keep them on.

Breastfeeding moms must take special care to drink plenty of fluids while exercising; if you get dehydrated, both you and your baby will suffer. Interestingly, a few studies

♥

FEEDING BABIES

Breastfeeding is ideal for backpacking. If you're mixing formula, make sure to have an excellent water filter. Water for formula can be kept warm at night by keeping it in your sleeping bag.

John Abraham — Calgary, Canada

have shown that babies may refuse breast milk immediately after their moms have exercised a lot. Evidently the milk tastes sour because of increased levels of lactic acid. However, this was never a problem for me

Breastfeeding mothers carry the ultimate advantage into the wilderness. They should make sure to drink plenty of fluids to avoid dehydration.

when Will was nursing, nor have I heard other mothers complain.

Formula

For formula-fed babies, powders are the easiest to use, and bottles with disposable plastic liners are more convenient and sanitary than bottles that have to be constantly washed in what may be less-than-optimal circumstances. *Never mix up formula or food with untreated water* (see Chapter 12). As for heating bottles, pack a thermos of hot water or a backpacking stove. We made it easy for ourselves: When we switched Will to formula, we didn't heat his bottles. Often we used warm water from the spigot, but he also drank them cold, directly from the refrigerator.

Baby Food

Those small baby food jars are an ideal size for outings, although the glass must be carried with care. Put them inside hiking socks for padding, for instance, or other clothing — then remember where you've put them when you unpack or sling the pack to the ground. Don't take risks with unrefrigerated leftovers — try to use an entire jar during one meal. You can also buy freeze-dried baby food if weight is an issue. Flakes of baby cereal are easy trail food; just pour what you need into a Ziploc bag and have safe water on hand. Many tiny tidbits, such as zwieback and Cheerios, are a snap to pack — just think of them as baby GORP.

Utensils and Accessories

Remember a baby-sized spoon, and a plastic, wipeable bib, along with plenty of paper towels or wipes for cleanup. For toddlers, take a sippy cup.

As for feeding and high chairs, they're not a necessity. On most car-camping trips when Will was an infant, we simply put his car seat on top of a picnic table and fed him there. On the trail, he sat in our laps. During one lunch on a White Mountain ridge, the three of us had a fine time as we sat in the shade, took in the scenery, and watched other hikers pass by.

On a few car-camping trips we took a plastic, portable high chair (ours is made by Safety 1st and cost about $20). This wasn't simply Will's traveling chair — it's all we used at

♥

P A R E N T - T O - P A R E N T

DEHYDRATING BABY FOOD

If your child is at the jars-of-mush stage and you have a home dehydrator, pour baby food onto a Teflex sheet and make a leather. You can quickly reconstitute this with a little boiling water.

Kate Gregory — Ontario, Canada

home, too. The seat buckles onto a regular chair and is a lifesaver whenever we travel or visit friends for meals. On a camping trip when he was almost two, Will got a thrill out of sitting at the picnic table like a "big boy" for snacks, but we enjoyed buckling him into his portable chair at mealtime — the restraint helped keep him still and occupied.

PAT BELL'S SKILLET BROWNIES

Veteran canoe camper and mother of four Patricia J. Bell recommends this family favorite. More of her recipes can be found in her book, *Roughing It Elegantly: A Practical Guide to Canoe Camping* (Cat's Paw Press).

1 box brownie mix
Water, as called for in directions

Use directions on the box for the amount of water, and ignore the called-for egg. Stir well and dump into a very well-greased skillet, preferably one with a non-stick finish. Cook over a brisk fire, stirring, especially after bubbles start to appear around the edges. Keep stirring; after a while the mix begins to resemble fudge. When the aroma is strong, the stuff can be considered done, and in the language lore of our house, "We'll eat it anyway!"

FOR ADULTS

365 FOODS KIDS LOVE TO EAT, by Sheila Ellison and Judith Gray (*Sourcebooks*).

✳ COOKING THE ONE BURNER WAY: GOURMET CUISINE FOR THE BACKCOUNTRY CHEF, by Melissa Gray and Buck Tilton (*ICS Books*). The best outdoor cookbook I've seen.

✳ GORP, GLOP & GLUE STEW: FAVORITE FOODS FROM 165 OUTDOOR EXPERTS, by Yvonne Prater and Ruth Dyer Mendenhall (*The Mountaineers*).

NANCY CLARK'S SPORTS NUTRITION BOOK, by Nancy Clark (*Leisure Press*).

✳ THE NOLS COOKERY: EXPERIENCE THE ART OF OUTDOOR COOKING, by the National Outdoor Leadership School Staff (*Stackpole*).

PLAY HARD, EAT RIGHT: A PARENTS' GUIDE TO SPORTS NUTRITION FOR CHILDREN, by Debbi Sowell Jennings and Suzanne Nelson Steen (*Chronimed Publishing*; originally published under

another name by the American Dietetic Association).

✳ THE WELL-FED BACKPACKER, by June Fleming (*Random House*).

FOR KIDS

✳ ACORN PANCAKES, DANDELION SALAD AND 38 OTHER WILD RECIPES, by Jean Craighead George (*HarperCollins,* grades 4 and up). Beautifully illustrated by Paul Mirocha, this intriguing book contains recipes for berry leather, berry milk punch, dandelion fritters, and violet soup.

THE BROWN BAG COOKBOOK: NUTRITIOUS PORTABLE LUNCHES FOR KIDS AND GROWN-UPS, by Sara Sloan (*Williamson*, grades 4 and up). There's more to life than peanut butter and jelly.

✳ COOKING ON A STICK: CAMPFIRE RECIPES FOR KIDS, by Linda White (*Gibbs Smith*, ages 7 and up). A must-have book for camping kids.

THE PEANUT BUTTER COOKBOOK FOR KIDS, by Judy Ralph and Ray Gompf (*Hyperion*, grades 2 and up). Although not a trail book, it's filled with plenty of edible ideas that can be taken on the road.

NATURE
DISCOVERY

*Another spring had come to the Chesapeake country. The weeping
willows were green again. The boy cut himself a long switch. He
broke a twig from a sassafras tree and sniffed its fragrance.*

*The creek was quiet but there was plenty to see. Periwinkles
slowly climbed the marsh reeds; clams stuck their noses out of the
mud; a turtle that was sunning itself on a log slipped into the water.*

Gilbert Byron, *Chesapeake Duke*

Like most tourists, I traveled to Sequoia National Park in California to see the magnificent Sequoias. Not all, however, come in search of grandeur. At one visitor center, I heard an intent foreign visitor inquire, "Where is the best place to see chipmunks?"

Nature's allure is in the eye of the beholder. And when the beholders are kids, especially young ones, their interests are likely to

The market is awash in gadgets designed to help kids observe nature up close *and* far away. Some, like this Magniscope, are reasonably priced and great fun (see "In Focus," page 71).

resemble those of a foreign visitor to a new land. What may be common and mundane to you may be extraordinary to them. Tonight Will exclaimed over a stray patch of clover in our yard as though they were as glorious as Rocky Mountain wildflowers.

Sadly, each generation seems to be further removed from nature than the previous generation. Our children probably spend less time roaming freely outdoors than we did as kids. They're busy with such things as computer games, soccer matches, and gymnastic meets. As parents, we need to make sure they have plenty of opportunities to explore and experience nature on their own.

START WITH WONDER

A good many adults rely on Thoreau's *Walden* as their bible of the natural world. For family adventurers, I recommend an essay by Rachel Carson first published as "Help Your Child to Wonder" in the *Women's Home Companion* in July 1956. After the author's death in 1964, Harper & Row published her article as a book called

✳ *The Sense of Wonder*. The Harper & Row edition is out of print, but the Nature Company has its own edition, available only through its stores and mail-order business, but *not*, unfortunately, in bookstores.

Carson, best known for her groundbreaking book *Silent Spring*, neither married nor had children, but her insights on introducing children to nature are both practical and philosophical. She starts her essay on a stormy night along the Maine coast: high drama she shared with her 20-month-old nephew, Roger:

> Out there, just at the edge of where-we-couldn't-see, big waves were thundering in, dimly seen white shapes that boomed and shouted and threw great handfuls of froth at us. Together we laughed for pure joy — he a baby meeting for the first time the wild tumult of the Oceans, I with the salt of half a lifetime of sea love in me. But I think we felt the same spine-tingling response to the vast, roaring ocean and the wild night around us.

Carson's eloquence continues, her prose as exquisite as the subject about which she writes. The heart of her message, which can be read in one sitting, is this:

If I had influence with the good fairy who is supposed to preside over the christening of all children I should ask that her gift to each child in the world be a sense of wonder so indestructible that it would last throughout life, as an unfailing antidote against the boredom and disenchantments of later years, the sterile preoccupation with things that are artificial, the alienation from the sources of our strength.

If a child is to keep alive this inborn sense of wonder without any such gift from the fairies, he needs the compan-

ionship of at least one adult who can share it, rediscovering with him the joy, excitement and mystery of the world we live in.

The reverse is equally true: If an *adult* is to keep this sense of wonder alive, a child is an invaluable guide. On a recent walk with Will, he saw

IN FOCUS

✐ During outings — and life in general — we want to give our children the ability to see beyond themselves, to appreciate the world's beauty and mysteries. But it's not so simple as "Won't you look at that? Isn't that a grand sight?"

With kids, props are a wonderful lure: magnifying glasses, microscopes, binoculars, telescopes. Not only do they give children a sense of purpose and help ward off boredom, they're a physical reminder that they're supposed to be *looking*.

MAGNIFYING GLASSES Kids love small things, small spaces. Help them find a cozy spot — by a tree, perhaps, or on the banks of a

continued on page 72

stream. Ask them to look and listen. How many different things can they find once they start looking closely? Look everywhere: up, down, around, over and under. Find bugs, flowers, plants, moss. Lift up rocks.

BINOCULARS Great for spotting birds, animals, treetops, vistas, or a family member in the distance. Increase use by playing your own ranger game: Who can spot a hawk? Are there people on that trail down there? Where's that squirrel going? Keep your own binoculars handy and give each child an inexpensive pair to avoid squabbles. Also, binoculars are better than telescopes for night skywatching with kids; telescopes have too narrow a field of view.

TELESCOPES Telescopes shouldn't be missed, but don't forget the old-fashioned method of stargazing. As one mother told me,

"Sometimes it's more fun to just walk down the road and lie down than to have all the equipment."

GEAR Start with inexpensive equipment made just for kids so there's less at stake if things are broken or lost. Educational Insights has several lenses for young explorers:

● Bright, lightweight 4x40 binoculars with a focus mechanism easily operated by small fingers ($10).

● The Magniscope, a handheld 30X microscope with a light and "MicroAquarium," a small attachment that allows water to be examined (under $20).

● The 19-piece MultiScope, which can be assembled as either a 30X microscope, telescope, or spectroscope, for turning a light source into a prism ($15).

● The Cosmic Observer, a compact 50X telescope, perfect for car-camping trips, with a short tripod and a light-up "star finder base" with moon and star maps, plus a built-in compass ($90).

the sunlight sparkling on a river and said, "Mommy, flashing lights."

LEARNING TO SEE

The best way to learn about nature is to step outside and open your eyes, then enhance the experience with books and teachers. For starters, try the writings of Tom Brown and Joseph Cornell.

Stop, Look, Listen

Have you ever fantasized about surviving off the land for a week — no backpack or gear, just you and your wits? I have. As a kid I loved to read survival dramas; as an adult, I'd like to learn more of the necessary skills and lore.

Tom Brown is an expert on the subject, and teaches others through his books and survival school in New Jersey. As he describes in *The Tracker*, he learned wilderness skills from an Apache medicine man, Stalking Wolf, the grandfather of a friend. Under Stalking Wolf's tutelage, Tom says he and his friend practically lived in the New Jersey Pine Barrens, rising, for instance, before dawn to lie still in the grass until birds swooped down to eat from their extended palms. They built their own cabin and learned to track, stalk, hunt, and survive.

Brown turned his boyhood passion for nature into a career, tracking missing people and criminals, teaching and writing. *The Tracker* reads a bit like a novel, the fulfillment of the dream many of us share of being completely at home with nature. His message: Open up your

Increase your children's vision by letting them use grown-up quality binoculars — under supervision. Teach them *always* to place the strap around their necks.

senses to nature; begin by sitting down, staying still, and simply observing.

Brown doesn't think occasional weekend camping trips or canoe outings are enough. He writes: "For most of us, it seems, Saturday is a mad rush to get to our wilderness destination and Sunday is a mad rush to get back. Very little time is actually spent *being* there. Very little time is spent experiencing."

Brown makes an excellent point. It's all too easy to become so focused on gear, snacks, guidebooks, packing packs and packing the car, mileage, and so on that we miss the proverbial forest. Sometimes the very things we think will help us, such as guidebooks, can become distractions, mere props. If you worry that such is the case with you and your family, just remember a simple lesson from first grade: Stop, look, and listen.

Nurture Nature Awareness

Joseph Cornell is an educator who

ARMED FOR ADVENTURE

✎ Kids love *stuff*, and there's plenty of adventure paraphernalia designed just for them. Some of the most imaginative I've come across are ✳ Wild Planet Toys' I.N. Gear items (I.N. stands for Investigate Nature). This colorful, hip expedition equipment is made for kids ages four and older.

Start with the *Trek Pak* "carry-anything belt," which includes a compass, magnifier, net, tweezers, activity cards, and collection cup, along with loops for other I.N. Gear items. The toys are available at Toys "R" Us, Natural Wonders, FAO Schwarz, as well as other stores. If I were a kid, I'd want 'em all:
ADVENTURE TOOL Modeled after a Swiss Army knife, this plastic version has a scooper, tweezers, magnifying glass, and serrated scraper.

BUGSCAPES At last, tiny condos for the insect crowd! These clever bug viewers come in different settings: city, desert, and kitchen.
CANTEEN COMBO The top of this canteen is a compass; the bottom has a storage compartment for snacks.
COLLECT-A-KIT Several compartments, tweezers, and a portable museum.
DISCOV-R–SCOPE A kaleidoscope with four compartments for filling with such finds as pebbles, sand, flowers, or leaves.
FIELD LIGHT Features a flexible neck for easy viewing.
MEGASCOPE A 2-in-1 telescope and microscope.
SIGNAL GLOVE Looks like a flashy biking glove, but has a sound alert, LED light button, and a "finger blast" whistle.
PERISCOPE 360 For underwater vision.

has developed a variety of nature activities for everyone from preschoolers to adults. Start with ✳ *Sharing Nature with Children*, a treasure of a book that describes 42 games and rightly bills itself as "The Classic Parents' and Teachers' Nature Awareness Guide." The games are simple and fun, with names like Wild Animal Scramble, Caterpillar Walk, Noah's Ark, and Wildmen in the Alders. If you're looking for activities for the backyard, a camping trip, or even a birthday party, look no further.

Cornell has developed a cottage industry of nature publications and products, all published by Dawn Publications (800-545-7475). He also founded Sharing Nature Foundation, through which he gives nature awareness workshops (14618 Tyler Foote Road, Nevada City, CA 95959; 916-292-3893).

Be forewarned: Cornell has developed his own jargon — handy for some but a turnoff for others, and his voice sometimes sounds like Mr. Rogers. Both Rogers and Cornell, however, offer a wealth of wisdom for families. I attended one of Cornell's workshops and enjoyed it.

There's a sequel to *Sharing Nature*, called *Sharing the Joy of Nature*, in addition to children's picture books, adult books, cassettes, and videos. I also highly recommend ✳ *Journey to the Heart of Nature*, an exceptional workbook for ages nine and up, an intriguing course of study and activities the whole family can share.

THE NAME GAME

As soon as children learn to speak, they want to know the names of things. Names are more than labels; they're our way of taking in and understanding the world, and, most certainly, nature.

Learning them can help your child become more observant. Once a child can identify such species as maples, elms, oaks, birch, and beech, for example, forests become more than just a collection of trees.

Such lessons are ideal during rambles, canoeing, or biking trips, keeping kids' minds active as well as their bodies. Once a child nears school age, these talks can be the starting point for examining the differences between, say, deciduous trees and evergreens, or among various evergreens — pines, spruces, and hemlocks. Carson gives specific advice on this subject in *The Sense of Wonder:*

child into a walking, talking little field guide, better to give him or her enthusiasm and an eye for detail and beauty. Once these have been tapped, vocabulary develops in due course. Help things along by:

Young Ben Wiltsie waits for action from a crawfish, or crawdad, captured in Lake of the Woods, Ontario, Canada.

When Roger has visited me . . . I have made no conscious effort to name plants or animals nor to explain to him, but have just expressed my own pleasure in what we see, calling his attention to this or that but only as I would share discoveries with an older person. Later I have been amazed at the way names stick in his mind . . . I am sure no amount of drill would have implanted the names so firmly as just going through the woods in the spirit of two friends on an expedition of exciting discovery.

As Carson suggests, thrill, don't drill. Instead of trying to turn your

- Waiting for signals that a child is interested: comments like "That's pretty," or "Hey, look at this!" You can also spark interest by pointing out things your child might miss.

- Giving a child a *reason* to remember a name. Instead of simply pointing out a woolly bear caterpillar, for example, explain that, according to superstition, the wider the caterpillar's brown stripe, the milder the coming winter will be. Explain that the prediction is often accurate, although scientists don't understand why.

- Scouring field guides for names and features that will catch your kids' attention, such as doll's eye (a plant with beady-looking, poisonous berries) or witches' butter (a bright yellow fungus). For instance, kids are apt to remember:

HELICOPTERS Throw the seeds of

maples into the air and watch them spin like helicopter propellers as they sail to the ground.

HONEYSUCKLE Your kids will love sucking its nectar.

JEWELWEED Also known as "touch-me-not," a plant whose seed pods "explode" with a harmless touch in late summer and early fall.

MILKWEED Its fruit pods are filled with silky, tufted seeds that look like cotton, but beware, its milky sap is somewhat toxic.

WATER LILIES While adults think of Monet and Japanese gardens and art, kids see them as boats, or stepping-stones for frogs and bugs. Show your kids their roots, which can be up to 10 feet long.

HOW TO SENSE THE WONDER

In addition to philosophical musings, Rachel Carson suggests a number of activities in *The Sense of Wonder*, including:

She and her nephew devised what they called "the Christmas tree game." Amid a crop of young spruce trees, Rachel would point to, for instance, a seedling and say, that must be a Christmas tree for the squirrels. She would then describe how the squirrels might decorate their tree and celebrate. An even smaller tree might be a Christmas tree for bugs, a bigger one a tree for the rabbits.

On nights from midsummer until fall, she and Roger took flashlights into the garden and hunted for members of the "insect orchestra."

On an October night she and Roger found a quiet place and listened for migrating birds. If the moon was full, they used a telescope to watch migrating birds fly across the face of the moon (a good pair of binoculars will also work). This is an exercise requiring patience, Carson warns.

♄

Deer share a common origin
with giraffes, who also have
cloven hooves. The deer family
(Cervidae) includes not only
deer, but caribou, elk, goats,
moose, and sheep. In addition
to having cloven hooves and
ruminant (four-chambered)
stomachs, these are the only
animals to grow antlers.

● Learning *with* your child. Take a
guidebook with you. And if you *still*
can't identify something that catches
your child's eye, remember enough
details so that both of you can track
down the identity once you're home.
In fact, the research may prove so
enjoyable that you'll want to find a
"mystery object" on every outing.

Field Guides

There are two schools of thought on
field guides for kids. Some believe
children should use those specifically
designed for them; others simply
hand over an adult book. Once a
child is old enough to consult a
guide, they reason, they're old
enough to learn to use adult guides.

Explains writer and naturalist
Rebecca Rupp, "I'd rather just go for
an adult book. The kids' guides are
smaller and simpler, but, sure as

shooting, you're going to come across
racks of birds that aren't in the guides.
That's frustrating, and you're going to
have to use the adult guide anyway."

I'm firmly in the middle camp on
this issue. Many children's guides
contain good information presented
in an entertaining and enticing
manner. Kids will be attracted like
hummingbirds flying to bright colors.
Meanwhile, parents can lead them to
more information and adult field
guides as needed.

Perhaps the best guides for kids
are the ✳ *Peterson First Guides*,
simplified versions of the famous
Peterson Field Guides, on the following subjects: astronomy, birds,
butterflies and moths, caterpillars,
clouds and weather, dinosaurs,
fishes, insects, mammals, reptiles
and amphibians, rocks and minerals,
seashores, shells, the solar system,
trees, urban wildlife, and wildflowers.
These books are simple enough to
entice a school-age child, yet informative enough for the entire family.
Your family may also enjoy:
● *Golden Guides*. Longtime favorites
on everything from rocks to stars, by
Golden Press.
● *Nature Club* series, Troll Associates. Paperback titles for elementary
school children, with titles such as
Animal Journeys and *Fossil Detective*.
● Usborne Books publishes a
number of notable series: *First
Nature* for ages 5 and up; *Mysteries &
Marvels* (ages 8–12), with titles
including *Reptile World* and *Plant*

Life; and Spotters' Guides for adults and children, on such things as cats, dogs, rocks, and trees.

If you really want to turn your kids on to nature, you'll need more than field guides, which provide only enough information for identification, along with some bare-bones details. To get to the real heart of the matter — the information that makes your kids think, wonder, and say, "Is that really true?" — you need books, activities, and outings crammed with "nature bait" for kids.

I'm especially fond of ✳ Tracker Packs (Thomson Learning, grades 4–9), with one volume on nature and the other on birds. They deserve an award for clever packaging; these guides are organized in loose-leaf binders and have built-in shoulder straps, which make them easy to tote on the trail. Tracker Packs are colorful, informative, and fun, a smattering of information that's not overwhelming.

Young naturalists will enjoy leafing through:

● My First Nature Treasury, by Lizann Flatt (Sierra Club Books for Children, ages 4–8).

● Dictionary of Nature, by David Burnie (Dorling Kindersley). 2,000 key words arranged thematically — a handy book for the entire family.

● The many books by Tom Brown. I especially recommend ✳ Tom Brown's Field Guide to Nature Observation and Tracking and ✳ Tom Brown's Field Guide to Nature and Survival for Children, both published

RELUCTANT NATURALISTS?

Don't push your kids. You can't force a kid to enjoy nature. If a kid's resisting, he's going to think of more and more reasons why he doesn't want to do this, and it's going to make things worse. If a kid's not interested, there's not much you can do until there's an open door or window. And once that window is open, don't stuff it too fast.

Paul Rezendes
tracker, photographer, writer
Athol, Massachusetts

for young children. They are for adults, teenagers, and adept readers with an interest in the serious study of nature. He has also written field guides to *Wilderness Survival, City and Suburban Survival, Living with the Earth, Wild Edible and Medicinal Plants*, and the *Forgotten Wilderness*.

To a child, even a gull can hold plenty of interest. Once you open your own eyes, you'll find that there is much to be learned about these ubiquitous, resourceful seabirds.

by Berkley Books. Despite the title of the latter, none of Brown's books is

DID YOU KNOW
Walking sticks are long, slender, plant-feeding insects that look like twigs, some as long as 7 inches. Once found only in the tropics and southern United States, they've migrated northward. A friend just spotted one in Vermont.

WILDLIFE

Kids love to see wild animals, whether it's a moose or a marmot. In the wild, though, you can't guarantee sightings. For that kind of certainty, you're better off at a zoo or drive-through park like Lion Country Safari.

Let's say you're in the Everglades, hoping to see an alligator. There's a fine line between building up excitement and interest in something you might see and setting the stage for disappointment if nothing turns up. With kids, it's always better to be surprised than discontented, so study up, be on the lookout, but promise nothing.

Increase your odds of seeing animals by checking with guidebooks and rangers to determine what you're likely to see and to pinpoint the best times and places for viewing, as well as potential dangers and precautions. Early morning and late evening feeding times are often best. Another key factor is seasonality. On a family trip to Novia Scotia, a friend discovered that few great blue whales and Atlantic puffins were around so late in the summer; in May or June sitings could be all but guaranteed.

Whether you're searching for rabbits, gators, whales, or other species, never get too close, and don't feed them. No matter how cute and harmless wild animals may seem, they can be dangerous (see

KID SCOUTS

When our son Jack was five, he longed to be a Boy Scout like his older brother, James. James told him, "You can't, you're too little." Jack shot back, "Well, I can be a Kid Scout." So we made up simple questions about seasons, native plants, birds, and ecological concerns, and when he answered correctly, we gave him small souvenirs or trail patches from park gift shops as a "merit" award for the trip.

Debra E. J. Robertson — Fresno, California

Chapter 12). Double-check with rangers about the current population. Sometimes one particularly frisky deer, raccoon, or other animal can cause problems at certain campsites.

LEARNING TO LOVE NATURE

Award-winning children's author Jean Craighead George spent much of her childhood exploring the banks and waters of the Potomac River. Her father, an entomologist for the U.S. Department of Agriculture, would frequently announce to the family: "Let's go up the river!"

"And up the river we would all go," George remembers. "We would fish and swim and fly hawks and collect and identify plants and butterflies. He taught my brothers and me which ones were edible, how to make stews from the clams and how to make fishhooks and lean-tos. It was a wonderful childhood.

"I look at kids today and believe they're missing half of life! They don't know what's out there. They really don't. That's a big gap in our understanding of ourselves. The way we come to understand ourselves is by identifying and knowing the other things on the earth."

If you don't see any wildlife, signs left by animals are the next best thing: tracks, scat, nests, claw marks on trees. Expert tracker Paul Rezendes shares such secrets in *Tracking & the Art of Seeing: How to Read Animal Tracks & Sign* (Camden House).

Birds

Beware, adventure fans. Bird-watching sounds like an ideal outing activity — and it can be — but sometimes the idea can flop. So warns Massachusetts Audubon Society scientist Robert Buchsbaum in his book * *Nature Hikes in the White Mountains* (Appalachian Mountain Club Books). Birds can be hard for kids to enjoy, he explains, because on hikes they're often seen

NATURE'S OWN ACTION HERO

When I was a boy in Scotland I was fond of everything that was wild, and all my life I've been growing fonder and fonder of wild places and wild creatures. . . . My earliest recollections of the county were gained on short walks with my grandfather when I was perhaps not over three years old.

John Muir
The Story of My Boyhood and Youth

The more I learn about John Muir, the more fascinated I become. His 76 years are filled with so many adventures, not to mention eccentricities, that he's an ideal subject for bedtime and campfire tales. And since he's one of the pioneers of the U.S. conservation movement, you can sneak any number of valuable lessons into the tales.

His legion of admirers has included the late Supreme Court justice William O. Douglas, who wrote a children's biography called *Muir of the Mountains* (Sierra Club Books for Children, ages 8–11). Adult readers may want to start with Linnie Marsh Wolfe's Pulitzer Prize–winning *Son of the Wilderness: The Life of John Muir* (University of Wisconsin Press). Muir himself wrote numerous essays and several books about his experiences, including * *The Story of My Boyhood and Youth, My First Summer in the Sierra,* and *Our National Parks.* Older kids will enjoy these as well as a short classic called * *Stickeen: A Story of a Dog,* an excellent choice for a family read-aloud. Stickeen was a small black dog who accompanied Muir on a trip to Alaska in 1880; he's one of those dog heroes as appealing as Lassie and Rin-Tin-Tin.

and not heard.

"Kids don't always like them," Buchsbaum says. "I'll be on a boat jumping up and down about the birds going by, and they hardly notice. But show them a slimy fish that they can get their hands on, or something like that, and they're hooked."

To pique a child's interest, Buchsbaum recommends pointing out "either big birds of open spaces and wetlands, such as hawks, herons, and ducks, or sassy, tame birds like gray jays and chickadees." (He's right about those jays. On several White Mountain summits, I've had personal experience with very friendly jays. They were so bold they practically ate from our hands.)

Often the best place to watch birds is at home, not on the trail. Set up a backyard or window feeder and keep the field guides nearby. Another option is going owling, venturing out at night to try to hear their calls. For inspiration, read Jane Yolen's classic picture book, * Owl Moon (ages 4–8), the story of a father and child walking in the woods on a winter night. Yolen offers these additional tips:
● Study up on owls and their habitat beforehand.

BIRDS OF A FEATHER LEAVE TOGETHER

I don't think we've ever gone out hiking deliberately saying, "We're now going to go look for birds." If we happen on something, that's great, but we've never been looking for birds, not seen any, and gotten frustrated. With little kids who get loud and excited, any bird with a lick of sense is long gone.

Rebecca Rupp, author of *Everything You Never Learned about Birds*
Shaftsbury, Vermont

● Listen to Audubon owl tapes so you can learn to distinguish their voices.
● Dress warmly.
● Remember, sometimes there's an owl and sometimes there isn't.

One of the best books I've come across, for both children and adults, is Rebecca Rupp's * *Everything You Never Learned about Birds* (Storey Publishing, ages 9–99). Open a page anywhere, and you'll find something interesting, including discussions of lore and legends, as well as project suggestions. Rupp is an excellent writer with an imaginative approach.

The following books will also help your birdwatching efforts: *Everybody's Everywhere Backyard Bird Book* (Klutz Press, ages 8 and

BIRDING TIPS FROM AN EXPERT

When I started writing the bird book, we began keeping a bird list on the refrigerator, so every time someone saw and identified a bird, they'd write it down. Pretty soon we had the binoculars and field guides out all the time, and were really paying attention. We spotted a pileated woodpecker, which are spectacular. It only takes one or two special birds to get your kids excited.

We've also had lots of fun listening to birdcalls on cassettes. Even the birds seem to find some of the calls hysterical. I always imagined that eagles had dramatic shrieks. But when we saw and heard one, we realized that our national symbol squeaks. Our boys were just appalled.

Rebecca Rupp, author of *Everything You Never Learned about Birds*
Shaftsbury, Vermont

up). This small, plastic-coated, spiral-bound volume is easy to carry into the field, and is packaged with an Audubon birdcall device.

The Great Bird Detective, by David Elcome (Chronicle Books). Few will be able to resist this extraordinarily clever guide in the form of a small loose-leaf "casebook." Plenty of useful information, fun facts, blank record sheets, and sections entitled "Detective's Database," "On the Case," "Snoop's Dossier," and "Stickers."

✳ *She's Wearing a Dead Bird on Her Head!* by Kathryn Lasky (Hyperion, ages 5–9). A fanciful yet fact-based account of the birth of the Massachusetts Audubon Society. A wonderful book!

Urban Roosts: Where Birds Nest in the City, by Barbara Bash (Sierra Club Books for Children, ages 6–10).

Bugs

You may never see a fox or a rabbit when you take your kids into the wild, but you can be pretty darn sure you'll see, and perhaps swat, some bugs. For instance, ants are everywhere, except cold places like mountaintops and the North and South Poles. Edward O. Wilson calls them "the little things that run the world." There are almost 9,000 recognized species; no doubt several are near, probably inside, your home. Have your kids note the differences among those you spot; encourage them to make drawings and keep notes.

Yes, insects are often a nuisance, but they're also one of the easiest living things for kids to observe. Buy a bug viewer or make your own. Instead of making your kids squeamish, stimulate their curiosity with:

✳ *Big Bugs*, by Jerry Booth (Harcourt Brace, ages 8–12). I love this one: a big book filled with information, great illustrations, and plenty of

EVERYTHING YOU NEVER LEARNED ABOUT BIRDS
Lore & Legends • Science &
Hands-On Projects
Rebecca Rupp
Illustrated by Jeffrey C.

Ben Wiltsie comforts an injured golden finch at Lake of the Woods, Ontario. The farther you trek from civilization, the more intimate — and memorable — your encounters with wildlife are likely to be.

activities. Want to bake Chocolate Chirpies? You'll need 1/2 cup of dry roasted crickets. You'll also learn how to track bees and build a caterpillar cage.

Creepy Crawlies Kid Kit (Usborne Books, ages 6 and up). Contains book and bug viewer with sliding magnifying glass.

PRESERVING AND PROTECTING

Most kids get healthy doses of ecology in school — today's topics seem to be Reading, Writing, and Rain Forest. Ecological boot camp, however, takes place during family outings, where habits are practiced and passed on, so make sure to practice what you preach.

Once on the trail, be on the lookout for subjects that encourage environmental conversations. Take, for instance, the subject of parks and trails that have been abused or overused. Remind your child that the woods are home to many animals, plants, and trees, then ask her to imagine the effects of hundreds, even thousands, of people tromping through her bedroom.

The essence of minimum-impact outings isn't complicated at all, as Karen Berger points out in *Hiking & Backpacking: A Complete Guide:*

Remember kindergarten?
Pick up your toys.
Clean up your mess.
Leave things as you found them.

The current mantra for people of all ages is: Leave only footprints, take only pictures. Once kids get the hang of that refrain, they can move on to more detailed verses of their own ecological anthem. You'll have to drill a few ideas into your children, some that initially seem confusing: Yes, we can pick flowers at home, but we mustn't pick wildflowers in parks. You're right, this does look like a great camping site, but we aren't allowed to camp here or we might cause damage.

From time to time plan a family outing that focuses on protecting and preserving: Visit a fragile alpine habitat, a polluted river or lake, an area that's been preserved or re-claimed, even a trash-strewn road-side. Each spot has lessons to offer. A national park, for instance, may demonstrate both the importance of preservation and the dilemmas of overuse.

When Will is a few years older we'll give him an ecology lesson on the nearby Nashua River. Not long ago its waters ran orange, green, or blue, depending on the activities of a paper mill that dumped waste there.

WET AND WONDERFUL WATER

✐ Whether it's a mud puddle, creek, pond, river, lake, ocean, sink, or bathtub, kids love to explore and play in water. When I was a kid, the creek behind my house in Richmond, Virginia, was better than any playground. Try to include as many water sites as possible in your outings (always respecting its inherent dangers, of course). Since about 70 percent of the earth's surface is covered with water, finding it shouldn't be much of a problem. Once there, be prepared for 100 percent of your child to be wet!

Water, by Frank Asch (Harcourt, ages 3–7). Simple text accompanied by gorgeous illustrations, tracing water from rain and dew to floods and oceans.

Water, Water Everywhere, by Mark J. Rauzon and Cynthia Overbeck Bix (Sierra Club Books for Children, ages 6–9). Photographs and a more advanced discussion of our "water planet."

Along came Marion Stoddart, a resident of our town who convinced politicians, mill executives, and other citizens to revitalize the dying waterway. Thanks to the efforts she started, the river now runs clear and is home to fish, herons, owls, and other wildlife.

Last summer Will took his first of many canoe rides there, and each year we can continue to care for the river by pitching in on special clean-up days. Lynn Cherry's wonderful picture book, ✳ *A River Ran Wild* (Gulliver Green, Harcourt, ages 6–10), traces the Nashua from its unsettled days through Stoddart's renewal campaign.

No matter where you live, people and history have changed the land, and there's a story waiting to be told, a spot that needs protecting. It's all well and good to know about the Brazilian rain forests, but families need to make conservation part of their daily lives. Find a way to become involved in your town.

For a sophisticated look at some of nature's special wonders, try

The Old Man of the Woods sports a handsome lichen beard. There is a fine line between keeping kids from removing too many "souvenirs," and unnecessarily preventing them from touching the world around them.

Between Earth & Sky: Legends of Native American Sacred Places (Harcourt, all ages), by Joseph Bruchac, a storyteller of Abenaki heritage. Included are short discussions of the Rocky Mountains, El Capitan, Mesa Verde, the Grand Canyon, and Nia-

RINGS AROUND THE TREE

Turn your child into a dendrochronologist (one who studies tree rings) with the *Tree Rings Hands-On Nature Kit* from Educational Insights (ages 9 and up). Included are a cross section from a ponderosa pine, an activity book, poster, pine tree seeds, and a magnifying glass. While there are a zillion general nature kits out there, this one is unusually well focused.

Rock can be fun to climb and walk over, as long as it isn't too slippery.
Big boulders like this one that are out in the sun are kept clean by rains and cleared by wind. They look bare and bald. But in the places where windblown dust and other debris collects, soil is created. And in that thin layer of soil, tiny plants and seedling trees

There's a miniature forest in this crack!

Crinkleroot's Guide to Walking in Wild Places, by Jim Arnosky, is one of the author's favorite nature guides.

gara Falls, all gorgeously illustrated by Thomas Locker. As Bruchac explains, this "is a book about some of the special places that are sacred to native people. It is also about learning *where* and *how* to look. When we learn this, we will not miss seeing the beauty that is around us as we walk between Earth and Sky."

Collecting or Stealing?

Kids love to collect. Rocks. Shells. Flowers. Bugs. You name it.

Fifty years or so ago, few people worried about the effects of collecting. Taking specimens home — even animals — was common practice, among naturalists as well as tourists.

Today, however, with more and more people flocking to the wild, the impact adds up. You may think one or two rocks won't be missed, but if everyone who visits takes something home, soon the effects are not only noticeable, but damaging. For instance, each year visitors to Petrified Forest National Park in Arizona pocket an estimated 12 tons of petrified wood. This, despite numerous warnings not to, and the fact that such criminal violation carries a minimum fine of $275.

Spell out the rules to your kids. Parklands belong to everyone, and must be preserved so that everyone, whether today or 100 years from now, can enjoy them. All things that live, grow, or lie in the park must stay there. If children still have questions about whether particular objects can be collected, suggest they ask a ranger.

Here's the word from Greg Caffey, assistant chief ranger at Petrified Forest National Park: "You can pick up things like rocks and twigs and look at them, but put them back. Don't take anything — period. Anything you take away changes the makeup of the park."

The restrictions may seem draconian, but they're important. If kids want to collect rocks or other things, they

Climbing on cliff-side Banyon tree roots, Oahu, Hawaii. Fortunately, for most children, climbing on yellow birch roots clinging to a granite cliff 10 miles from home provides equal excitement.

WILDLIFE FACT OR FICTION?

Nature folklore abounds, from the bands on woolly caterpillars that purportedly predict the severity of the coming winter to the English superstition that porcupines milk cows at night. Kids love this kind of lore regardless of its accuracy. I still remember the first time someone held a buttercup under my chin and said that if the yellow reflects on your chin, you like butter. Brush up on ancient and modern beliefs with *Wildlife Folklore*, by Laura C. Martin (Globe Pequot Press).

?

DID YOU KNOW

Animals have their own highway system. The main routes are called trails, which sometimes serve several species. Tom Brown has found trails he believes deer have been using for more than 200 years. Less frequently used paths are called runs; they connect trails to areas where animals can eat, drink, or rest.

need to do it at home, on their own turf.

You might be able to soften the blow by telling them the story of the Polynesian fire goddess, Pele, believed to inhabit the crater of Kilauea Volcano in Hawaii Volcanoes National Park. Visitors here are told that it's unwise to take away pieces of lava because the loss upsets Pele and will result in bad luck. A friend of mine couldn't resist, despite the warnings, but soon found that ill fortune did seem to haunt her. She mailed the lava rock back, only to discover that she is one of many guilty souls — parcels of rocks arrive at the ranger station every day!

Smooth

TIGER SWALLOWTAIL 1½ in
The newly hatched caterpillar is brown, white and looks like a bird dropping; as it matures, however, the larva becomes smooth and green, enlarged in the head. 2 orange eyespots and a yellow band. caterpillar may be hard to find because it usually feeds high in the treetops, making shelter by folding the edges of a leaf together. It feeds on tree leaves, including willow, cherry, tulip tree, poplar, basswood, and birch. Just before pupating, the larva may turn brown. The chrysalis is suspended from a twig or other support for overwintering. The egg is round and yellow-green. The adult is one of our most familiar butterflies. It is a very large (up to 6 inches) high-flying insect, yellow with black tiger stripes. The female has a dark form in which the yellow is mostly replaced by black. The long "tails" on its hindwings give the family its name. The Tiger Swallowtail is found in the eastern half of the United States including most of the Great Plains. The similar Western Tiger Swallowtail is found west of the Rockies.

** _ISH SWALLOWTAIL** To 1½ inch
_ spicebush and sassafras _ _ry woods, gaps

TIGER SWALLOWTAIL

SPICEBUSH SWALLOWTAIL

90

NATURE ROUNDUP

There is such an overwhelming number of nature books for kids, that I'm reminded of that Mae West quote: "When I'm good, I'm good, but when I'm bad, I'm very bad." So it goes with children's nature books — while some are fabulous, others are downright boring.

Two of my favorite nature writers for children are Jim Arnosky and Jean Craighead George. Arnosky's many books provide sound information while teaching kids to observe, enjoy, respect, and reflect, all in an entertaining, yet evocative manner. Also an artist, he created Crinkleroot, a cheerful nature guide appearing in several books, such as CRINKLEROOT'S GUIDE TO WALKING IN WILD PLACES, and separate guides to birds, trees, butterflies, and animal tracking (*Simon & Schuster*, ages 4–10). Crinkleroot also has his own show on PBS, *Backyard Safari*.

Don't miss Arnosky's many other books such as SECRETS OF A WILDLIFE WATCHER (*Lothrup*, ages 8 and up) and IN THE FOREST (*Lothrup*, ages 6 and up), a gorgeous picture book the entire family can enjoy. In NEARER NATURE (*Lothrup*, ages 10 and up), Arnosky shares his reflections on a year spent tracking wildlife and tending to his Vermont farm.

Jean Craighead George is the author of more than 100 nature-related books for children, including picture books, nonfiction, and novels. She is best known for JULIE OF THE WOLVES, about a girl lost in the Arctic who befriends a pack of wolves, and MY SIDE OF THE MOUNTAIN, about a boy who lives in a hollowed-out tree for a year. Also check out ONE DAY IN THE WOODS (*Harper-Collins*, grades 4–7), about a girl's adventures, and two nonfiction series: ONE DAY IN THE (ALPINE TUNDRA, DESERT, TROPICAL RAIN FOREST, etc.) (*HarperCollins*, grades 5–7) and THE THIRTEEN MOON series, detailing the lives of 13 different animals (*Harper-Collins*, grades 3–7).

Some of the very best nature experiences simply happen, without any planning. However, a bit of structure can add excitement as well as variety to family outings. Scouting handbooks are a particularly good resource for nature-related games and "theme" hikes. In addition to scouting manuals, you'll never run out of information or inspiration with:

FOR ADULTS

✳ HANDS-ON NATURE: INFORMATION AND ACTIVITIES FOR EXPLORING THE ENVIRONMENT WITH CHILDREN, edited by Jenepher Lingelbach (*Vermont Institute of Natural Science*). The best nature activity book I've come across; this one contains more substance than the others. It's chock-full of creative activities, scientific information, puppet show scripts, and lists of suggested reading for children and adults.

continued on page 92

✳ 365 DAYS OF NATURE AND DISCOVERY: THINGS TO DO AND LEARN FOR THE WHOLE FAMILY (*Abrams*).
LET NATURE BE THE TEACHER, by Lucille N. Gertz (*Habitat Institute for the Environment*). This book is filled with activity suggestions from Gertz, director of children's programs at a Massachusetts nature center.

FOR KIDS

✳ THE KIDS' NATURE BOOK: 365 INDOOR/OUTDOOR ACTIVITIES AND EXPERIENCES, by Susan Milford (*Williamson Publishing*, ages 8 and up).
LOOK WHAT I DID WITH A LEAF!, by Morteza E. Sohi (*Walker*, ages 4–10). A craft book that explains how to use leaves to make collages. Sohi explains how to collect leaves in a low-impact way, and also provides a short field guide.
✳ NICKY THE NATURE DETECTIVE, by Ulf Svedberg (*R&S Books*, ages 4–10). This blond-haired girl is the heroine of one of the best nature books I've seen.

COLORING BOOKS

The National Wildlife Federation and the National Audubon Society have teamed up to produce an excellent series of PETERSON FIELD GUIDE COLORING BOOKS (*Houghton Mifflin*, ages 4 and up), on subjects ranging from birds to wildflowers.
Running Press has a START EXPLORING series (ages 4 and up), with volumes on forests and insects.

AND MORE...

NATURE KITS

EXPLORING NATURE (*Educational Insights*, ages 8 and up). Perform 21 experiments in this Nature Observation Lab.
NATURE WATCHING, by Paul Sterry (*Running Press*, ages 8 and up). This combination book and activity kit contains a naturalist's tray, insect observatory, tweezers, and three pull-out animal and bird identifiers.

CD-ROMS

EXPLORE YELLOWSTONE (*MECC*, Mac and Windows, ages 8 and up). Explore areas of the park, watch QuickTime movies, read the field guide, take a ranger's quiz.
✳ ONE SMALL SQUARE: BACKYARD (*Virgin*, Mac and Windows, ages 8 and up). Based on the Scientific American book of the same name, this exceptional CD-ROM allows kids to explore a three-dimensional ecosystem from every angle, in every season, above and below ground.

GAMES
AND
ACTIVITIES

And that was the beginning of the game called Poohsticks, which Pooh invented, and which he and his friends used to play on the edge of the Forest.

A. A. Milne, *The House at Pooh Corner*

Mom, I'm bored.
There's nothing to do, Dad.

Words to make a parent tremble. Kids don't even have to say them — just start to fidget, squabble, or mope. Whining sets in (if it hasn't already) and bigger trouble is likely to follow.

How to respond?

The worst, but most frequent, parental response is: "How can you possibly be bored?"

As a kid, I got used to entertaining myself; my two brothers are at least 10 years older than I am, not exactly playmates. Reading has always been a favorite, and when we went on trips, I'd cram an entire suitcase full of books and games. Inevitably, I took more than I needed.

Ben and Nick Wiltsie entertain themselves, if not their patient dog, Khampa.

Now I'm packing similar assortments for Will to stave off boredom in restaurants, on vacations, and especially during long car rides or plane trips. Sometimes I feel like a Happy Meal factory, doling out trinkets, both old and new, at the first sign of restlessness.

When kids are footloose outside, however, there's usually no need for such props. After all, the outdoors is an endless playground. Maybe you have one of those pricey, plastic playhouses in your backyard — we have a hand-me-down. Will plays in it from time to time, but things like pebbles, dirt, and bugs are bigger draws.

The upshot? Don't be too quick to pull out activities. Let your kids explore. They'll find

Paloma Painter

Sue Chef

Fannie Firefighter

their own fun. That's when they start using their imagination and inventing their own games, like Pooh and his Poohsticks. Once kids get busy building mud villages, making stick people, watching bugs, and assembling dandelion chains, you can sit back and relax.

Use the suggestions in this chapter as a grab bag of ideas for those moments when the natives are truly restless. In addition, there are more activities in Chapter 5, Nature Discovery. Each activity chapter also discusses strategies for keeping kids amused.

GETTING IN THE MOOD

On Will's second Christmas, when he was fourteen months old, my parents gave him a small wooden camper, a truck toting four peg people, two tents, a picnic table, and a canoe. Toys like this are a great way to build children's enthusiasm for camping and other outings.

Cruise toy store aisles with an eye for the outdoors. Nature is a huge theme for toy makers, and entire jungles of plastic animal figures are available. Many items in Disney's Pocahontas line, for instance, feature a tent and canoe, and there's the *Pocahontas Nature Guide: Woods and Wildlife*, by Gina Ingoglia (Disney Press, ages 7 and up). I've also had my eye on a Sesame Street camper set as a potential gift for Will.

If you've got some money to spend, check out Timiny Kids — boy and girl dolls distributed by International Playthings — you can get a top-rate camping play set that includes a nylon flap tent, two sleeping bags, two mattress pads, two backpacks, a backpacking stove, and

MUSIC AND GAMES FOR THE ROAD OR TRAIL

✍ The most popular on-the-road entertainment is music, whether homegrown or on the radio, tape, or CD. Several cassettes contain good trail or campfire songs and games — think of your car trip as a rehearsal for the trailside show:
● *Campfire Songs Car Songbook and Audiocassette* (Running Press). The goofball DJ of this sing-along collection is Uncle Bumpy Roads, whose play list includes "We're Tenting Tonight," "Down by the Riverside," "Do Your Ears Hang Low?," and "Good Night Ladies." If your kids like this one, they'll also like *Uncle Bumpy Roads Laugh-Along Car Jokebook*.
● *Nancy Cassidy's Hullabaloo* (Klutz Press). This set includes a tape, spiral-bound activity book with sturdy pages, and markers.

Songs include "Arise," "Rise and Shine," "Johnny B. Goode," and "Whoopy Ti Yi Yo." On the trail, use them for motivation: For instance, personalize the lyrics and turn "Johnny B. Goode" into a fight song for a tired hiker: "Go go, go [Steven], go go go! Go [Steven], go go go!"
● Klutz Press publishes a series of cassettes and songbooks called *KidSongs*, many of which are camp, scouting, and school classics.
● Valentine Productions in Norcross, Georgia, produces several cassette tapes of games, including *Games for the Road* and *More Games for the Road* for kids ages 5 and up. The first, for example, includes 23 games such as "Round Robin Story" (a good campfire activity) and a counting and memory game called "How Many Snakes" (excellent for hiking). Call 800-544-8322.

kitchenware. The same distributor markets Tibaby Doll, which kids can tote in its own backpack baby carrier.

A number of Playmobil figures and sets have outdoor themes as well, including cross-country cyclists, a sportsman's cabin with magnetic fish, family campers, a fast-water canoe, and horses and a pony ranch.

Turn your child's room or play area into a wildlife and exploration center, and your resident explorer will be ready to hit the trail.

TAKE THE TRAUMA OUT OF TRAVEL

"Getting there is half the fun."

Whoever coined that phrase was definitely childless.

For many families, getting there (and back) is the toughest part of all. Long trips, whether by car, train, bus, or plane, can be monotonous and confining, especially for kids.

Will is a good traveler, and getting better all the time. We take at least one eight-hour car ride each year, to see Jim's family in Maryland. Will made his first pilgrimage at Christmas, when he was two months old. Six months later we drove 16 hours to West Virginia for my parents' 50th anniversary celebration. In those early days, he slept a lot. Several times I practically forbade Jim to stop for gas because the interruption would awaken Will, but Jim overruled, insisting fuel was essential. Whenever Will was awake, I sat beside him in his car seat, handing him squeaky toy after squeaky toy, board book after board book.

Now he loves to watch the highway, peering at cars and trucks, two of his favorite things. When he's restless, I get in the back seat with him so we can read or play. Thankfully, the toys and books I hand him have become more interesting to me, their handler. They should get more interesting each year as Will's attention span increases, and when he eventually learns to read.

When that time comes, the first game I'll teach him is "Alphabet," the family favorite when I was a child. In this game, which everyone no doubt already knows, each player races to complete the alphabet by watching for letters on passing signs. To get elusive letters like J, Q, or X, we counted on the fairly frequent signs for Howard Johnson's, Quaker Oil, and exit.

Car Diversions = Trail and Camp Diversions

Think of the car as the modern-day campfire. Aside from the dinner table — which for some families is a hit-or-miss proposition — it's the one place families regularly gather without many other distractions. During long car rides there's time for reminiscing, singing, telling stories, and playing games.

Car and camping trips are also a great place to rediscover the joys of reading aloud. You'll be surprised at

GEAR TALK

THE GAME OF ALL GAMES

The best piece of recreational equipment you can take on *any* family vacation is small and lightweight and can be found in every house: a deck of cards.

Preschoolers can play "52 Pickup" and simple matching games. But once a child reaches age six or so, a whole world of delights await.

I spent hours playing "Spit," "War," and "Go Fish" with my friends, more time at home playing solitaire. We also all joined in for games of double and triple solitaire, revealing a competitive side of my grandmother I'd never seen before.

A book of card games is helpful for explaining new games and settling rule disputes. I can still picture the one I had, a small red paperback called *50 Solitaire Games for Children*. A few of today's batch include *The Klutz Book of Card Games* (which comes with a deck); *A Book of Cards for Kids*, by Gail MacColl (Workman, ages 4–9, also with its own deck); and a Level 3 easy reader called *Let's Play Cards! A First Book of Card Games* (Aladdin).

Two more great time-passing activities: card tricks and building houses of cards.

self read *Charlotte's Web* adds another dimension to its magic.

Many pastimes, such as "20 Questions" or "I Spy," work equally well while traveling by car, plane, foot, canoe, or bike, or lounging around a campfire. Hand games, such as thumb wrestling and "Paper, Scissors, Rock," are fun backseat diversions, as well as end-of-day campsite amusements.

To take a song from the road to the trail, for instance, make

When packing for any trip, whether car camping or backpacking, include for each child a few well-worn favorites like this comic book Nick Wiltsie is re-reading on the shores of a ranch pond in Wyoming.

how many stories and books will entertain the entire family, including adults. When your voice gives out, use books on tape. On a recent drive with Will, he stayed busy with a Winnie-the-Pooh booklet and tape, listening over and over again. Try classics like *Stuart Little*, the perfect traveling story. And hearing E. B. White him-

slight alterations to lyrics, such as changing the words of "100 Bottles of Pop on the Wall" to "100 Bottles of Bug Spray," or changing, "The Wheels on the Bus" to "The Wheels on the Bike."

Similarly, alter the theme of word games: "ABC Cities" becomes "ABC Mountains" or "ABC Rivers," in which you take turns naming rivers in alphabetical order, or naming as many rivers that begin with a certain letter, say "M." "Twenty Questions" and "I Spy" work well no matter where you are, at a beach or on top of Pike's Peak.

A game guaranteed to keep everyone on their toes is called "Don't Say That." Agree on a forbidden word, such as "I" or "my" or "tree." During ensuing conversations, try to trick other players into saying the prohibited word. Anyone who says it gets a penalty point.

Try some popular, portable trivia with the * *Brain Quest* series (Workman), decks of question-and-answer cards for a variety of ages and interests, ranging from toddlers to sixth graders, on sports, English, math, geography, and "weird stuff." *Brain Quest Extra for the Car*, for ages 7–12, contains backseat games and 1,100 questions and answers about America. Will enjoys the preschool deck, useful on our last trip to Maryland.

Today's bible on traveling with kids of any age is * *The Penny Whistle with Kids Book*, by Meredith Brokaw and Annie Gilbar (Simon & Schuster). Jam-packed with ideas, it offers suggestions for simple, fun games, stretching exercises, road trip recipes, and many useful resources, such as travel guides for kids, travel kits and activities, and children's museums across the country. Whether you're staying in a tent or a four-star

resort, this is an extraordinarily useful book.

The key to traveling is keeping kids busy. You can easily make a fairly inexpensive travel pack for your child, a backpack stuffed with surprises like coloring books, activity books, puzzle books, small toys, and snacks. Colorforms, stickers, stamps, and art supplies also work well.

My favorite store-bought kit is * *Kids Travel: A Backseat Survival Kit*, by the editors of Klutz Press. The book itself travels well; it's spiral bound with heavy cardboard covers. Included are games (with boards, playing pieces, and dice), car rituals and road games, hand games, word games, quizzes, instructions on palm reading, mysteries, tricks, songs, secret decoder wheels, and a 100-page activity book. Many are also fun in camp.

Another good kit is *Travel Fun* (DK Books, ages 5 and up). Included are game cards, an activity book and stickers, a magnetic game board, wipe-clean games and crayons, and a cat's cradle cord.

Card-game-turned-roughhousing at a High Sierra, California, campsite. With views like the one through this tent window beckoning, sibling tussles become almost endearing.

OUTDOOR FUN

Two weeks ago Will and I went to Chuck E. Cheese's for the first time. I hope it was our last. There, gathered under one ungodly noisy roof, was *everything* parents like to gripe about.

> Crowds.
> Commercialism.
> Manic moms and tots.
> Entertainment overload.
> Not to mention bad food.

It was even too much for Will, who made no protest when we left.

I'd rather spend an hour in the woods any day, even a rainy one. I think he would, too. We don't need flashing lights, tokens, or cardboard pizza. In fact, we don't need much more than an interesting spot.

Low-Tech Rec

Before you load up on gear, games, and glitz, don't underestimate the allure of the simple. While fads like Power Rangers, Ninja Turtles, and Pogs come and go, some things endure. Here are activities that don't cost a dime:

CLOUD GAZING Lie on your back. Look up. Imagine. Does that look like a horse? A car? You name it.

DIRT WRITING If you miss your answering machine, campsites are often the perfect venue for leaving messages, often things like: Hi mom, Katie was here, or Lance loves Lydia. You see these messages along trails too — just be sure not to hurt vegetation. Use the dirt as a game pad, too, for things like hangman or tic-tac-toe.

GRASSLAND BAND Turn a piece of grass into a whistle. Find a long, wide (this is important) blade, press it lengthwise between the sides of your thumbs, blow into the space below your knuckles. Keep the grass as taut as possible, readjusting until you find a position that works. You can also blow into the top of an acorn to make a whistle.

HAND SHADOWS Shine a flashlight and make a bunny, or any number of things, on the tent wall. Essential skills like this stick with you all your life — I can still make the head of a German shepherd. If you want to go beyond Basic Bunny, get *Shadow Games: A Book of Hand & Puppet Shadows* (Klutz Press).

HOPSCOTCH Find a rock for tossing and use a stick to draw in the dirt.

STONE SKIPPING For advanced stone tossers. Andy and Opie used to do this during the credits for Mayberry R.F.D. My husband is an expert, just waiting for Will to be old enough for

GRAB IT AT A GARAGE SALE

✎ Everybody loves a surprise, especially a bored child. It's helpful to have a secret stash of toys, books, and games for car trips and rainy days.

Instead of buying new stuff, recycle. Yard sales are a great place to pick up quality toys, books, and clothes, often for a dollar or less. Since Will came along, I've become a fanatic. The sales are a treasure hunt, offering not only bargain prices, but the thrill of unexpected finds. He now has several pairs of cross-country skis and poles, in varying sizes.

I've got a box of small toys and activities for our next vacation and car trip, including a viewfinder and slides, puzzles and games, a plastic bug set, Curious George books, and a lacing game — each item cost less than a dollar.

Look for ads that specify toys for sale. The number-one tip for success is get there early, first thing. Good things go fast.

lessons. Once you find a flat, round stone, Jim tells me, the secret is wrist action. Fling the rock as you would a small Frisbee, and hop, hop, plop!

STONE TOSSING There's a small fire pond down the hill from our house, and Will regularly heads for it like a fish going for water. Even a puddle will do.

SWIMMING Whether it's a pool, pond, lake, or ocean, many kids could spend the entire summer in the water. The goal: Stay in until your fingers are wrinkled and your lips blue. Ever play "Marco Polo"? It's a game of tag in which the person who's it keeps her eyes closed and periodically says, "Marco." Everyone answers "Polo," until "it" manages to tag someone.

TAG Another perennial favorite. We played endless versions, including freeze tag and TV tag. Just don't get too noisy for the neighbors, and don't trample fragile areas.

TREE CLIMBING One of my favorites.

Not just the climbing, but the sitting, watching, and musing. Kids can transform each limb into a personal fort.

WADING Great for a hot day, but kids don't care what the temperature is.

Easy, All-Time Favorites

Here are more classics, good for the trail, canoes, and camp. You'll need a little equipment, but not much; most equipment is small enough to fit in a backpack pouch.

When showing your kids the ropes, you're likely to be transported back to your own childhood. In case you need to brush up your skills, Klutz Press publishes guidebooks for many of these activities, many with the necessary items, such as a yo-yo or marbles. Workman Publishing also has several similar kits, including a jump rope and marbles.

BALLS Bring several, in different sizes. A game of catch, perhaps kick-ball, softball, or whiffle ball.

Take a Hike!, a board game invented by five-year-old hiker Derek Nelson, is a great hit with young kids (see page 104 for details).

BUBBLES Good for all ages. Today's bubble-blowing equipment comes in an amazing assortment.

BUCKETS Bring a sand shovel and net, and you're ready for sand, dirt, or water fun. Avoid squabbles by bringing a bucket for every child.

CAT'S CRADLE I did this for hours and hours as a kid. All you need is some string; a guidebook is useful.

FRISBEE Good for a simple game of catch or a Frisbee football match.

HACKY SACK These footbags are sold in outdoor stores everywhere.

JACKS Word on the street is that today's plastic jacks are more difficult to use than the old-fashioned metal kind, but still fun.

JUMP ROPE Cinderella, dressed in yellow, made a mistake, and kissed a snake . . .

KOOSH These soft plastic doodads weren't around in my day, but now they're a standard of modern childhood.

MARBLES Mine were hand-me-downs from my older brothers, a treasured collection I carried in a velveteen bag. A set satisfies a kids' urges to collect, trade, and play games.

NETS Vital for collecting on land (butterflies and bugs) or in water (fish and frogs).

PICKUP STICKS An excellent game of concentration and dexterity.

YO-YOS Can you walk the dog?

BORED? TRY A BOARD GAME

When it's raining cats and dogs, or everyone simply needs a quiet moment in the car or at the campsite, bring out the games. Toy stores carry travel versions of many favorite games, such as *Clue*, *Hangman*, and *Battleship*. These games are also useful on ferryboat rides and even whale-watch trips, in which you can have little to do for several hours.

University Games makes a series of travel-size and card games, including *Checkers*, *Cribbage*, *Chess*, *Truth or Dare*, *Go Fish for Letters*, and *The Sierra Club Matching Card Game*, in which players build pictures of endangered species. My favorite is *Old Bachelor*, featuring career characters such as Edna Editor, Josephine Judge, Sue Chef, and Consuelo Cardiologist.

Ocean Animals Clue Game (Dawn Publications, 2–30 players) is a versatile deck of cards based on activities from Joseph Cornell's book *Sharing the Joy of Nature*. The 70 animal and clue cards come with instructions for six different games, one of which is good

continued on page 104

old-fashioned *Concentration*.

If you're car camping and have room, take along board games with outdoor themes:

FOR AGES 7 AND UP

∗ *Mountaineering Game* (Family Pastimes, 2–6 players, but can be played alone). As in real mountaineering, players work as a team to reach the summit and descend. The board contains a photograph of a peak, with illustrations showing base camps, trouble areas, and supply spots. Watch out for frostbite, crevasses, snow slides, cliffs, snow blindness, and more.

∗ *The Sierra Club Game: The Family Game of Adventure and Exploration* (University Games, 2–4 players). You'll learn about nature and explore North and South America using trailblazer tokens, explorer chips, and explorer logs.

FOR AGES 4-8

∗ *Take a Hike!* (University Games, 2–4 players). No reading is required in this delightful game invented by five-year-old Derek Nelson. Derek was laid up with a broken collarbone when he saw an announcement for the annual National Young Game Inventors Contest sponsored by University Games.

Derek based his winning design on his two favorite hobbies: hiking and collecting. "When I go on a hike," he explains, "I like to collect bugs and pine cones and leaves and put them in my box, which is kind of like a rainbow, just a little fatter."

In *Take a Hike!* players move across the board's forest scene, trying to fill hiking bags with "critter stickers," and be the first hiker back at camp. You've got to love a game with little hiking boots for playing pieces.

FISHING

For several years of my childhood, my family lived in West Virginia, across the road from the Greenbrier River. Each of us had our own fishing pole, kept lined up in the garage. I was proud of my pole and loved to fish.

Kids are never too young to get in on the act. Last summer, several months before Will's second birthday, we visited Howard Mosher, a novelist who lives and writes in Vermont's Northeast Kingdom. Howard has a passion for many things, chief among them fishing.

A few minutes before dinner,

Howard peered closely at Will, stood up, and announced, "It's time we took that boy fishing."

His tone was urgent, as though only minutes remained to immunize our son. After getting the go-ahead from Howard's wife, Phillis, that dinner could wait, we headed for a nearby river.

Fishing is probably the best camping pastime ever invented. The gear is lightweight and simple, the process endlessly diverting, and the rewards considerable, especially when a trout stream is within casting range.

Howard did all of the actual fishing, catching a Will-sized beauty about two inches long, but Will loved tromping through the grasses. Jim and I were busy holding back Will — he wanted to be *with* the fish, swimming.

An inexpensive, plastic, toy fishing kit, complete with fish, is a good starter set. I bought one in a grocery store; Will likes to use it in his kiddie pool. On the trail he's just as happy with a stick, which he dips into streams and ponds, announcing, "I'm fishing."

Once kids are old enough to use a real hook, child-sized fishing rods and reels are available in sporting goods stores. Michael J. Rosen has written an excellent guide, ✳ *The Kids' Book of Fishing* (Workman, ages 8 and up), which comes with a bobber, fishing line, hooks, and sinkers, plus a coupon worth $5 toward the purchase of a Zebco spincast reel and rod combination. Rosen's writing is intriguing, full of prac-

FAMILY FISHING

I always say: The family what fishes together, swears together.

When our four children were young, we sometimes did some fishing during our canoe camping trips. The important thing about fishing and children is to stress safety. When you're fishing in a boat, sit down and stay put. Parents need to be aware of the balance of the boat, and life vests are in order.

I love trolling around the lake in the evening. Trolling has its hazards, though; lures hook on things. My husband actually acquired a fly rod and a spinning reel on separate occasions this way.

One of the fishing experts here advocates taking off all but one set of the treble hooks on artificial lures, and I'm strongly inclined to agree. It's a safety factor: Getting a fishhook out of someone's flesh is an ugly, painful business. And removing the hooks from the lure makes it so much easier to remove the lure from the fish.

Patricia J. Bell, author of
Roughing It Elegantly:
A Practical Guide to Canoe Camping
Eden Prairie, Minnesota

tical advice, hands-on suggestions and activities, and environmentally sound instruction.

To further whet your child's angling appetite, get *Kids Incredible Fishing Stories,* "personally verified and retold" by Shaun Morey (Workman, ages 8 and up). There's a 3-year-old whose first catch was a 4.5-pound trout, pronounced one of the best catches of the year in a Sierra Nevada tackle shop. A 6-year-old caught an Alaskan salmon that outweighed her by 24 pounds. And a 13-year-old boy single-handedly landed a 925-pound blue marlin.

Regardless of your catch, your kids will have fun. As Philip Brunquell notes in his book, *Fly-Fishing with Children: A Guide for Parents* (Countryman Press): "Between the shared congratulations over fishes landed and the mutual condolences over fishes lost, there can emerge a common ground of appreciation and understanding."

While you may regard fly-fishing as an esoteric art suitable only for teenagers and adults, Brunquell says that with adult guidance, most kids can begin by age 10, many by age 8. He says there are two essential requirements for the sport: visual motor skills to lay out a fly line, and the judgment to avoid hazardous water conditions.

JOURNALS AND ARTWORK

We need to start a hiking and camping journal, Jim told me the other day — and he's right. We've already missed two summers, and part of a third, of recording Will's outdoor adventures.

Journals are a time-honored tradition at huts and shelters along the Appalachian Trail. These registers

A mother coaches her daughter in fly casting. Don't ever mistake fishing for a "boys-only game." Some of the best natural fly fishers are women.

PHILIP BRUNQUELL'S 10 RULES OF FLY-FISHING FOR PARENTS

1. Rig all tackle the night before.
2. Begin with bluegill.
3. Fish as you would have your children fish.
4. Know the specific water you are fishing before bringing your kids to it.
5. When you are teaching your kids how to fish, don't fish yourself.
6. Provide safe, alternative activities for the child who needs a break from fishing. This need is not a crime.
7. Carry a first-aid kit and know how to use it.
8. Patience is the golden virtue. Corollary: Don't be disappointed if your kid does not cast like Lefty; neither do you.
9. Enroll your child in an organization with high conservation standards, such as Trout Unlimited and the Federation of Fly Fishers.
10. Share your knowledge with disabled children, and encourage your children to do the same.

are a place for messages, poems, art, gripes, jokes, and, well, anything that comes to mind. Making and reading entries is relaxing at the end of an arduous day.

Never make family journals a chore — spontaneity is key. Encourage kids to draw, write jokes, poems, stories, as well as capture the day's adventures. Everyone can make an entry each day, or you can take turns, with one person doing the honor one day, another the next, and so on. Structure is helpful for some; keep records of birds, animals, plants, and trees identified, streams crossed, mountains climbed, weather conditions. Each evening, around the campfire or during a relaxing moment, read the latest entry and reminisce about the day's events. It's a fun way to pass the time, a great way to share impressions, and a souvenir you'll always treasure.

Use a spiral notebook or blank books, available in many designs and styles. Several children's travel journals are also available, which include journal pages as well as games and activities:

Kid's Vacation Diary (Marlor Press, ages 6–12).

The Travel Bug: A Travel Journal for Kids 7–14, by Linda Schwartz (Learning Works).

PHOTOS AND VIDEOS

Take them. Lots. They're the best souvenir you'll ever have, and a good gift for others.

At our house, we seem to go through photo and video cycles — for a while we'll snap and film like crazy, especially during holidays or family visits, and then we won't touch the

---

TIPS FROM A JOURNAL PRO

✎ "Journals are such a compact, modest way of working," Hannah Hinchman says. "They've always appealed to me because of their small scale and privacy. You don't have to be intimidated because you're not creating art for display."

The Wyoming resident started keeping a journal at age 17, when she found a blank book and was working at a nature center. Since then she's made a career as an artist, essayist, and naturalist. Her book *A Life in Hand: Creating the Illuminated Journal* (Gibbs Smith) contains a wealth of journal-keeping pointers. She has several especially for families:

● Make sure the journal is a family project, a joint effort. I'm very hesitant about encouraging young children to keep journals. If they're asked to do this, it may

cameras for weeks.

With all the other gear you have to haul on family outings, you might be tempted to leave the camera and video equipment at home. Don't, if you can help it. If nothing else, buy one of the disposable cameras, which is compact and lightweight.

Start some special hiking, camping, or biking photo albums, so you can see your family progress over the years. One of the best pieces of advice I've heard comes from John Stoops, a backpacker and father of four in Portland, Oregon. He says: "Take plenty of pictures but be sure to make them 'people' pictures. Your scenery shots won't compete with those of Ansel Adams. Mount Rainier will still be there 20 years from now, but your son won't be 11 again. You're not really taking pictures; you're saving memories."

Photo Tips

Here's some advice from outdoor photographer Gordon Wiltsie, father of two, based in Bozeman, Montana:

● Don't do much posing. Make the camera as invisible as possible. Instead of having people line up, capture everybody being natural and having a good time.

seem like a *task*. They may get a bad feeling for it and not want to keep a journal later, when the real impulse to record your life comes.

● I believe kids should be weaned from writing on lines as soon as possible. Lines carry a whole lot of baggage involving narrowed ways of thinking and seeing. By all means have only a blank book and use decent tools: some fairly precise pens, some technical pencils.

● Try to include drawings, or at least my idea of images, which also includes maps, diagrams, and other things besides what we usually consider drawings. I'd also encourage people, kids especially, to trust their eye when they draw. When I started keeping a journal, I had never thought of myself as skilled, or on the path to becoming an artist. I didn't go to art school until I was 30.

PACK A PANORAMA

Disposable panorama cameras are terrific. Before they were available, I used my regular camera, taking two or three different pictures from the same spot, but changing my direction. After they were developed, I would tape these pictures together to form a panorama. Often, however, the photographs wouldn't quite match. The panorama cameras solve the problem nicely.

John Stoops — Portland, Oregon

● Try to take "storytelling" pictures, where the kids are in the foreground, but there's also an interesting background, so other people don't get bored looking at your photos. Look for a nice scene, then put yourself into a position to catch both the scene and your child.

● Pay attention. Kids are always moving and someone always has his eyes closed. That's the biggest challenge of all: really watching. You have to watch through the camera to catch that instant when everybody's in the right position.

● Take lots of pictures. Most people shoot far too few. When your kids are bouncing around, take five or six shots instead of one — you're more likely to get a decent shot. It's cheaper to take lots of pictures than it is to repeat your vacation and try again.

● Always use the flash. It's important all the time, especially on bright,

sunny days. The flash fills in harsh shadows on people's faces, brightening them up and making the scene look more natural.

● The prettiest photos are usually taken shortly after the sun comes up and shortly before it sets. Taking pictures in the tent is fun, although it takes a wide-angle lens to work. Campfire shots are great. It's fun to have the campfire, the scene, and the family sitting around.

Kids and Cameras

If you want to encourage kids to study their surroundings, give them a camera.

Last year I watched three preschoolers and two fathers set off on a short backpack to a base camp. The youngest wore a Fisher Price toy camera around his neck, while the older two had real cameras. They were all raring to go, ready to shoot.

Wiltsie says kids are ready to have their own cameras at about age seven or eight. Before that, he says, "It's pretty much a waste of film." You can choose from many inexpensive point-and-shoot cameras, and disposables are also a good choice for kids. Workman also publishes *My First Camera Book*, by Anne Kostick, for children ages 4–8, which includes a small reusable fixed-focus camera.

Some guidance is in order, Wiltsie says. "One of the things kids tend to do with a camera is point it at absolutely anything and go click, click, click, and burn up a whole roll of film. When they're beginning, have them ask before they take a picture. Have them explain what they want to do so that they understand it's a creative process. After you've done that for a while, they'll learn to respect the fact that film isn't free."

So remember this double standard (but don't tell your kids): Parents need to take plenty of pictures to get a few good shots, but children should be restricted, or you'll have some hefty photo-finishing bills.

Wiltsie adds some more tips on outdoor photography you can share with your children:

⬤ Action shots can be tough for beginners. Automatic cameras don't deal well with things that are happening fast.

⬤ You need a long lens to get good animal shots, and plenty of patience. Wait until an animal does something interesting, rather than just standing there. But don't get too close, which is dangerous. If an animal is way off in the distance, don't even bother taking a picture, unless it's a really exciting species. A photo of a deer across the meadow at Yellowstone isn't going to be exciting. (I can attest to this from bitter experience. Want to see my whale-watch photos? Whales are exciting in person, but mere ocean specks in my photos.)

⬤ When photographing flowers, use a close-up attachment or switch, if your camera has one. Simplify the background. Flower photos often look best when the background is blurry.

Time out for some watercolor painting, Big Pine Canyon, Sierra Nevada, California. A few choice art supplies weigh little and give kids a reassuring taste of home projects right in camp.

RAINY DAYS AND LAZY MOMENTS

There's no escaping the fact that a rainy day in a small tent is no fun, especially with bored, restless kids. Sometimes it's time to head to an interesting nearby village, check out a museum, some shops, or a pizza joint, or, occasionally, pack up and check into a motel or go home.

Unless it's truly pouring, the best activity is to get outside in spite of the rain. Hike. Play. Jump in puddles. As long as kids are warm enough, don't let a little rain keep you tent-bound — everyone will be much happier to be moving. Be careful, however, because it's easy to get chilled when wet, even when the weather's warm.

If you're stuck inside a tent or

cabin, coloring, other arts and crafts, and reading are staple ingredients for a successful day, or for any day when everyone needs a quiet interlude.

Jigsaw puzzles are another good choice. Try Educational Insights' *Pieces of Knowledge* series, with world maps featuring birds, wild animals, or fish of the world (ages 5 and up). Kids learn what each species looks like, its name, and where it lives. F.X. Schmid has a 550-piece map of the United States showing national parks, along with brief descriptions. Schmid has more puzzles with outdoor themes, of varying difficulty, including an ant village, mountain and park scenes, and wild animals. There's even a glow-in-the-dark puzzle featuring wild mammals of the United States.

AROUND THE CAMPFIRE (OR CANDLE)

If you're an idealist like me, when you envision your family camping, you don't think of rainy days or outhouses, you imagine everyone gathered around the campfire, the flames casting a golden glow on a gaggle of smiling faces.

Such tranquillity isn't hard to achieve. Even if you're in an area where fires are prohibited, a candle can give focus and radiance to your gathering. The important thing is being together, outdoors.

If you stay at a campground offering evening ranger talks, take advantage of the show. They're almost always interesting and informative.

If, on the other hand, you're in charge of your own entertainment, give this part of your day a certain rhythm, like that of a metronome losing speed, or a clock in need of winding. Start off fast, then wind down. The kids can burn off any leftover energy early on, then — one hopes — sit, settle in, slow down, stop. A good end-of-the-day game is "Charades," but do this early, since the competition can make the adrenaline flow. Many kids love to perform skits; your campsite makes a wonderful stage. Let your children rehearse while you prepare dinner, then sit down to the drama.

Use marshmallows and cocoa as a transition to a quieter time. The roasting usually starts out active, but, as everyone fills up, take time to reflect on the day. Bring out the family journal. Talk about each person's favorite activity, worst moment, and so forth, and discuss plans for tomorrow.

Let the conversation — or silence — flow. Listen to each other, but take time to hear the fire, the woods, and the wilderness around you.

Tales

Traditionally, campfires and marshmallows go with ghost stories.

Beware!

With kids along, you may pay a price, and have to stay up all night warding off those spooks and specters.

When I was in first grade, my friends and I often gathered outside after dinner to tell each other scary tales. I don't recall the particulars, except that they always featured a hidous creature, a trail of blood, or a creepy noise, then a long section of "step by step, closer and closer it came. . . ."

To be honest, I can't remember these stories keeping me up at night. But I wasn't camping; I returned home, to my safe, cozy bed.

Avoid ghost stories with young children, and tell them with caution to older children, especially if they're new to camping or sleeping in their own tents for the first time.

Kids love stories, real stories, especially about their parents' child-

Spring snow shower, Beartooth Mountains, Wyoming. Inclement weather is the big downer for camping families. But the right gear and the right attitude can hold those foul-weather blues at bay. If bad weather persists, don't be above striking camp and heading home early.

hoods, and about themselves when they were younger. You can also make up stories, especially with a game called "Pass the Story." The first person (usually the best storyteller) starts telling an original story, talking for a while to set the stage. Then he says, "I pass the story to . . . ," who then takes over. Another twist is to first agree on the name of the story and then begin.

A superb read-aloud choice is ✳ *Grandfather Tales* (Houghton Mifflin), a classic selection of southern folk tales collected and retold by Richard Chase. He dedicated the book to all the grandfathers and grandmothers who told him wonderful stories. Here are Appalachian versions of King Lear, Robin Hood, Cinderella, and Hansel and Gretel.

Short story collections are another fine source. Try *Stories to Tell a 5-Year-Old*, selected by Alice Low (Little, Brown), which will also entertain older listeners. Included are classics such as "Rumpelstiltskin" and "The Sorcerer's Apprentice," along with more modern tales, including one by Beverly Cleary. Particularly nice for outdoor telling are

Music can pull kids into a positive frame of mind when all else fails. If you don't have much of a voice, bring a harmonica or jew's-harp along.

"A Curve in the River," about a boy who puts a message in a bottle, and "The Fish That Got Left in the Tide Pool," by Margaret Wise Brown.

Spend some time with ✳ *Juba This and Juba That* (Little, Brown) and you'll feel like a campfire professional. Virginia A. Tashjian has compiled "stories to tell, songs to sing, rhymes to chant, [and] riddles to guess." You get not only the words, but the choreography for action rhymes such as "Miss Polly Had a Dolly" and music and instructions for novelty tunes like "John Jacob Jingleheimer Schmidt."

If you do opt for ghost stories, you'll be inspired by two volumes

PICK A FAMILY SONG

🖉 In Belgrade Lakes, Maine, Elizabeth Snuggs, Ed Charles, and their two children have a "family song." The tradition started when Charles went to the Middle East during the Gulf War. To help ease the separation, they decided to pick a song that they could sing at designated times; the choice was

"Somewhere Out There" from *An American Tale*.

The tune remains a favorite. Everyone chimes in during hikes when their energy flags, or when they reach a summit. Each family member has a special part to sing.

"We stand at the top of a mountain and Joey starts off," Dr. Snuggs says, "and we continue. It's a wonderful tradition."

published by Globe Pequot Press: * *Campfire Chillers: The Classics* (edited by E. M. Freeman) and *Campfire Chillers: The Short and Scary Ones* (edited by Rebecca K. Rizzo). Another good choice is the "Scary Stories Boxed Set," which includes three collections illustrated by Caldecott Medalist Stephen Gammell: *Scary Stories to Tell in the Dark, More Scary Stories to Tell in the Dark,* and *Scary Stories 3* (HarperCollins, grades 5 and up). Each book is available separately and also as a cassette recording.

Whatever selection you decide on, take heed from a note at the beginning of *Grandfather Tales*: "No, it'll not do just to read the old tales out of a book. You've got to tell 'em to make 'em go right."

Music and Songs

I love to sing, but I'm a terrible singer, a truth I realized in sixth grade during the middle of a short solo in church choir. From that moment on I've mouthed the words whenever forced to sing in public. Except on the trail or around a campfire, that is. This sort of singing isn't so much about harmony and pitch as

FAMILY BAND

During one family's annual backpacking trip in the Sierras, the group ran into some rain, and 15 people took shelter under a large overhang. They built a fire, had lunch, then one of the brothers started a rhythm that got everyone involved. Some people hit rocks together, some just hit their legs or hands, others used sticks. They kept repeating the rhythm during the rest of the trip, and by the end of the week, were ready for the stage!

it is about spirit, enthusiasm, and togetherness.

Singing can give kids energy or calm them down, whatever the mood of the moment, whether you're cooped up in a car, lagging on a trail, or relaxing around a campfire. Like magic, it's equally useful when spirits are high or low.

Anyone who's ever been a student, camper, or Scout has a built-in repertoire. Singing is one of the things I remember most vividly about being a Girl Scout and a summer camper, especially that lonely first night when we sang "500 Miles" (from home). Will is starting to build his own list of favorites, which currently includes "Jingle Bells" and "A Peanut Sat on a Railroad Track."

Rehearse at home with your children's cassette tapes, or watch the Sharon, Lois, and Braun video *Sing around the Campfire* (ages 2–8, dis-

---

SONGS OF SUMMER

✐ Jane Yolen's *Songs of Summer* (Boyds Mills Press) is a picture book filled with wonderful tunes for any family outing, including "Lightly Row," "Canoe Round," "Walking Song," and "The Foot Traveler." Yolen got help from her son, Adam Stemple, with the musical arrangements — he's an adult now, a member of a rock band.

"My own children learned these songs from me on our camping holidays," Yolen says, "which took us from the coast of Maine to the West Virginia hills, across the Continental Divide to California's Donner Pass. It is amazing how history and moonlight can affect a song."

The family sang in the car and around campfires — but not, she confesses, in campgrounds when others were close by, because they felt embarrassed.

"I was the designated lullabyer," Yolen adds. "I put all three kids, and my husband, to sleep on our camping trips. But I didn't just sing lullabies, I sang from a rather large repertoire of folk songs. The longer anyone stayed awake, the more songs they heard! I'm not sure it was a great inducement to sleep."

Yolen says her favorite campfire songs are:
- "She'll Be Coming Round the Mountain"
- "Kilgarry Mountain"
- "Hush Little Baby, Don't Say a Word"
- "All the Pretty Little Horses"
- "The Old Woman Who Swallowed a Fly"

FOR ADULTS

✳ 365 OUTDOOR ACTIVITIES YOU CAN DO WITH YOUR CHILD, by Steve and Ruth Bennett (*Bob Adams Inc. Publishers*). This book is jam-packed with a range of activities that will appeal to kids ages three and up. The authors also wrote 365 TV-FREE ACTIVITIES YOU CAN DO WITH YOUR CHILD. TRAVEL GAMES FOR THE FAMILY: 100 WAYS TO ENTERTAIN KIDS OF ALL AGES FOR HOURS, by Marie Boatness (*Canyon Creek Press*). More good ideas.

FOR KIDS

Puzzle, coloring, and activity books of any sort are good for car trips and quiet hour during camping trips. WHERE'S WALDO is good fun; Candlewick publishes several Waldo activity and sticker books. Candlewick has an ingenious, intricate line of "gamebooks," including THE MAGIC CRYSTAL: A WILDLIFE ADVENTURE GAME (ages 8–12) and ONE GREEN ISLAND: AN ANIMAL COUNTING GAMEBOOK (ages 3–5).

DK Books publishes a variety of puzzle and sticker books for children of all ages, including its SNAP SHOT NATURE STICKER PUZZLE BOOK for ages 3 and up.

Usborne publishes wonderful "puzzle adventures" for various ages, with a comic-book-style story and puzzles on each page. Try PUZZLE JUNGLE (ages 5 and up) or AGENT ARTHUR'S ARCTIC ADVENTURE (ages 8–13). Adults will enjoy the fiendishly difficult "advanced puzzle adventures," such as

MYSTERY ON MAIN STREET (ages 12 and up). DRAWING FROM NATURE, by Jim Arnosky (*Morrow*, grades 5 and up). A gifted artist and naturalist shares his secrets. KIDS LEARN AMERICA! BRINGING GEOGRAPHY TO LIFE WITH PEOPLE, PLACES & HISTORY, by Patricia Gordon and Reed C. Snow (*Williamson*, ages 8 and up). Each state has its own two-page spread of fun facts. Keep this in the car for road trips.

✳ THE KIDS' SUMMER HANDBOOK, by Jane Drake and Ann Love (*Ticknor & Fields*, ages 8 and up). This wonderful book is brimming with the joys of summer. Full of activities and craft suggestions for the beach, home, or woods, after dark, hiking and camping, and rainy days.

✳ MOUNTAIN MAZES, by Roger Moreau (*Sterling Publishing*, ages 8 and up). If you like mountains and you like mazes, you'll love this book. Included are mazes of the world's greatest mountains, such as Rainier, Kilimanjaro, McKinley, Aconcagua, and Everest. Conquer the "seven summits" and never leave your chair. Also included are short descriptions of each summit and climbing histories. OODLES OF FUN WHILE YOU WAIT, by Pamela Klawitter (*Learning Works*, ages 8 and up). Games for the car, tent, or campfire. RIDE & SEEK, by Linda Schwartz (*Learning Works*, ages 6 and up). A travel pad with six different search games.

continued on page 118

BEST-BET READING

continued from page 117

ROUGH SKETCH BEGINNING, by James Berry, art by Robert Floczak (*Harcourt,* ages 7 and up). An unusual and beautiful picture book exploring creativity inspired by the natural world.

USBORNE BOOK OF CAR TRAVEL GAMES, by Tony Potter (*Usborne*, ages 8 and up). USBORNE BOOK OF AIR TRAVEL GAMES, by Moira Butterfield (*Usborne*, ages 8 and up). Colorful, imaginative games, puzzles, and activities. A creative change from the usual travel fare.

tributed by Educational Insights, also available in cassette and compact disc). With the help of children and an elephant character, this musical trio goes on a camping trip and sings such standards as "Flea," "Fly Mosquito," "Up in the Air," "Junior Birdsmen," and "Fish & Chips & Vinegar."

When it's your turn to sing around the campfire, add your own music by clapping your hands, whistling, tapping sticks together, or using whatever's on hand — as long as you don't bother your neighbors. Don't forget to try some rounds. Some campers bring guitars; our friend Mike serenades us with his flute.

Harmonicas are another good choice — they're spirited, soulful, and easy to pack in. If you're tone-deaf, try *Harmonica for the Musically Hopeless*, by Jon Gindick (Klutz, includes harmonica and cassette tape). Before you know it, you'll be riffing and bending while your children sing their hearts out.

CAMPSITE FUNDAMENTALS

"How come housework is fun in this little cabin?" [Twig] asked. "I hate it at home."

"Maybe it's because we can see what we're accomplishing. It's just the right scale."

"Or maybe it's because we have only one mug apiece and it's easy to clean," said Craig.

Jean Craighead George, *Journey Inward*

How do you turn your family into happy campers? And keep them that way?

Without the right gear and knowledge, camping can be miserable, an exercise in self-deprivation. Properly done, it's comfortable and exhilarating. It's also a vacation, even though plenty of work is involved.

As with all vacations, parents need to perform a delicate balancing act — preserving enough routines to make children feel secure and the days pass smoothly, while diverting

STONEWORKS GAME

A good activity while adults are busy set-ting up camp: Have kids use little stones to make stone walls and create little vil-lages on the ground. Our girls had lots of fun doing this.

Jerelyn Wilson — Brattleboro, Vermont

from the norm enough to inject a cer-tain amount of spontaneity and fun. The good times come easily, though, since mundane tasks are more fun outdoors, whether setting the table or washing dishes.

I don't remember *learning* to camp. Somehow, though, I picked up skills along the way, on Girl Scout trips and family excursions. It's a lifelong apprenticeship: I'm still learning each time I venture out with Jim and Will. Different roles — child, adult, mother — call for dif-ferent methods.

It's no secret that children learn by imitation. As long as parents enjoy themselves and use safe, low-impact camping methods, kids will pick up expertise, almost by osmosis.

I hope that, like me, Will doesn't remember camping lessons. Instead, I'd like him to recall helping his dad build a fire, pulling our stash of food high into the trees, or laughing as we pitch the tent.

THE FIRST NIGHT OUT

As always, Mom and Dad should know what they're doing before pulling out the tent and sleeping bags. If you've never camped before, go camping with a friend or family who has. You'll learn more in 24 hours with an experienced camper than during 24 weeks of poring over a manual.

Even if you've camped your way around the world, at some point your kids will be novices. You may be ready for a week or more in the wild, but better to go slowly, initiating your children — and you in your role as camping parent — with just a night or two.

For many, the first campsite is the backyard. Mine was in Billy Garten's driveway, next door, in first grade. His dad's pickup truck had a cab with

GEAR TALK

DON'T FORGET CAMP SHOES

If you've been wearing hiking boots all day, your feet deserve an end-of-the-day break. I generally use lightweight tennis shoes, but you can also buy fancy camping booties. Water shoes are often good for kids in camp, and they're perfect shower shoes if your campground has a bathhouse.

bunk-bed cots inside, so we hauled out sleeping bags, flashlights, and our timid selves. Once darkness fell, we didn't last more than an hour. Such is the essence of childhood adventures.

But it's sleeping outside, not camping. For that, parents should be partners. Commit yourselves to spending the entire night outside, unless illness or foul weather intrudes. Stay away from the house, away from the enticements of faucet and fridge. It may help to remove yourself from temptation and go to a nearby campground or campsite.

The basic plan: Head to a campsite, set up camp, cook a simple meal, sleep outdoors, get up and eat breakfast, break camp, go home. Throw in a short hike and some campfire tales. Keep things simple and concentrate on fun. Since you're not far from home, a solution to any problem isn't far away.

Next, you'll be ready to venture out farther and longer. The hardest part of camping is making and breaking camp, so once you're out, you might as well stay a few nights,

Make a sign, if need be, but make sure they're followed:

✓ NO SHOES

✓ NO FOOD

✓ NO FIRES

Shoes bring dirt, food brings animals, and fire brings disaster.

Rule number one of camping with kids: Stop hiking and pitch your tent EARLY! In fact, much earlier than you think necessary, to give yourselves time to settle in, relax, cook, and explore.

getting full benefit of your efforts.

Meanwhile, back at home, your kids can still have fun setting up tents in the yard and sleeping out with friends. It's super reinforcement for real camping adventures.

IN CAMP

Here's the most important piece of camping advice I can give you. Arrive at your campsite early so

CAMPSITE DIVERSIONS

Our seven-year-old has always been easy at campsites because he finds so much to look at. His favorite camp chores are getting water and collecting sticks for the campfire. He also likes riding his bike and playing at the edge of the water, catching frogs and tadpoles, stuff like that — we always get a site with water frontage for our canoe. We have a ring toss game that has been fun for many years. A favorite activity for both Chris and his five-year-old brother is the hammock. Paul strings it up and both Chris and Steven love to swing in it.

Donnie Funch — Groton, Massachusetts

you'll have plenty of time to set up, get settled, and enjoy yourselves. If you don't, you might as well stay home or check into a Holiday Inn.

A common mistake is to spend much of the day hiking, biking, or canoeing, trying to cram as much as possible into 24 hours. You may be having such a good time that nobody wants to stop. But you're likely to pay later, with hungry, tired children, approaching darkness, and a mad scramble to make camp.

Remember when on a camping trip that being at your campsite is a major focus of the day.

Choosing a Safe Site

That first hour in camp can be a dangerous one. Now that you're "home," busy pitching tents and unpacking, it's easy for parents to let their guard down. Meanwhile, children are naturally excited, eager to see what's what. This is just the time when they can wander off or get into trouble.

Although the only surefire safeguard is adult supervision, all sites are not created equal. Kids love to help choose, and should be given a say. But while they've got their own agenda — good climbing trees, a path to explore — it's up to you to survey for potential hazards:

● Beware of cliffs, steep drop-offs, hills, rivers, lakes, and creeks. Some of these features, such as a creek, provide great entertainment as well as potential danger, so parents must make the call based on their children's age, temperament, and need for supervision.

● With young children along, especially toddlers, check sites for trash, particularly glass and tin, and other debris they might put in their mouths, as well as sharp roots or stumps they might fall on.

● Tent stakes and guy lines are easy to trip over. Remind kids not to run near them, and to watch out.

● Babies, toddlers, and preschoolers need constant supervision when camping, just as they do at home. For parents, there's no escaping their needs, even during vacations. One parent must often baby-sit while the other gets things done — one of many reasons why it's handy to camp with other adults.

● Establish rules and boundaries for

kids of all ages. Young kids shouldn't go out of sight or away from the campsite. Older children may be allowed to visit designated areas — set a time for their return or for an adult to check on them. The buddy system is always a good idea. While campgrounds may seem like safe places full of friendly campers, remember that they're strangers. Even older children should be closely supervised.

● Many families give children whistles when hiking, to be used if they're lost or in need of help. They're a good idea in camp, too, but make sure kids understand they're only to be used for emergencies (see Chapter 8, "Hiking," and Chapter 11, "Lost and Found").

♥
PARENT-TO-PARENT

COOKING SAFETY

Cook on a stove rather than a fire: It's quicker and easier to keep the children away from it. Don't let young kids near fire pits or stoves even when they're cool. It will be years before they can handle "sometimes yes, sometimes no." We were surprised how quickly Beth and Aimee learned to stay away. They repeated "burn" after us and stayed away when they were one and one and a half.

Kate Gregory — Ontario, Canada

● When car camping, trunks are an ideal place to keep things you don't want your kids playing with: stove fuel, lighters and matches, knives,

GATHER AROUND THE CAMPFIRE?

✎ While campfires are the highlight of many family camping trips, they're not always permitted. Some areas are too fragile, conditions may be too dry, or heavy usage and abuse of resources may have forced a ban.

Even when fires are permitted, they're not *always* fun. On breezy evenings, as the song goes, smoke gets in your eyes, and kids may have little tolerance for the resulting sting.

Try going without — you may be pleasantly surprised by the different sights and sounds you'll see and hear, everything from wildlife to stars. If you still want a warm glow, try a candle.

When you build a campfire, play it safe:
● Wood and stick gathering is great fun for kids of all ages. Be certain, however, that such collecting is allowed. In some places you need to bring or buy wood. When you can gather your own, explain that only dead wood can be used and supervise the search.

continued on page 124

GATHER AROUND
continued from page 123

- Appoint one adult as keeper of the matches or lighter; keep them stowed out of easy reach.
- Teach older children proper building and handling techniques. Have young children stand a safe distance away from campfires and stoves. Make sure they're mindful of boots and shoes, too — prop up your legs and the soles may melt.
- Keep kids away from fire grates and watch for campfire sparks, which can ignite clothing.
- Don't let your kids throw things into the fire.
- Absolutely no roughhousing near fires.
- Sticks for roasting marshmallows and hot dogs are cooking tools, not swords. Take them away if misused.
- Teach kids about the importance of putting out fires and monitoring the embers.

Set strict, clear rules for campfire behavior early, and never waver. Otherwise, one of camping's greatest pleasures can quickly turn sour.

axes, medicine, and so on. Think of the trunk as a large safety chest.

Kids and Fire

Fires are like babies and toddlers. Never leave them unattended.

Even though you've already taught your children not to play with matches at home, camping trips are a good time for a refresher course. Open fires are irresistible for many kids. Not just for looking, but for building, setting, poking, even touching.

Different families take different approaches to fire. Older, responsible children may be allowed to help participate in all phases, including tending. Some children can be trusted to poke and prod a bit, but the issue can get sticky among siblings of different maturities. Often the safest bet is a strict "hands- and sticks-off" policy. Set your own limits and stand by them.

Young Helpers

Most little kids like to help. Even if they don't, camping is your chance to get them in the groove. They're likely to be more willing to pitch in outdoors, where teamwork seems more important, where problems and solutions are more immediate.

Will loves to assist with such things as unloading the car and pitching the tent. With supervision, he can dole out tent stakes, fill a water bucket, and carry sleeping bags. Each year he becomes a more

accomplished camper.

Such tasks can almost always be accomplished more quickly without pint-sized help. At home, when chores start to pile up, I fantasize about the amazing feats I could accomplish during a weekend, or even a day, without Will. Remember, though, that the whole point of family camping is letting kids be part of the act. You'll keep them happy, teach them camping skills, and foster a general sense of responsibility.

The routine will go more smoothly if you think of your tent not only as shelter, but as the family amusement center. Kids of all ages love to play in tents. They're a natural playpen for babies, and a conve-

they do at home: sleep or watch the rest of the family. Make them part of the action by giving them a spot in the midst of things.

Never leave a child in a child carrier unless it's on your back. You may be tempted to plop your child there momentarily, but child carriers are not freestanding and overturn easily. If you have some energy left after the day's activities, you can get a lot accomplished with a child in a carrier on your back. Your baby will be

Life under the sky is an opportunity to require your children to pitch in with various chores, including clean-up. (Be sure to use biodegradable soaps.)

nient diaper-changing station. They're great playhouses for older kids whose parents need a break or have work to do.

Young babies easily assimilate into camp life. They like to do what pleased with the ringside view.

Mobile babies and toddlers present the toughest challenge. If not confined, they need constant attention, taking one adult off the job. Some families surmount this problem by bringing a playpen or port-a-crib. We did this once, but Will stayed in it for such a short time that the next time we left it home.

On one car-camping trip last summer, I was the designated Will-watcher, but there were several instances when Jim needed a hand. During these times we let Will play in the car. We left the windows partway down (so he had plenty of air, could call for us, but not fall out), the keys in our pockets, and the emergency break on. Will was always in our sight, and found the new play space thrilling.

Here are some ways you can put young helpers to work:
TODDLERS Carry light loads to and from car; gather small sticks; hand Mom or Dad items such as tent stakes, utensils, buckets; remove rocks and other debris from the spot where the tent will be pitched.
PRESCHOOLERS Can do all the chores toddlers can do, plus spread

♥
PARENT-TO-PARENT
SAFETY ALERT
A lot of the stuff you bring camping — medication, stove fuel, shampoo — should be kept out of the reach of children. But there are no high cupboards in a tent, and no locking bathroom cabinets either. Train your children not to get stuff out of packs by themselves, and try to bring things in childproof containers whenever possible.
Kate Gregory — Ontario, Canada

sleeping bags, pads, and ground covers; simple cooking tasks, such as pouring water that isn't hot; building real or pretend fire rings with stones.
6- TO 8-YEAR-OLDS Attention spans can sometimes be short when it comes to chores, but kids this age can really start to help, not hinder. Many are excellent assistant chefs and tent pitchers; they make eager trash patrollers and water haulers. A good challenge is getting a sleeping

GEAR TALK
COOKWARE

✐ Scour yard sales or stores for inexpensive cooking and eating utensils, such as a spatula or frying pan, to be used specifically for camping. Store it with the other camping gear and it's always ready to go. You'll avoid the oops-I-forgot-the-serving-spoon syndrome. In your kitchen cookware box, store a frying pan, cooking pots with lids, spatula, serving spoon, knives, hot pads, matches, salt and pepper, dishwashing liquid, pan scrubber, sponge, towels, coffee-making equipment, bowls, plates, eating utensils, cups, and napkins.

In bear country, a combination of airtight (therefore odor-tight) containers and bear-bagging — hanging all food from the branch of a tree some 20 feet off the ground — is highly recommended.

They still need supervision with stoves and fires.

For more suggestions for keeping young campers busy, see Chapter 6, "Games and Activities."

Animal Proofing

Food should never be eaten or stored in tents, where it will attract wild visitors. It's important to stress this to kids, who love to stash things away, munch, and produce enormous quantities of crumbs.

There's a fine line between laying down the law and scaring kids. One father told me about a well-meaning ranger who dropped by to warn about a hungry bear.

"It turned out that the bear hadn't been around in months," he said, "but it was one of those things that rangers tell people. We wouldn't have left food out anyway, but the kids were up all night looking for the bear."

When you're car camping, keep food in the trunk — along with anything else you don't want your kids into. In the backcountry, food must be suspended from trees. Teach your

bag into a stuff stack.

8 AND UP Some of the very best campers, good at almost all chores. Some can pitch tents on their own, prepare simple meals and desserts.

GEAR TALK

LEAVE NO CRUMBS

An extra ground cover or tarp makes an excellent area for kids of all ages to play and eat. Any spills can be easily wiped, crumbs can be shaken off and disposed of instead of left as litter. Your kids stay cleaner and leave no trace.

kids these safeguarding techniques; reassure them that all will be well. With young, easily frightened children, don't mention bears, just raccoons, squirrels, and mice.

WHEN NATURE CALLS

Jay Nelson was picking up his seven-year-old daughter at school in a San Francisco suburb when a bulletin board caught his eye. On display were photos from a recent seventh-grade trip to Yosemite. His mouth began to water as he reminisced about the backpacking trips he used to take before his kids were born. It was high time, he decided, to take Blythe and her six-year-old sister, Arianna, camping.

"Wouldn't it be fun to hike there?" he asked Blythe.

She wrinkled her brow, then looked up and said, "Only if you bring a toilet."

The reaction puzzled Nelson, who says neither of his daughters is generally phobic about dirt, water, or sweat.

Across the country in New Hampshire, Rick Wilcox has a very different problem. Wilcox is a world-class mountaineer, head of the White Mountain rescue service, and owner of a gear store. His son and daughter, slightly older than the Nelson girls, can look out their windows and see the mountains.

Not surprisingly, Wilcox's son loves to play in the woods — and is used to relieving himself outdoors. Soon after he began first grade, his

---

THE BATHROOM BEAR

Director Buzz Caverly has many tales to tell about Baxter State Park, Maine; one of his favorites involves a camper and a bear who met "cheek to cheek" in an outhouse at Chimney Pond Campground. The woman had no idea that a bear had gone through a trap door in pursuit of some trash illegally dumped by a lazy camper.

"Just about the time she sat down on the seat," he relates,

"Brother Bruin looked up, saw something strange, and reached up with his nose and touched it. About that time a yodeling scream came out of the outhouse and the door came completely off its hinges as the woman came flying through.

"You know, she's still traveling, and the bear was so scared that the last we heard he'd gone through customs on the Canadian border."

The moral? *Never* put garbage into an outhouse.

SCAT TRACKING

When I lead a Scout trip, I carry the trowel for digging cat holes. This way I can keep track of who has had a bowel movement during the day. Constipation can be a problem because of diet changes. However, the bigger problem is usually an unwillingness to pass wastes away from the conveniences of home.

Ray Dahl — Kearns, Utah

teacher informed Rick that his son was urinating on the playground. Rick went home and explained that at school, the practice isn't acceptable, and he must go inside to use the bathroom.

"Why?" his son asked.

Any family that ventures outside, away from bathroom facilities for more than an hour or two, must face the bathroom issue. There's no getting around the fact that peeing outdoors is easier for boys than for girls. About the only time I wish I were male is when I'm hiking and have to relieve myself, especially in winter.

Better to be outside, though, than to be on a congested highway with a three-year-old who announces, "I have to go. NOW!"

Latrines and Outhouses

On the trail, these come in all shapes and sizes. One log-cabin loo along the Appalachian Trail in Maine boasts curtained windows, a mirror, and a washbasin. Few are so classy.

Use them nonetheless. Keep popular hiking areas well traveled, not well *used*. However, sometimes campground caretakers prefer that outhouses be used only for pooping, not peeing, so they don't fill so quickly. Inquire at each site.

Inspect facilities before your kids go in. Some outhouses are filthy or home to flies, spiders, or wasps. Young children often need a helping, steadying hand. If the air inside is thick, teach kids to hold their nose and breathe through their mouth.

A friend once gave me a package of toilet seat covers made for campers and hikers. Heck, I'm not that fussy, but if they'll improve your child's attitude, give them a try.

Potties

If you own a child-sized potty, either in use or stored away, take it car camping. They're handy for kids too young to visit the outhouse on their own, since going back and forth can be a major excursion, especially if you're busy with cooking or other camp chores. I've heard of families who keep them inside their tents for late-night nature calls, but I think a potty takes up too much valuable space. It's easy enough to keep it just outside the tent, and either use it there or pull it in as needed, then (carefully) shove it out.

For finicky kids who gripe about outhouses, try putting a portable potty seat over the opening. For finicky adults, portable adult camping toilets are also available, some simple and inexpensive. Luggable Loo is one brand — I love the name. However, I've never felt a need for these contraptions — we've always made do with outhouses and the woods.

Jay, I hope you can lure your girls away from their twentieth-century comforts, convince them that squatting isn't the end of the world. Show them how liberating it is not to depend on the niceties. But if all else fails, let them bring a potty. Beats looking at pictures and wishing you were there.

Kids in the Woods

Parents need to teach their children not only where to go, but how to do so in an ecologically responsible way. As always, parents must first know the correct techniques — well, inside out. When there's no bathroom or outhouse available, here are the basics:

- Never relieve yourself near a water source, trail, or campsite.
- Bury human waste. Dig a 6-inch-deep hole with a small trowel, then cover the hole when you're done.
- Groups of 10 or more should dig a latrine, about 10 inches wide and 10 inches deep, then cover it when they move on.
- Always keep some toilet paper (not a whole roll) in your pack, whether you're dayhiking or backpacking. Pack out all associated man-made products, including toilet paper, sanitary pads, tampons, and

diapers, in plastic bags of appropriate size (double-bagging helps).

- No matter where you are, keep a flashlight near the tent door for nighttime bathroom trips. Tell young kids to wake you up if they need to go.

The outdoor bathroom bible is *How to Shit in the Woods: An Environmentally Sound Approach to a Lost Art* (Ten Speed Press), written by Kathleen Meyer, a former river guide. It's full of *every* detail you need to know — women's issues, Arctic conditions, advice on intestinal upsets — in addition to being well written and laced with humor.

Accompany kids on nature calls until they're not only knowledgeable about but comfortable with the outdoor routine. Let them help choose the right spot: a certain tree for boys, a sheltered spot for girls. Show them how to beware of hazards like briars and poison ivy.

Boys and girls may need to hold your hand or arm to keep their balance when squatting. They may also need assistance to keep from soiling their pulled-down pants in the process. Cindy Ross and Todd Gladfelter, authors of *Kids in the Wild*, give their daughter the comfort of sitting on a small log over a hole. When such an improvised seat isn't available, Gladfelter holds her in his arms over the hole.

As a parent, you're an old pro at reminding your kids to use the bathroom. Require pit stops before bedtime and during breaks.

DIAPER CLEANING AND BOTTOM AIRING

When our girls were young we used cloth diapers when we canoe-camped. I scraped and rinsed and put them in plastic bags so things didn't get too foul before we finished the trip and got to a Laundromat. In the woods, kids can go naked a lot. It really worked, and we had a great time!

Jerelyn Wilson — Brattleboro, Vermont

Problems and Attitudes

Keep track of your children's output.

One sure sign of dehydration is decreased urination. Children resistant to going in the woods or who are simply preoccupied may become constipated: certainly uncomfortable and sometimes harmful.

Take seriously any of your child's fears and concerns about the "wild toilet," and try to deflect them with humor. Bathroom jokes are often a hit; history and nature lessons can divert attention and tension as well. Discuss the bathroom habits of animals, look for scat, talk about pioneers, ancient civilizations, Native Americans, Mayflower pilgrims, and the time-honored usage of pages torn from old Sears catalogs.

Diapers

On day trips or car-camping trips, diapers aren't any more difficult than they are at home. Take whatever you normally use, cloth or disposables; flush or bury fecal matter; and pack out soiled diapers in double plastic bags. For a "changing table," we carry the foam pad from our diaper bag and, as Will has gotten bigger, rest his head against the pack during changes.

Disposables can be thrown in trash receptacles; *never* leave them in outhouses. They don't decompose, and someone will eventually have to dig them out. I've been in mountain huts on cleanup day, and it's not a pretty sight.

Diapers are a challenge (or, more precisely, a pain) on extended backcountry trips. Burying or burning disposables is envi-

Disposable diapers are fine on overnights or when staying at campgrounds, but they're inappropriate for longer treks. That's when cloth diapers — which can be cleaned, dried, and reused — come in handy.

ronmentally unsound. Even where fires are permitted, burning is an inefficient use of resources. You'd need a bonfire to get rid of a pile of soaked diapers.

The sad fact is you must carry diapers out. Just imagine the weight of one day's worth of soiled disposables, and you'll get the picture.

Unless you have the luxury of pack animals, cloth diapers make far more sense. Ross and Gladfelter, who *do* travel with llamas, still prefer cloth diapers. They can be air-dried, thus reducing their weight. They can also be washed and reused.

We used cloth diapers when Will was a baby, and found diaper liners a big help in cleaning up bowel movements. We also used Velcro cloth cover-ups. However, these occasionally leak, and don't stay put with active toddlers, who either wiggle out or unfasten them.

Instead of Velcro cover-ups, Ross recommends coated nylon pants. She also used vinyl pants, but found that they become stiff in cold weather.

Try to avoid extreme cold, wet conditions with children in diapers: They'll be exposed every time a change is needed.

Bedwetting Campers

As one mother told me, "That's why God invented pull-up pants!"

If your child has a bedwetting problem, or if an accident is the least bit likely, play it safe and pull out the pull-ups. Be sure there's no shame

involved. If you meet resistance, explain that this is standard camping procedure, to keep the sleeping bag clean and dry.

When a bag does get wet — diaper leakage is another problem — today's synthetic bags are much easier to dry than the cotton flannel bags you probably used as a kid. Remember, if you put a child in a down sleeping bag, down takes forever to dry. Blot as much urine as possible, then turn the bag inside out to dry, preferably in the sun. When car camping, turn a wet bag inside out and put it on the hood of the car. Once you return home, remember to wash the bag before stowing it away.

GENERAL HYGIENE

Expect dirt. Lots of it.

If your campground has shower facilities, you've got it made. But even if it does, that's probably the last place your kids want to go.

Ben and Nick Wiltsie clean up during a backpacking trip. Maintaining evening rituals on the trail is reassuring to kids and helps them unwind as bedtime approaches.

They work reasonably well, provided the sun is shining.

There are some routines your kids can never avoid. Don't forget tooth brushing, for instance, but do so a short distance away from camp, and away from water sources. Hand washing should also be a rule before meals and after bathroom breaks, in camp or on the trail. Always inspect your kids for such things as ticks, bug bites, and poison ivy (see Chapter 12).

You can usually give kids a break unless they're filthy. A sponge bath gets rid of most grime. Baby wipes are also a necessity for all ages. When the layers start to build, I find it useful to remind myself that we can plunk Will in the tub the minute we get home.

We always take along a bucket to use as wash-up sink, for both people and dishes, changing the water often. We have a lightweight, collapsible bucket for backpacking. Always use biodegradable soap, and keep soap away from water sources.

Sun-heated camping showers are fun. Some are simple, inexpensive water pouches; others have adjustable nozzles and even shower curtains.

BEDTIME

Get your gear ready for bedtime well ahead of time, so you won't have to fumble in the dark. Unroll sleeping pads and bags, and get out pillows, sleeping clothes, flashlights, toiletries, and any favorite stuffed animals. Practical advice, yes — but these comforts also turn a tent into a home, especially for children.

Stick as close to your nighttime routine as possible, and you'll all have a happier tomorrow. Campers tend to go to bed early. They get up early, too, especially when the birds start singing and daylight streams through your tent. We replicate our at-home toothbrushing and storytime rituals; a favorite stuffed animal and a few cherished books are standard gear.

Will, Jim, and I are all late sleepers, but that isn't the case when we camp. Unless Will gets to bed early, he's likely to be grumpy. When he was a baby we could put him to bed inside the tent, then step outside and relax. Now that he's a toddler, one of us usually lays

Extra-sweet dreams. There is nothing cozier than a tent for two, and nothing to compare with the blissful sleep induced by days (and nights) on end spent out in the open.

with him or reads until he falls asleep. New surroundings can be frightening, especially on the first night.

Give younger kids fair warning that once they go inside the tent to go to bed, they can't go outside until morning, unless nature or some other

emergency calls. On our most recent trip I forgot to explain this to Will, who wanted to roam in and out. When I informed him that he couldn't, he announced, "I want to go home." We got over the mini-crisis after some crying and comforting, but it could have been avoided.

Send older children inside their

SLEEPING SOLO

Seven-year-old Chris has never been afraid of the dark, either at home or on camping trips. In fact, on our first trip this summer Paul brought along his old pup tent, and Chris slept in it alone. We didn't hear a peep out of him until morning. He was also quite enthusiastic about learning how to put it up. He wants to do it himself.

Donnie Funch — Groton, Massachusetts

tent at a designated hour, making allowances for giggles and flashlights.

Sleeping Arrangements

On our camping trips this summer, I looked forward to the coziness of the three of us snuggling together, Jim and I sleeping with Will tucked between us. But it didn't happen quite the way I envisioned. Instead, Will decided to sleep in the opposite direction, with his feet, not his head, near ours.

Oh well, as long as everyone's comfortable, any arrangement will work. Kids can sleep head to head, feet to feet, head to feet, or, as Jim says, in a pile in the corner like cordwood. Tired kids usually pass out, hardly aware they're sleeping on the ground.

With parents, the story can be different, filled with tossing and turning, moaning and groaning. It's vital to make yourselves comfortable. Use a quality mattress pad, and the bigger the better, especially when car camping.

When you start feeling like Mother Hubbard and her brood, give older kids their own tent. Prepare for some adjustment time: Anxious kids may need reassuring, and even overnight visits from Mom or Dad at first. Even if your own kids are at ease on their own, their friends may

NAPPING TIPS

✎ It can be virtually impossible to make a child settle down in a tent during the day, babies being the exception.

If your child needs a nap, they're best taken on the move: while being toted in a child carrier, canoe, bike trailer, or car. That's good news for parents, since it means activities don't have to come to a stop in the middle of the day.

If your child returns to camp tuckered out, you may want to at least insist on quiet time. Reading aloud, listening to tapes, coloring, or calm play with toys — suggest a variety of activities, as long as kids stay in the tent. The peace will be restorative for all.

need comforting, especially if they haven't camped before.

On several camping trips, my friend's 13-year-old wasn't keen on sharing a tent with his mom, and he thoroughly enjoyed the backseat of her Thunderbird.

If the wind roars or the rain pours during a car-camping trip, you may also want to move into your car. Sport utility vehicles and vans make nifty sleeping alcoves as long as ventilation is adequate. A "camper top tent" (about $100, available through Campmor) attaches to the rear of certain sport utility vehicles.

Easing Nighttime Jitters

About the time everyone is safely tucked into sleeping bags, owls, raccoons, and bats begin their nightly prowling, causing your cheery young camper to suddenly start to shiver and shake.

Everyone has fears — they're part of human nature. But kids' fears come in double, often terrifying, doses. They often peak between the ages of three and six, when children may not be able to verbalize their fright, leaving parents with few clues about the problem.

The first time I showed Will lightning bugs, he buried his head in my shoulder, pleading, "Inside! Let's go inside." When I eventually calmed him down enough to glance at the flickering lights, he asked, "Lightning bug won't drink my juice?"

In Will's eyes, here was a horde of

♥
PARENT-TO-PARENT

THE BIRDS AND THE BEES

Some folks ask us a rather delicate question related to sleeping arrangements. They ask us how they can *sleep together* when kids are in the same tent.

Get some imagination! You can sneak out of the tent into the moonlight when the kids are asleep (highly recommended); you can go off for a paddle to a secluded beach in the afternoon, leaving your children with friends you've brought along; or you can encourage your friends to take your kids on a *long* hike after dinner. Let's just say our friend's daughter was conceived on a camping trip and leave it at that.

Kate Gregory — Ontario, Canada

invaders, a threat to his fruit juice. Let's face it: Nighttime can be scary. Here are a few ways to help everyone breathe easily through the night:

● Make sure *you're* not afraid. If you're nervous, your kids will pick up your vibes.

● Prepare your family as much as possible. At home, your child is used to certain sounds: barking dogs, passing cars, perhaps sirens. Camping noises are scary because they're new. They won't be if you listen to the CD or audiocassette *A Guide to Night Sounds* (NorthWord Press, 800-336-5666). You'll hear everything from whippoorwills to owls, alligators to coyotes. A 40-page booklet is also enclosed.

● Avoid scary campfire tales with young children. They can be fun for older kids, but only if you're sure they can handle them. See Best-Best Reading for more soothing story suggestions.

● If your child becomes frightened during the night, listen closely. Try to have him voice his fears. Don't start reassuring until you've let him speak. If both of you hear something, investigate. If the fear is imagined, humor him by looking outside the tent, but with a light touch, letting him know you both realize nothing's out there. Reminisce about your own scary moments as a child. The worst thing you can do is chastise, tell your child to buck up and be brave. As T. Berry Brazelton advises, let kids regress and be babies for a moment. Humor is always helpful: When one of those lightning bugs landed close by and then flew away, I told Will he was going to look for his mommy.

● Be prepared to sleep with your child. The idea of separate adult and children's tents may sound fabulous, but when the moment of truth comes, your kids may need you. With a parent within reach, the world outside the tent becomes a much friendlier place.

With any luck, your kids won't ever be frightened as long as they're in your tent. After all, Mom and Dad are within arm's reach. What could be more comforting?

HOMESICKNESS

Here's a riddle for your kids: What animal never gets homesick?

No matter how long you travel, whether it's a week or a year, your child will experience stabs of home-

---

TECHNIQUE TIP
BRRRR!

It's tough to get up on a cold morning, especially for kids. Have them tuck their clothes into their sleeping bag to warm up. Then have them get dressed inside their bag. You may get some giggles, or at least a smile, in the process. Even when it's not cold, it's handy to store clothes this way and save space in the tent. Serving a hot beverage immediately also helps get everyone moving.

sickness, even with you, the parents, right at hand.

We recently camped next to a Canadian family with two children, a boy and a girl, ages seven and ten. One night the boy sat at the picnic table and announced, "I miss my family."

"But we *are* your family," his mother said.

The boy explained that he missed his grandparents, cousins, friends, and pets. Even though he was having a swell vacation, at certain times, especially in the evening, he longed for the familiar faces and routines of home. Homesickness is normal, most likely to crop up at nighttime or during boring moments and downright unpleasant times.

Regardless of the cause of the complaint, take your child's woes seriously; never be dismissive. Acknowledge that you, too, sometimes miss the comfort of home and friends, that

Mornings dawn early in camp, so there is plenty of time for cuddling before everyone is up and at 'em.

you'll eventually be back, that the joys of the trip ultimately outweigh any sadness, and that one reason to travel is to look forward to returning home.

The answer to the riddle? A turtle, who brings his house along. Ask your children to imagine themselves as turtles — what friends or things from home would they carry with them? Their answers may provide clues about what they miss, and need, most.

THE MUSEUM OF FAMILY CAMPING

🖉 What were sleeping bags like in 1895? Tent trailers in 1947? How about a pair of 100-year-old folding binoculars that also serve as a magnifying glass and compass? Who's in the Family Camping Hall of Fame?

You can see all this and more at the Museum of Family Camping at Bear Brook State Park in Richmond, New Hampshire. There's a videotape of camping in the Model T era, videotaped yarns and tall tales told by seasoned campers, and many vintage photos, magazines, and books.

The museum opened in 1993,

continued on page 140

MUSEUM OF FAMILY CAMPING
continued from page 139

dedicated to the efforts of Roy B. Heise, who came up with the idea and organized a mobile display. Heise died in 1991 after spending a lifetime collecting camping memorabilia. Because the museum doesn't have room to display its many items, plans are under way to relocate and build a larger facility.

Contact the Museum of Family Camping, 100 Athol Road, Richmond, NH 03470; 603-238-4768. Open from Memorial Day to Columbus Day.

MORNINGS

Start each day with a good idea of your schedule, and whether you have to push. Have a big hike planned? Heading home, or to another campground? Is there time to putter? Or, if you need to jump-start the day, announce a race to see who can get dressed first, promising extra marshmallows for the winner's cocoa.

Ideally, everyone wakes up in racing form, bright and chipper, ready to help with breakfast. Maybe this happens when folks like the Cleavers camp, but don't peek into our tent first thing in the morning. I'm likely to be lying there, avoiding leaving my cozy cocoon sleeping bag, trying to figure how long I can put off going to the bathroom. Will is probably jumping on top of me, shouting, "Let's go!" Jim varies from one extreme to another, either out and about, or sound asleep.

Before this moment of truth arrives, decide who's going to get breakfast, who tends the kids. Jim is typically our camp chef while I'm on Will-duty. One morning, when Will was a toddler, we walked round and round the campsite loop greeting other campers. Our constitutional was easier than staying back at the campsite, where the main attraction for Will was dirt and our cookstove.

Make a point to give everyone a few chores, preferably something crucial like doling out hot cocoa powder or oatmeal mix. Young campers can also set the table (perhaps make a pine-cone centerpiece), wash dishes, roll up sleeping bags, stuff clothes into duffel bags.

It's wonderful when kids can be responsible for packing their own clothes and gear, but make periodic inspections, being sure, for instance, to separate wet clothes from dry ones. When it's time to take down the tent, give everyone a role, even if nothing more than a pole to hold.

Older kids can take advantage of free time to play, but make sure they stick close by. As with making camp, it's easy to become distracted when breaking camp and lose track of your brood.

Leave Only Footprints

Once you're packed and ready to head out, ask your children to be detectives. Do you have everything? Are there any signs of your stay? Gather trash and make a game of it. Who can find the most? First one ready gets to start off leading the day's hike.

❖

BEST-BET READING

FOR ADULTS

BACKWOODS ETHICS: ENVIRONMENTAL ISSUES FOR HIKERS AND CAMPERS, by Laura and Guy Waterman (*Countryman*).

CAMPING AND BACKPACKING WITH CHILDREN, by Steven Boga (*Stackpole Books*).

✳ CAMPING HEALTHY: HYGIENE FOR THE OUTDOORS, by Buck Tilton and Rick Bennett (*ICS Books*). All you need to know to keep your camping trips happy and healthy. Tilton is the founder of the Wilderness Medicine Institute.

✳ HOW TO SHIT IN THE WOODS: AN ENVIRONMENTALLY SOUND APPROACH TO A LOST ART, by Kathleen Meyer (*Ten Speed Press*). An invaluable guide.

KIDS IN THE WILD: A FAMILY GUIDE TO OUTDOOR RECREATION, by Cindy Ross and Todd Gladfelter (*The Mountaineers*). Practical, field-tested advice, including a detailed discussion of cloth diapers in the backcountry.

✳ NOLS WILDERNESS GUIDE, by Peter Simer and John Sullivan (*Simon & Schuster*).

SEX IN THE OUTDOORS, by Robert Rose and Buck Tilton (*ICS Books*). A humorous look at a common camping skill.

THE SIERRA CLUB FAMILY OUTDOORS GUIDE, by Marilyn Doan (*Sierra Club Books*).

FOR KIDS

ARTHUR'S FIRST SLEEPOVER, by Marc Brown (*Little, Brown*, ages 3–7). Arthur the Aardvark invites some friends to camp in the yard, but the gang gets scared.

EVERYONE POOPS, by Taro Gomi (*Kane-Miller Books*, ages 2–8). A simple, straightforward book for young kids, bound to make older kids snigger. Might help squeamish children overcome outdoor-bathroom phobia.

✳ KIDS CAMP! ACTIVITIES FOR THE BACKYARD OR WILDERNESS, by Laurie Carlson and Judith Dammel (*Chicago Review Press*, ages 7–12). A treasure chest of easy, fun activities, everything from making trail food to homemade tents.

THE OUTDOOR ADVENTURE HANDBOOK, by Hugh McManners (*DK Books*, ages 7–12). Step-by-step, illustrated instructions for a variety of camping skills.

SLEEP OUT, by Carol and Donald Carrick (*Clarion*, ages 4–8). While on a solo camping trip, Christopher is sure he hears a wolf.

AN USBORNE GUIDE: CAMPING AND WALKING, by David Watkins and Meike Dalal (*EDC*

continued on page 142

Publishing, ages 8 and up). An excellent step-by-step guide with plenty of illustrations, detailed information, and activities.

FOR NIGHT OWLS

✳ DISCOVER NATURE AT SUNDOWN: THINGS TO KNOW AND THINGS TO DO, by Elizabeth P. Lawlor (*Stackpole Books,* for older children and parents). Detailed nature notes and suggestions for exploring.

FIREFLIES FOR NATHAN, by Shulamith Levey Oppenheim (*Tambourine Books*, ages 3–7). In this picture book, Nathan's grandparents let him use his father's old firefly jar.

NIGHT IN THE BARN, by Faye Gibbons (*Morrow*, ages 3–7). Four boys camp in a barn and get scared, only to discover that the ghost is the narrator's dog.

✳ NIGHTPROWLERS: EVERYDAY CREATURES UNDER EVERY NIGHT SKY, by Jerry Emory (*Harcourt Brace*, ages 8–12). A super book full of fun facts and activities.

NIGHTTIME IN MY BACKYARD, by Donald M. Silver (*W. H. Freeman*, ages 3–7). A pop-up book with intriguing details.

PART III: HIT THE TRAIL!

HIKING

"Daddy, it's a beautiful day for a mountain."

Alicia Heymann, age 4
atop Mount Watatic, Massachusetts

Of all the outdoor adventures at your family's fingertips, hiking is the easiest. You don't need special equipment, just a place — anyplace, really — to explore. On many hikes everyone can come along, regardless of age or ability.

That's the good news; now for the great news: No matter where you are, with a little bit of imagination, you'll never run out of hikes.

Think diversity.

Hikes can happen anywhere, not just on trails and mountains. Beaches are perfect places for toddlers to run; you can trek through neighborhoods and city parks.

When desperate, even as unlikely a place as an airport will do. Will and I once had a long layover in Charlotte, North Carolina, so we hiked the corridors and explored a stair-step "mountain" in the central terminal. During that long day of travel, our "hike" was just what both of us needed.

Hiking parents must carry a whole bag of tricks for keeping their young charges charging along the trail. Sometimes that means a shoulder ride, but do make it brief — or you'll be looking for someone to carry you.

autumn day, a friend treated me to a wonderful birthday hike and cooked a cheeseburger lunch at the summit. Halfway up we met a group of senior citizens from Delaware. Several spry ones charged straight up the rocky slopes. Others looked wobbly and tired; they weren't summit-bound, but, regardless, were happy to have come as far as they did.

On the way down I noticed a rock with a message scratched on its surface: *Hurry up, Dad!* I couldn't help smiling,

Back at home, as I've already mentioned, we're lucky enough to live near Mount Monadnock, in New Hampshire, one of the world's most popular hiking spots. One recent

thinking that one day Will might write my husband such a message.

One mountain pleasing so many people — young, old, and in between. Somewhere amid all that

New Hampshire granite, Mount Monadnock must be smiling.

HOW TO PICK A TRAIL

Where to go? How far? Consider: DISTANCE FROM HOME The closer, the better, unless you like Car Rides from Hell. A trail needs to be particularly exciting to justify a long ride, especially anything longer than an hour or so for preschoolers.

Before Will came along, Jim and I loved to get up early, drive several hours to the White Mountains, hike all day, stop at a restaurant, and, finally, arrive home long after dark. With Will along, a flight to Siberia would be easier. At least we could take turns hiding in the bathroom. TRAIL LENGTH This is the $64,000 question. To be safe, pick a round-trip distance, then shorten it. Even by half if your kids are young — better to keep them begging for more.

One rule of thumb is that a child can travel the same number of miles as his age: That is, a two-year-old can hike 2 miles; a five-year-old, 5 miles; and so on. I know of several five-year-olds who can hike 5 miles, but the rule seems overly ambitious for beginners, especially if much elevation gain is involved.

Until your child has had some practice, it's safer to plan on mileage equal to his age minus two. This means that an average three-year-old can probably handle a mile with no problem; four-year-olds, 2 miles; and

so on. Don't count on much mileage for two-year-olds and under; be thankful for what you get. And remember that guidelines aren't always useful: Some children can't hike so far, others can go farther.

Once you're trail-bound, remember that you need to go back. When things are going well, it's often tempting to go just a little farther than planned. Soon after Will turned two, we took a wonderful beach walk. Will moved right along; in fact, he *ran.* Nobody wanted to even think about turning around. When we finally did, however, Will's energy instantly evaporated. He raised his arms to be carried; Jim and I took turns lugging him back. Many toddlers and preschoolers seem to be born with this sort of precise trail-timing.

CHANGE IN ELEVATION Err on the side of flat. Mountains are exciting, but nothing is harder on families than an overly steep trail. That goes for offspring and parents alike, especially parents hauling gear, children in backpacks, or both. Will weighed

In some respects, babies are the easiest hiking companions, once they become accustomed to child carriers. To do so, take them along early on walks around your neighborhood.

You can often drive to a high point and *then* start hiking. This gives you the best of both worlds: the excitement of a summit without the work. Remember, though, if you hike *down*, save enough energy to hike back *up*.

about 30 pounds at age two, a tolerable load on level terrain. As soon as we hit hills, however, I turned him over to Jim.

POINTS OF INTEREST Pick a trail with the same scrutiny you'd give to choosing a museum or a Disney World ride; read trail descriptions as

---

TECHNIQUE TIP

HELP YOUR CHILD UP THE MOUNTAIN

Is your child lagging, but too old to be carried? You can "pull" him along with a walking stick. Hold one end while your child holds on further down — somewhere in the middle — never near the end. The stick is parallel to, not touching, the ground. Now pull!

"You're not actually carrying them," says Dr. Elizabeth Snuggs of Belgrade Lakes, Maine, "but you're carrying some of the weight for them."

However, as Dr. Snuggs notes, use extreme caution so that the end of the stick doesn't injure your child.

Another hiking father reports that he also uses this method — sometimes with two sticks — with great success, especially when he barks and pretends to be a sled dog. His sons love to yell "hike," the musher's word for "go," and "max," his boys' personal signal for speed.

"My guys can be ready to drop," he says, "but this gets them going."

you would travel guides. And do your scrutinizing *before* leaving home.

The first thing you need is variety. A long "highway-like" trail will be boring for everyone, even if it eventually reaches a spectacular spot. Keep the group motivated with waterfalls, streams, bridges, boulders, log crossings, and the like.

Sometimes just a word or two is enough to make an area exciting. On the edge of a South Carolina beach, for instance, we called a patch of live oaks a "tree tunnel." That did it — Will wanted to go through again and again.

Create your own diversions by turning hikes into safaris, "moose hunts," or "turtle treks," for instance. Even if you don't spot your "prey," spotting clues — footprints, scat, a nest or den — is fun. If you don't see anything, ask your child to invent an animal and show you where it lives.

Older boys and girls might enjoy incorporating a favorite book into your day. Fans of *My Side of the Mountain*, for example, can pretend to be Sam Gribley searching for a tree to call home.
REFUELING AREAS As one

START 'EM OFF WALKING

If a child is old enough to hike at all, let him start out hiking and then decide when he's ready to get into the carrier. This gets the child more "involved" with the hike, gives him the idea that the goal is to hike the whole way, and also gets the "mule" warmed up for the task ahead.

Mike Marion — Nashua, New Hampshire

mother says: Keep feeding them. With your family along, you can never snack or rest too often. Sometimes the best part of a hike is stopping. How about lunch by a stream on a sunny day? A snack on top of a boulder?

Scan trail descriptions and the trail itself for such four-star rest and picnic spots. Many children have a knack for finding great locations on

The best way to keep even a reluctant child hiking is to pick a trail with an appealing destination. A pond never fails to do the trick.

CHILD CARRIER HAPPINESS

I have *very* wiggly, independent children, but we have never had trouble getting them into their carriers. That is the only way they know to hike. I just do lots of preparation to make sure they have fun. I think of games to play, we sing songs and practice ABCs and counting. We count the birds, we count the trees. I make sure we have lots of healthy snack foods. We let them grab pine needles overhead and they love to grab handfuls of leaves. When we take a break, we let them run around.

Laura Dahl — Kearns, Utah

their own, so assign them the task of hunting — it's the perfect diversion for hungry hikers.

Whenever you pass a good site, consider stopping even if you're not ready. It's a law: Once you pass a perfect picnic spot, you won't find another until long after everyone is starving.

Also remember that hiking rewards don't always have to be *on* the trail. Will your drive take you by an ice cream stand or snack shop? We're partial to one New Hampshire trail solely because it's near an old-fashioned general store with out-of-this-world homemade cookies. Now *that's* hiking!

WEATHER AND SEASONS Try to avoid the tribulations; begin by getting youngsters hooked on the highs of hiking. When they're older, they might be willing to hang tough. Although you may not mind forging ahead through wind and rain, your troops may go on strike.

Keep an eye on weather forecasts a day or two before a hike, then get an update that morning. Some busy trailheads have daily weather postings, but don't count on any.

TECHNIQUE TIP

CHILD CARRIER BLUES

Don't give up. The first time I put my daughter in a child carrier, she screamed the entire time. My heart went to my toes because we're a camping, outdoors family.

The next day she and I took off alone. I talked to her and she got used to it. I realized that as long as I kept moving and didn't stop, she was fine. When I needed to stop, I learned to keep moving or swaying.

Later, when we hiked with the rest of our group, I kept going slowly when they stopped. They could quickly catch up to my daughter and me after their break.

Dr. Elizabeth Snuggs — Belgrade Lakes, Maine

Kids should fill their own small packs with a water bottle, a few favorite toys, and snacks, like the one this hiker is clutching. A walking stick, found along the trail, is also a great idea.

Also, for every trail, there is a season. A glorious walk one month may be a mosquito jungle the next. Spring rains or snowmelt may make streams impassable, trails a gloppy mess. Avoiding the mud season is more than a matter of keeping your boots clean; your muddy footprints can seriously damage the trail. Some areas — Vermont's Long Trail is one — close at such times.

Know the dates of hunting season — and don't hike where hunters are allowed. In the fall, for instance, shots can be heard right in our neighborhood, and we are forced to avoid many of our favorite trails.

Be inquisitive if you're on unfamiliar turf. I'd never heard of black-flies until I lived in New England, but as a southerner I knew where to look for snakes and chiggers.

Gear

For most hikes, you need nothing more than basic adventure gear (see Chapter 3):

- Sturdy footwear
- Daypacks
- Adequate clothing

A HELPFUL
COMPANION

Let your child bring along a favorite toy. For quite a while our daughter, Jen, brought her Care Bear.

Debbie Bockus — Hubbardston, Massachusetts

Sun block is especially important for children's tender skin. They'll enjoy carrying their own if the packaging is imaginative.

- Food and snacks
- A first aid kit

In addition, pack a small, lightweight diversion or two to amuse children if they need a rest. Keep them as an emergency surprise, anything from a small book or field guide or deck of cards for older kids to a tiny doll, car, or a few Legos for younger ones.

Your son or daughter may also try to add toys to the equipment pile. One or two can sometimes be a big help, but make sure they don't haul much. Once they hit the trail, their treasures are likely to suddenly weigh a ton.

Walking Sticks

They can be a real help and most kids love them. They're a boost for tired bodies going uphill; coming down, they help maintain balance and footing.

For heaven's sake, don't buy one; half the fun is in picking out your own special stick along the trail. If your child gets tired of using a walking stick, toss it aside. There's likely to be another later on, if

needed. However, make sure everyone understands that only sticks, dead ones, are fair game.

If you happen to be skiers, ski poles also make excellent, lightweight walking sticks. Some hikers like to use two on steep sections.

Walking sticks are also useful for minor trail maintenance. Show your children how they can use a stick to flick small branches off to the sides of the path.

Finally, children are children and sticks are sticks, which means watch out for sword fights. Make it clear that if your child doesn't use a walking stick safely, away it goes.

Sore Feet and Blisters

Nothing can ruin a hike faster than aching feet. The pain can be especially tough on children, who aren't usually known for being stoic. I like to compare the problem with diaper rash: It's inevitable if you're not careful, but with foresight and a few preventive steps, you shouldn't have to worry.

RULE 1 DON'T GIVE YOUR CHILD NEW HIKING SHOES ON THE MORNING OF ANY HIKE. Young hikers need good footwear, but it should be well broken in at home and around the neighborhood first. And for many hikes, a worn-in pair of sneakers is just fine (see Chapter 3).

RULE 2 SOCKS ARE JUST AS IMPORTANT AS SHOES. Avoid cotton, which absorbs moisture and causes blisters. Cotton tube socks are popular, but they're not for hiking.

Buy socks made of synthetics or wool, depending on the weather. Also equip your children with a pair of thin synthetic wicking liners to wear underneath as added protection against blisters.

RULE 3 TREAT ANY FEET COMPLAINTS SERIOUSLY. STOP AT ONCE! Blisters are best treated *before* they form. The moment a child mentions trouble, check it out. If you don't, *everyone* will soon be sorry.

Also, urge your son or daughter to tell you immediately about foot trouble; tell them this is one area where forbearance is not warranted.

Once there's a hot spot, something needs to go between it and whatever is causing the

✔
HIKING MILESTONES

• First hike in a child carrier
• First time walking along a trail
• First hike without a child carrier
• First mile
• First summit
• First "big" mountain or long hike
• First time above treeline

friction. Many people immediately haul out the moleskin, but white athletic tape, and even duct tape, works better. Friction is caused by pressure, and thick moleskin just increases the pressure. Tape is more effective because it's thinner. It also stays in place better than Band-Aids, another common fix.

If you or your child repeatedly has trouble with one spot, such as a

If your child complains of foot soreness STOP. Remove her boot, and tape the hot spot. If you don't, a bad blister is bound to ensue. Treated early, this bane of hikers can be prevented.

WALK SOFTLY WITH A MUDDY BOOT

My wife and I teach our children to travel "softly," to stay on the trail even if it's muddy or full of horse manure. It can actually be kind of fun because the kids get to be dirty and it's all right with Mom and Dad.

Ray Dahl — Kearns, Utah

heel, tape that spot at the start of each hike.

RULE 4 IF BLISTERS OCCUR, TREAT THEM. Don't pierce them. A blister's fluid is the body's way of protecting an irritated area and helping it heal. What's more, pierced blisters are also more susceptible to infection.

Now's the time to bring out the moleskin or mole-foam. Cut a hole in the padding the same size as the blister. This "doughnut hole" goes over the blister, keeping pressure off while cushioning the surrounding area.

RULE 5 IF YOUR CHILD IS IN PAIN, TURN AROUND. The hiking won't be fun for anyone, and unpleasant memories may cause your child to balk at another hike. Turning back isn't a sign of failure, just common sense.

MIND YOUR MANNERS

The laws of the trail are simple, just extensions of the same courtesies you teach your family in everyday situations:

BE RESPECTFUL Treat the outdoors just as you would someone else's house. After all, the wilderness *is* home to bugs, plants, birds, and animals. No littering or otherwise damaging the environment. Resist the temptation to pick the flowers or feed the animals.

While hiking, point out the various ways hikers affect the wilderness, and have your family think of ways to help the trail, such as removing litter. Show how walking on the edge of a trail erodes and widens it — by sticking to the middle, even if there's a puddle, your family can help preserve the wilderness.

BE THOUGHTFUL Let other hikers pass if they need to; make sure you step aside and don't block the trail. On the other hand, don't crowd anyone else. Keep your distance or pass.

DON'T MAKE TOO MUCH NOISE Exuberance is wonderful, but too much of a good thing will chase all the wildlife away or ruin someone else's hike.

As Peter Whittaker advises, "Listen to the mountains." Observe a moment of silence from time to time. There's always something to hear.

SHARE Public lands are for everyone, but if another party arrived at a choice area first, don't move in and take over. Look for another spot.

You'll also want to remind your family of the one clear and simple rule for all outdoor activities: *Leave only footprints*. In certain areas — Mount Washington's Alpine Garden comes to mind — hikers who stray off the trail damage delicate, sometimes extremely rare vegetation. Other fragile areas include bogs, mossy spots, and places above treeline. Forewarn your kids about such spots before you begin a hike, so they can look forward to seeing and protecting their delicacy.

Even on less rarefied terrain, explain that such things as bridges and bog crossings aren't there just for the sake of convenience, but also to protect the surrounding area.

Of course, wilderness is for exploring, and you don't want to give your family the impression they're in a museum where nothing can be touched. As long as you're not in a fragile area, make a point from time to time of venturing a short distance off the trail to look at an interesting tree, for example, or a huge boulder. No matter where you are, walk softly.

Family Safety on the Trail

The most important safety advice I can offer is: STST. That stands for: Stay Together and Stay on the Trail. Keep track of your hiking party like a mother bear attends to her cubs: *Let nothing come between you.*

If a youngster bristles at the rule, to help him or her save face, explain that you're worried only about *yourself* — if Mom or Dad gets tired or injured, you want to be sure you can call for help.

Even when hiking with adults only, we usually assign one person in the group to be "point," a term bor-

PARENT-TO-PARENT

AVOID THE
BIG PICTURE

It's important to break the trip up into small segments for children. Tell them we're going to head up around the bend to a stream, then go on from there. Don't say: We're going to hike for eight hours today and go x number of miles. That would blow their miles. Don't give them the big picture.

Rick Wilcox — North Conway, New Hampshire

rowed from military patrol lingo. The point navigates and leads the way, while another person acts as "sweep." This rear guard makes sure no one gets left behind. The system works well for families or groups of families, and is essential whenever a few adults lead a group of young hikers. Also, giving a child a chance to be point from time to time gives him a boost and sense of importance.

If someone has trouble, the sweep helps him or her along and alerts the rest of the group if the pace needs adjusting. To keep the group intact, the point and sweep should periodically touch base with each other. Also, at any crossroads along the trail, everyone in the front of the pack waits for the rest to catch up. This ensures that parts of the group don't wander off in different directions.

As children get older, especially once they hit age 10 or so, they're likely to want to run ahead. They may

Summer Wuerthner may be ready for some short "hikes" and explorations, but, if miles are to be covered, a stout carrier is still very much in order; as are plenty of water and a variety of snacks.

white spots. Build on these lessons over the years, so your child can recognize trail junctions and read a compass and map (see Chapter 11).

If you're confident of your child's abilities, give her a bit of free rein, but ask her to stay within close earshot, if not eyesight. That way everyone will know immediately if problems arise.

WHISTLES Whistles are much easier to hear than shouts of "Help, help!" and every child should have one, to be used only in an emergency. If your child is lost or injured, he should blow it, but then and only then. Hand out the whistles at home, where kids can blow them to their hearts' content, getting the whistling urge out of their systems before they hit the trail.

CODE WORDS Before you begin hiking, agree on a family code word to use in case you become separated.

need privacy, or at least the illusion of privacy, especially if other friends are along. However, make it a rule that they stop at any and all trail signs or junctions. Of course, this means that your child can be counted on to recognize and notice these junctions.

It's almost never too early to begin trailblazing lessons. Start by pointing out trail signs and blazes. Even toddlers will enjoy spotting the yellow triangles, for instance, or

With our friends and family, the word is "Mahoosuc," to commemorate a wonderful hike we took through Mahoosuc Notch, Maine, a boulder-strewn gap reputed to be the toughest mile of the Appalachian Trail.

We shout "Mahoosuc" if anyone gets separated from the rest of the group and wants to check position or progress. We try to stay within a "Mahoosuc" of one another — and whenever we hear our code word, hurry in that direction.

A distinct whistle — a short pattern of notes or a bird-call imitation — can also be used. While younger hikers will love shouting a code word, teens and preteens may find it less embarrassing to whistle.

This sort of password is much more effective than relying on yells of "Mom!," "Dad!," or "Katie!," for instance, since any number of people might shout the same thing. Out on the trail, voices aren't always easily recognizable.

Be sure everyone agrees on the same signal, something another group is unlikely to choose. Let your child pick a word and then practice using it

FAMILY HUDDLE

At the start of every hike, just before beginning the trail, we would all form a huddle. Dad would say, "Here's the plan! We're going to hike to Suchandsuch Mountain, we're going to eat lunch, soak our feet in ice water, maybe get to the summit and eat again, and look for Martians on the way! So be careful!"

Debbie Bockus — Hubbardston, Massachusetts

A cold dip in Big Pine Creek, Sierra Nevada, California. There's nothing like the promise of skinny dipping in a remote stream to motivate a child to hike his best.

early in your outing; he probably doesn't need to be asked twice to yell.

Finally, unless you're *more* than certain of what you're doing, don't wander far off marked trails. Bush-whacking can be fun; getting lost isn't.

Take a Deep Breath

After all this talk about minding manners and trail safety, it's time to

HIKING AND ART

When I was 11, my family, along with my friend Susie's family, took a trip to Mount Washington (New Hampshire). We climbed halfway up the mountain, swam in a river, crossed a rickety bridge on foot, and ate the best sundaes ever. Susie and I had crayons, colored pencils, and paper with us and we drew pictures of everything we did. They were some of the best drawings I'd ever created, probably because they were about things I'd actually done.

Mary Jane Begin
children's book illustrator
Talking with Artists, Vol. 2

cut loose. Most children instinctively know how to have fun wherever they are. It's we adults who sometimes need help.

No doubt you've seen Backwoods Dictators on the trail: moms and dads screaming at their brood to go faster, go slower, be quiet, or stop sniveling. We all reach our breaking points from time to time, but before you yell at your child to, say, keep moving, get down on your hands and knees and find out what's so darn fascinating. Let your children dictate the pace sometimes.

Here's your chance to be a kid again — skip stones, tell jokes, sing — that's the best way for everyone to enjoy the trail.

FINDING YOUR FAMILY'S STRIDE

For all the joys of family hiking, it's often a math problem.

First, there's length. Some legs in your family are probably long, some short, and some in between. They go at different speeds.

Then there's distance. Your goal: to get from Point A to Point B and back again. Your son has the same goal, but his Point B is different from yours — about only 20 yards from Point A.

Now what?

DON'T SLOW DOWN — STOP!

"Nature was always a mystery to my father," writer Jean Craighead George recalls. "As an entomologist, he would sit and watch a spider for hours. . . . He had us all doing that — just sitting and looking and thinking.

"People who hike a lot and just walk really don't see. You've got to go in there and sit down and sit still. Pretty soon, if you're part of the landscape, animals and birds will begin to come around you. Just sit — that's what we did."

How do you keep your family together *and* happy?

Common advice is to adjust to the speed of the slowest hiker. Any preschooler will be delighted, but the rest of the group will be champing at the bit.

On some outings you'll want to compromise, to hike together as a family. Some may have to slow down, others speed up. You can put dawdlers in a child carrier and cool the jets of the older siblings.

But happy mediums usually aren't.

Sometimes it's equally important *not* to hike together.

Older brothers and sisters need to be challenged to go farther than before, to reach the next highest peak. Otherwise, they'll get bored watching younger siblings pick dandelions.

At the same time, your little one needs to build stamina and explore on his own terms. An older child's enthusiasm may be infectious and

Sometimes pacing means splitting up, allowing an eager six- or seven-year-old to move ahead with Mom while a younger sibling dawdles with Dad.

spur him on, but sometimes the youngest needs to feel like he's King of the Hill, not Mr. Tagalong.

Age isn't the only consideration. Your 9-year-old may dream of Everest

TECHNIQUE TIP

DOWNWARD BOUND

I learned this trick for going downhill from my sixth-grade math teacher. It helps you cover more ground and seems to take some impact off your knees.

Have you ever seen race-walking events? People walk very quickly and wildly gyrate their hips. Try this as you hike down, rotating your hips and lengthening your stride.

Ray Dahl — Kearns, Utah

while your 10-year-old loathes hiking.

What's the solution to all of these math problems?

Sometimes you need to divide into Set A and Set B. Mix and match according to everyone's speeds and needs. One or both parents can take one child on an outing; leave the other behind. Or bring everyone along, but one parent stays behind with one child while the other two speed ahead.

Pacing

No matter who's in the group, remind everyone of the tortoise and the hare.

Your children are likely to start off running like the hare. But if they

AGES AND STAGES

HIKING

INFANTS (NEWBORN—6 MONTHS)

Should be carried in front carrier because of lack of head and neck control; enjoy motion of hiking; fussiness and unpredictable schedules make short outings easiest.

BABIES (6 MONTHS—1 YEAR)

Gain sufficient head and neck control to use backpack-style child carrier; enjoy sights, sounds, and motion of hiking; regular schedules make longer hikes more feasible.

TODDLERS (1—3 YEARS)

Ready for first steps on the trail, but still must be carried much of the way; these "micro-hikers" enjoy short steps and small details — bugs, leaves, rocks, sticks; watch their every move.

3- TO 4-YEAR-OLDS

Coordination improved; stamina unpredictable; keep the child carrier handy.

4- TO 6-YEAR-OLDS

Improving stamina; transition time away from child carrier; highly inquisitive about the natural world.

6- TO 8-YEAR-OLDS

Thrive on physical activity; improved sense of balance helps climbing; increasing awareness of distance and time can be helpful on the trail.

8- TO 10-YEAR-OLDS

Increased stamina means it's mountain time; ability to understand compasses, maps, and trail guides can be motivating.

10- TO 12-YEAR-OLDS

Growth spurts and preadolescent "attitudes" make some less physically active; others gain strength and endurance and are raring to go; growth spurts may increase clumsiness; increased awareness and responsibility make the beginnings of real "trail sense" possible.

burn themselves out, the tortoise will soon pass them as they sit on a log huffing and puffing.

Help your kids find a pace they can maintain. They should be able to keep talking with no heavy breathing.

Teach them to slow down when going uphill, to shorten their stride when they feel tired, and to stop when necessary. You may find it helpful to

text continued on page 162

BABIES

"My wife and I just had our first child. We love to hike and don't want to give it up. Can we take our baby on the trail?"

Your hikes will definitely be different, but babies make great little hiking partners. Since you're the "legs" of this partnership, you can move at your own pace. Traveling with a toddler is more difficult by far.

You can't be overly fastidious when it comes to your baby's biggest trail worries: temperature, sun, hydration, and bugs (see Chapters 3 and 12). Babies can't tolerate cold, heat, sunburns, or bug bites as well as adults can. The fact that they're being carried and not moving makes them even more susceptible to these hazards.

Start taking your baby on walks in a front carrier in mild climates as soon as possible. True hikes will be most pleasurable once your child is on a schedule and has enough head control to switch from a front pack to a backpack-style child carrier, usually at about five or six months.

Now begins the golden age of hiking with babies. They're still light enough to be easily carried, and, in most cases, their schedules are dependable. Hike and walk

often — at least once a week — so your daughter will get used to being on your back.

By now your daughter will also be alert enough to enjoy the scenery. Point out animals and trees and discuss them; even if your daughter doesn't understand the words, she'll enjoy hearing your voice. She'll also like some toys and teething materials strapped to the child carrier. Eventually, the motion of being carried will lull her to sleep.

As always, be attentive to hunger, thirst, and diapering needs. Make sure your baby gets plenty to drink on hot, sunny days (see Chapter 4). Breastfeeding moms don't need to carry extra gear, but they need to drink extra fluids when exercising. For bottle-fed babies, powdered formula works well on the trail, as long as it is *never* mixed with untreated water, which could make your child sick.

Whenever you feed or diaper your baby, allow for some playtime out of her carrier. She needs a chance to stretch her legs, too.

continued on page 160

Avoid extreme conditions and check your baby often, even if the weather is fine. The fact that a baby isn't complaining isn't always a good sign. A quiet child may be suffering and in danger. Be familiar with the warning signs of hypothermia, dehydration, and heat exhaustion (Chapter 12).

As long as you and your spouse monitor your baby's needs vigilantly, the three of you can hike as far as you want.

TODDLERS

"Our son used to love riding in his child carrier, but ever since he turned two, he wants no part of it. We try to let him walk on his own, but we don't get far."

How far can your two-year-old hike?

As far as he wants to.

Sad to say, it's almost easier to move a mountain than it is to budge a determined two-year-old.

There's no getting around the fact that toddlers are at an awkward age for hiking. They're too heavy to be carried far. And, like your son, they usually want to walk on their own, but don't have much stamina.

Let's face it: True hiking requires skills your son hasn't yet developed — physical coordination and a sense of both focus and time. Even if your boy was physically able to keep up with you and your spouse, he'd be distracted by a million things along the way. Nor does he have a clue about minutes, hours, and mileage — so you can hardly explain that you've got 4 more miles to hike

and it's going to be dark in an hour. And if he could understand these concepts, toddlers are hardly known for being reasonable.

The best way over these hurdles? Short outings are ideal. Instead of spending a lot of time and energy hiking to and from a pretty place, just go somewhere close and enjoy it. Select trails less than a mile long. Once at your destination, have a picnic and let your son explore to his heart's delight. If one of you needs more exercise, one adult can be on toddler duty while the other goes farther along the trail. If you're still yearning for a "real" hike, go on separate, adult outings.

Some toddlers don't mind child carriers; their lucky parents can haul them as long as their backs can bear the burden. However, if you don't encourage a child to walk on his own from time to time, he'll never develop the stamina needed to become a real hiker.

For all the challenges toddlers present, you'll be hard-pressed to find a group of more inquisitive and joyful hikers. Since practically everything is new and exciting, you don't have to go to great lengths to find diversions along the way. You may be surprised at how much you enjoy their knee-high discoveries.

PRESCHOOLERS

"Our three-year-old loves to hike, but she always runs out of steam. She ends up in tears and my arms nearly fall off when I carry her."

Let your daughter hike as far as she can, but keep the child carrier on your back. Until she's a bit older, it's a good insurance policy, even if you never have to use it.

"Our son is nearly five and still likes to be carried. How can my husband get him off his back?"

Can you blame him for not wanting to leave a cozy perch with a bird's-eye view? Wouldn't you like to be carried from time to time, given the opportunity? His lack of stamina may not be just a trail issue. How much walking does your son usually do each week? If you're still carting him around in a stroller, get him on his feet.

When hiking, try to be low-key but firm — you don't want to turn him off hiking before he's even given it a try. Start with short, flat hikes — a mile or two — *but don't give him the option of being carried. Leave the child carrier at home.* Give yourselves plenty of time for all the breaks, snacks, and exploring your son needs. If he lags, challenge him to a race. Another child who's raring to go may also spur your son on, so consider bringing a friend.

Think of your outings as a training program for your son. Advance from flat, neighborhood walks to strolls with hills. Once you've made progress on the home front, hit the trail again. Eventually your child carrier will be left in the dust.

SCHOOL-AGE CHILDREN

"I know my 6- and 10-year-old girls are physically capable of hiking the 4- and 5-mile trails our family explores. But sometimes they get bored."

You're right, your girls are old enough to be bona fide hikers. If you're sure they're not tired, hungry, or thirsty, it's time to get creative. Try field guides, a scavenger hunt, and plenty of songs, stories, and games (see Chapter 6).

Your older child may enjoy being "trail leader." Teach her to use a compass and put her in charge of the trail map and guide.

"My eight-year-old loves to hike so much that he's always running ahead. I hate to dampen his enthusiasm, but I'm afraid he'll get hurt or lost."

Your fears are well-founded. Your son is too young to be charging ahead, well out of sight. At the very least, he should stay within earshot. Lay down the law.

"My 11-year-old boy often complains about knee pain when we hike. What's the problem?"

Could be any number of things — or nothing — but take his complaints seriously. While physicians don't consider "growing pains" as an official diagnosis, it's important to acknowledge that adolescents undergo major changes, both physically and emotionally.

One not-so-common possibility is Osgood-Schlatter disease, an inflammation that affects teens, especially boys, during growth spurts. It is caused by repeated stress on the knees during activities such as hiking or running; the symptoms are pain and swelling around the bone protruding about an inch or two below the kneecap. Osgood-Schlatter disease isn't serious;

continued on page 162

decreasing activity usually solves the problem.

Whatever the cause of your son's discomfort, a visit to the doctor may be warranted if ice, ibuprofen, and rest don't soon relieve the pain.

TEENAGE GIRLS

"*Our 13-year-old daughter has always led the way on family hikes, but recently she's been lagging. What could be slowing her down?*"

Your daughter's lowered energy may be due to adjustments her body is making to the onset of menstruation. If she has her period during a hike, she may simply be uncomfortable from cramps. However, weakness and fatigue may also be a sign of anemia, so have a doctor check the level of iron in her body.

text continued from page 159

count out loud to get them in rhythm: one, two, three, four, one, two, three, four.

An even more important lesson is to teach young hikers to slow down on *downhill* sections. They can charge down gentle inclines, but they need to hold their horses on steeper stuff. Show them how easy it is to trip on tree roots and loose rock, gravel, or soil. Explain that really steep sections are like ladders — you need to turn around to descend safely.

Breaks

What's the best way to keep kids moving?

Stop.

Often.

Here are four commandments for hikers of any age: Walk. Eat. Drink. Rest. With your family along, run through the list at least once an hour, sometimes more.

Once all that is done, have your kids drink some more, even if they're not particularly thirsty. Remember, kids need to replace fluids more quickly than adults do, because they lose them more quickly.

Just as you change diapers before they begin to leak, it's essential to schedule breaks before your child is in dire need. Otherwise, you'll be forced to take longer breaks to allow your child's metabolism to fully recover.

Rest stops are one of the best hiking incentives around. Just point to the top of the next hill and promise a cheap bribe, such as candy bars or fruit juice. If the trail is particularly steep, however, fuel up at the bottom, and take more breaks — sometimes just a minute or two for breath catching — on the way up. Stop, too, when the scenery beckons — a scenic ledge, for instance, or a stream perfect for soaking sore feet.

Don't forget to snack on the return half of the trip. Any whines you may attribute to end-of-the-day crankiness may actually be hunger pangs. Don't worry too much about spoiling dinner; concentrate on getting to the end of the trail.

ADVANCED TRIPS

You're all ready for bigger and better hikes. Once your child becomes an enthusiast, the tables may turn: Now you're the one who's likely to have a hard time keeping up.

Pick some challenging trails; set a family goal. Many hikers in New England climb all 48 of New Hampshire's 4,000-footers. Jim and I scaled them before Will was born; perhaps we'll do them again together when he's older.

That's just what the Bockus family of Hubbardston, Massachusetts, did. They started in 1979 when son Chris, 7¹/2, and daughter Jen,

3¹/2, still had to be carried part of the way. They weren't looking for a project, just a mountain easy enough for everyone to handle. Instead, they got 48! Eight years later they finished their last peak with a mountaintop celebration and surprise commemorative mugs for Chris and Jen.

"Those were the best family sharing times we had," Debbie remembers.

Stream Crossings

Most crossings are short, shallow, and fun; some children love them more

GEAR TALK

BABY TOYS

Want to keep your baby happy on the trail? Discovery Toys has a plastic chain that works beautifully and can support lightweight rattles or chewing keys.

Be sure not to use anything that might choke or strangle your child. Carabiners are definitely not a good choice. I have found that my teething babies scream in pain from the hard metal. Also, the gates can open and pinch their lips.

Laura Dahl – Kearns, Utah

Stream crossings can be as fun (and benign) as this one over Coyote Creek in the Sierra Nevada, California. But deep or fast-flowing water can be hazardous; take your time to find the safest crossing.

than anything else on the trail. I know of one four-year-old girl who sprang to life at the sight of mud; her trail job was to figure out the best way through or around.

However, crossing deep or fast-flowing water can be dangerous, especially for families. Potential hazards range from the merely inconvenient (wet socks) to hypothermia and drowning.

Check on trail conditions *before* you start out. Some trails may be a bad choice during spring thaws, for instance.

Once you reach a tricky crossing, turn back if it appears dangerous. It's better to avoid serious risk, even if you have to backtrack, go out of your way, or chalk an unfinished outing up to experience.

If, on the other hand, a crossing appears manageable, first check it out yourself while the youngsters stand on shore. You may be able to hop on rocks or use a log as a bridge.

Take off your daypack and your child's pack (even a fanny pack) so that if anyone falls in, the pack won't drag him down. Take packs across yourself; in some cases, you can throw them. If possible, stand in the middle of the stream to give everyone a hand, even a lift. A ski pole or walking stick may help with balance.

Neither you nor your children should cross barefoot; you risk cutting your feet or slipping on a rock.

❤

PARENT-TO-PARENT

VARYING VIEWS

During one Colorado hike in which we climbed to 12,000 feet, we had spectacular views, but they were of little interest to our four-year-old. The novelties under her nose mattered most to her: the stick that could be a fishing pole, the flower, the rock, the critter poop.

Rob Kleine — Phoenix, Arizona

Instead, take socks off to keep them dry, then cross in your boots.

Snow and Ice

Want to get young hikers on the trail? Promise to show them snow and ice in June.

If you're not near the Rockies or

❖

BEST-BET READING

FOR ADULTS

AMC NATURE WALKS series, by various authors (*Appalachian Mountain Club*). Various short walks perfect for families. One of my favorites is Robert N. Buchsbaum's NATURE HIKES IN THE WHITE MOUNTAINS, which has enticing trail descriptions.

✳ BEST HIKES WITH CHILDREN series, by various authors (*The Mountaineers*). Regional guides with descriptions of trails well-suited to families.

✳ THE COMPLETE WALKER III, by Colin Fletcher (*Alfred Knopf*). The granddaddy of all walking books.

✳ A FAMILY GUIDE TO ROCKY MOUNTAIN NATIONAL PARK, by Lisa Gollin Evans (*The Mountaineers*). A complete and clearly presented guide to a spectacular spot.

✳ HIKING & BACKPACKING: A COMPLETE GUIDE, *Trailside* series, by Karen Berger (*W. W. Norton*). Everything adults need to know *before* they hike with kids.

FOR KIDS

IN THE WOODS: WHO'S BEEN HERE?, by Lindsay Barrett George (*Greenwillow Books*,

continued on page 166

B E S T - B E T   R E A D I N G
continued from page 165

ages 4–8). In a story presented as a guessing game, a boy and girl explore a trail and follow clues various animals have left behind.

✳ MOUNTAINS, by Seymour Simon (*Morrow*, ages 8–12). Breathtaking photos and a clear explanation of how mountains are formed.
SHEEP TAKE A HIKE, by Nancy Shaw, illustrated by Margot Apple (*Houghton Mifflin*, ages 2–4). Three sheep get into lots of trouble, but their adventures will amuse the very youngest hikers.
SUMMIT UP: RIDDLES ABOUT MOUNTAINS, by June Swanson, illustrated by Susan Slattery Burke (*Lerner Publications*, all ages). These silly riddles are best told on the trail.
TAKE A HIKE! THE SIERRA CLUB KID'S GUIDE TO HIKING AND BACKPACKING, by Lynne Foster, illustrated by Martha Weston (*Sierra Club*, ages 9–12). Hand this one over and your kids may be telling *you* what to do.

✳ TO CLIMB A WATERFALL, by Jean Craighead George, illustrated by Thomas Locker (*Philomel*, ages 3–8). A gorgeous book, narrated in the second person, about the wet and wonderful hike "you'll" have.
THE TREE IN THE ANCIENT FOREST, by Carol Reed-Jones, illustrated by Christopher Canyon (*Dawn Publications*, ages 4–10). You don't have to travel far to see plenty; here's one tree and the multitude of life that surrounds it.

other high peaks, that can be tough. But even here in New England's White Mountains, snow can be seen on Mount Washington, in Tuckerman's Ravine, in the summer. There's also another White Mountain spot called Ice Gulch, where certain caves protect ice year-round.

As much as kids love snow and ice, remember that it can be life-threatening. A 13-year-old boy was killed in Baxter State Park, Maine, when he slipped on some ice while trying to make a snowball. Summer snowfields on steep mountainsides are well-packed and stable, which means it's easy to start sliding out of control. Hiking on such terrain becomes mountaineering, requiring a greater degree of knowledge and experience.

Stick to flat patches of snow where you can toss a few snowballs and have a picnic nearby.

CAR
CAMPING

And then I heard it. Loud, uncontrollable and inhuman: the unmistakable sounds of my brother and sister laughing themselves silly.

Suddenly a flashlight beam lit up the night. It was aimed at me. "You were right, John," said my mother. "This is going to be a vacation none of us ever forgets."

Dyan Sheldon, *Harry on Vacation*

H

ave car, will camp.

As a kid, I couldn't understand why car camping was so popular. I assumed it meant spending the night in the car, which sounded uncomfortable.

Now that I understand the term, it's still an oxymoron. Don't most of us go camping to escape things like cars?

True, but even I have to admit that a car is a giant security blanket, a link to home for kids and parents

The ubiquitous American station wagon packed to the ceiling with all of the camping essentials.

alike — not to mention a grand convenience.

Go almost anywhere, take anything you can cram inside. If there's a problem, either big or small — left the toothbrush behind, ran out of diapers, need some ice cream, illness, or foul weather — you can get what you need, find a motel, or go home. Don't be a purist unless you want to.

Car camping, especially with children in tow, is car comfort.

CAMPGROUND KARMA

Campgrounds are like hotels and motels: Some are four-star facilities; others are dumps. There are mom-and-pop campgrounds, sites in state and national parks, and private camping meccas ready to serve hundreds.

I've been in beautiful campsites so secluded I might have been backpacking. Moose and deer strolled by yards from our tent. Others were hellish — not much more than parking lots full of campers, tents, and recreational vehicles (RVs) packed like sardines. More solitude and communion with nature could be had by holing up in a Manhattan hotel room and reading a few chapters of Thoreau or Edward Abbey.

I've stayed in campgrounds with immaculate facilities; others were dilapidated, even odd. One memorable place was obviously open, although the few campers there seemed to be having a private party in a battered VW bus. We couldn't find the caretaker but stayed anyway — it was late. Our visit had a bizarre, slightly eerie feel.

Just as there are all kinds of campgrounds, there are all kinds of campers. Let me state my bias: Jim and I tend to be backwoods minimalists. We want peace, quiet, woods, the fewer amenities the better. All we really need is a spot for our tent and a water source. The rest — picnic table, outhouse, fire ring — is extra. Usually we prefer state or national park campgrounds, where facilities are usually clean, safe, and relatively minimal. Some of the very best campgrounds are private, but unless you know the place or are armed with strong recommendations, quality is a crap shoot.

A good many families like to pretend to camp, but aren't about to leave their microwaves and cable TV behind. They cruise in RVs, hunting for the campers' version of Disney World, complete with outdoor movie screens, Olympic-size swimming pools, miniature golf, and video arcades. In fact, there is a campground across the street from Disneyland. Could that possibly be camping?

Some couples change camping styles after becoming parents. Friends of ours who used to seek panoramas now want playgrounds. As long as their two boys are amused, they get some time to themselves.

Will hasn't made great changes in our camping style. We do less backpacking and more car camping, but in the same types of places. So far, he thinks just about anywhere we pitch a tent is dandy.

A BONA FIDE FAMILY OF CAR CAMPERS

My family did a lot of camping. We couldn't afford much, so my father built his own car-top tent that attached to the top of the family station wagon. It folded down for travel, up for camping. Three of us slept on top in the tent and the other three slept below in the back of the car. The old tent got worse-looking on every trip. It finally bit the dust — it flew off the top of the wagon in northern Minnesota after leaking like a sieve the night before during the heaviest rain I have ever experienced. Our entire family mourned its loss like it was one of the family. In a sense I guess it was — there were so many emotions wrapped up in that leaky, musty, shrunken canvas.

Lorna Olsen — Fargo, North Dakota

FINDING NIRVANA

Irvin C. "Buzz" Caverly had been looking forward to taking his wife and two granddaughters camping in New Hampshire. As director of Maine's Baxter State Park, he was taking a true busman's holiday. But he came home disappointed because so many campgrounds, both public and private, had no buffers between sites.

"I missed all the restrictions we have at Baxter: on pets, CDs, and radios," he explains. "Even though we could still hear the snap and crackling of our campfire, we couldn't hear owls hooting out in the woods or other night sounds, such as coyotes.

As a single mom, I used some unusual methods to get my 8- and 10-year-old daughters interested in the outdoors. Once I took along a couple of their friends and threw a Mary Kay cosmetic party during a camping trip. They loved it!

To those who question whether that is what you are "supposed" to do in the outdoors, all I can say is that on the same trip, they also learned quite a bit about hiking, pitching camp, camp cooking, and identification of various edible plants and mushrooms. And they began what I believe may turn out to be a lifelong love affair with the outdoors.

Ellen Lanterman — Pine, Colorado

Instead, we heard domestic sounds."

So how *do* you find your little corner of car-camping heaven?

The more you camp, the more you know what to expect. If you don't know an area, get a recommendation from someone you trust, then drive through the facility yourself. Once you know what to look for, you'll know in a matter of minutes whether this is the place for you.

NUMBER OF SITES First, grab a guidebook; some basic detective work is easy enough. After the first clue, whether an area is private or public, the next telling sign is number of sites. Generally, the smaller the better, the more chance for peace and privacy. Fifty or fewer spots is ideal; 100 may be fine. We recently camped on national forest land with 87 sites, but the campground was so hilly and woodsy that it felt much more intimate. However, tranquillity isn't possible with several hundred families nearby, not even in the midst of Sequoia National Park, one of my favorite places.

RVS AND TENTS Also note the number of sites with hookups, which tells whether RVs are catered to. Avoid RV parks at all costs. It's tough to enjoy a wilderness experience when your neighbors are watching *Seinfeld*. If such a place is your only option, inquire about a "tents-only" section.

Before you shout "snob," let me assure you I can tolerate RVs under certain conditions. Several were at the national forest campground just

---

GEAR TALK

THE WELCOME MAT

A small rug at the entrance of your tent helps keep debris out. Don't let kids wear their shoes inside; they can sit on the mat to take them off. Don't leave shoes or boots outside overnight — rain or dew may soak them.

mentioned, but since no hookups were available, they weren't intrusive. Less noisy than many neighbors, in fact, since these campers were inside.

BUFFERS As Caverly noted, buffers between sites are hugely important. There's one New Hampshire state park I avoid at all costs. It's at the doorstep of some of the best hiking in the White Mountains, but the 97 sites are so close together that it's usually impossible to get a decent night's sleep. So we drive 15 miles to a national forest campground with 60 sites, nicely spaced and woodsy. The difference is night and day.

SITE LOCATION Whenever choices are available, I love to hunt for just the right campsite. Take, for instance, camping at Sequoia. We knew the camping areas were like zoos, but decided to try them anyway, to maximize our time on the park's trails.

Since it was late September, there were openings, and we circled various loops repeatedly, until our efforts paid off — we found a site offering a semblance of privacy, on top of an incline leading down to a river. That evening we sat by the river, looked up at the moon, and felt worlds away from other campers.

The exact location of your site can make or break your stay. In effect, you're on a mini real estate excursion, searching for a home away from home. Some families like to be near bathrooms, but this often means more noise, less privacy. Secluded, or

CAMPGROUNDS vs. MOTELS

I think camping with young children is much easier than spending a night in a hotel or motel.

Entertainment options are practically nonexistent in hotel rooms. Our two girls are invariably attracted to the phone, water glasses, and the wastebaskets. Climbing on the furniture and bouncing on the bed are also "fun." At campsites chosen with children in mind, the outdoors offers lots of entertainment and area for exploring.

Sleeping accommodations vary from one motel room to the next, but our tent "bedroom" always looks the same. We get to sleep in our own sleeping bags and in the same configurations. Since kids thrive on familiarity, this seems to make the bedtime routine go more smoothly.

In short, we feel free when camping, but confined in motels.

Rob Kleine — Phoenix, Arizona

close to playground, or lake? Sunny or shaded?

Refine your wish list the way singles labor over personal ads. Ours reads: Secluded, woodsy, tents-only site wanted for all-night stands. In the heart of prime hiking and biking trails, with a pond nearby. Hilly terrain preferred. Cleanliness and quiet a must, flush toilets and showers a bonus.

Enjoy the hunt, but don't be inflexible. Life, as you know, doesn't always bring us our heart's content,

Car camping is car comfort, right down to the ever-useful tailgate. For kids and parents alike, the car is a giant security blanket and a link to home.

Utah, 61 miles from Bryce National Park and 74 miles from Zion National Park.

"We like to think of ourselves as the park that time forgot," says interpretive ranger Anji Porter of Cedar Breaks.

"About 600 people a day visit us," Porter says. "That's a far cry from Zion, which can get that many people in a half hour."

This is canyon country, a giant natural amphitheater, made of rock and shaped like a huge coliseum, 2,000 feet deep and more than 3 miles in diameter. One visitor said, "If Cedar Breaks were anywhere but in this region, it would be picked as one of the world's greatest scenic wonders." Given its location, however, folks rush past to see Zion, Bryce, and the Grand Canyon.

The campground is small, with 30 tent and trailer sites, open from June through September. There are rest rooms, running water, a visitor's center, and evening ranger programs, but no RV hookups.

whether it's romance or camping. Sometimes it's worthwhile to lower standards, just to get the kids settled for the night. Compromise doesn't always mean catastrophe.

TALES OF THREE CAMPGROUNDS

What are you likely to encounter at various campgrounds? Here's a sample of three spots, each offering vastly different camping experiences.

✐ A SMALL JEWEL If you want to avoid the crowds at major tourist attractions, look for smaller parks nearby, just slightly off the well-beaten path. Take, for example, Cedar Breaks National Monument,

You can't reserve a site at Cedar Breaks; they're available on a first-come, first-served basis. Porter says they are generally full on July and August weekends, but weekdays remain "fairly empty."

"The campground is very laid back," Porter says. "Just come prepared to relax."

Contact the National Park Service or Cedar Breaks National Monument, P.O. Box 749, Cedar City, UT 84720; 801-586-0787.

✎ BACKCOUNTRY PARADISE For wilderness lovers, Baxter State Park in Millinocket, Maine, is a backcountry Disneyland, full of endless attractions — and one of my favorite places.

In fact, a man named Maurice "Jake" Day was once artist-in-resi-dence here. Later, when he worked with Walt Disney, he used the region as inspiration for the backdrop drawings in *Bambi*.

Baxter State Park is best known as the northern end of the Appalachian Trail. Most through-hikers finish their trek at Baxter Peak, atop 5,267-foot Mount Katahdin. But the 201,018-acre park also contains countless other pleasures, bequeathed by former governor Percival P. Baxter to the people of Maine on condition that it "shall forever be left in the natural wild state."

For Director Caverly, Baxter's mandate is gospel. It means preservation and protection always come first, recreation second. There are nine campgrounds, seven accessible by

---

A CAMPING LEXICON

Savvy campers read between the lines of campground directories:

TYPES OF CAMPGROUNDS

● Public Campgrounds: Typically on parklands and run by a variety of public agencies, these are what you want. There may not be many or any man-made frills, but the natural frills are first rate: lakes, mountains, trails, views. In addition to state and national parks, look into national forest and Bureau of Land Management property, where you can camp for free or a token fee.

● Private Campgrounds: These are the ones to inspect carefully, since quality varies so greatly.

TYPES OF SITES

● Group Tenting: As opposed to sites for families or a small group of friends, these are large, open sites for crowds. If you're having a family reunion or are with a school, scouting, or church group, using these sites is a good way to keep

continued on page 174

CAMPING LEXICON
continued from page 173

costs down. Avoid them otherwise
— too many people, too much
commotion.

● Open: Some campgrounds are
basically meadows, offering no privacy, no matter how large the sites.
I try to avoid open sites, but sometimes the landscape allows nothing
else, at beaches and in deserts, for
instance. Semi-open is tolerable;
one campground I like offers open
sites on the edge of woods, which
affords some privacy and means a
sunny, warm site when the weather
is good.

● Primitive: Pit toilets and a
picnic table, but that's about it. No
showers, and perhaps no drinking
water, just a stream from which
water must be purified.

● Remote: Also called walk-in
campgrounds. Just for backpackers; too bad you can't take
your car.

● Resort: For those faux campers
I mentioned who want entertainment, but not the wilderness-style
type. Prices are usually three-to-
four times the price of a national

park site — say, $30 versus $10
per night, with charges for hookups
that can rack up your tab even further. Steer clear of these campgrounds; leave them for RVs. If
you're in the mood for a resort,
leave your tent at home.

● Wooded: Just what I like.
Wooded sites provide a natural
buffer from other campers, and
sometimes make you feel as
though you're backpacking.

TELLTALE SIGNS
● Buffers: What you need between
you and the campers next door.
Some campgrounds, even public
ones, are woefully short of them.

● Hookups: The lifeline of RV
campers, these give them water,
electricity, sewage, and cable TV.

● Showers: Typically coin-oper-
ated. Some public campgrounds
have them, some don't. They're
nice, but you can usually live
without them.

● Toilets: These come in two styles
— flush or pit (outhouses). I have
to admit I prefer flush toilets over
outhouses, but for me, wilderness,
not plumbing, is a priority.

car, several group camping areas,
plus remote campsites. Access is
restricted to 1,000 to 1,200 campers
per night in the park's tent sites,

lean-tos, cabins, and bunkhouses;
limits are also placed on the number
of dayhikers. There are pit toilets, no
RV hookups, and no treated water.

"We like to think of how Governor Baxter's mandate affects everything we do," Caverly explains, "from constructing a toilet, laying out a campsite, or building a building. We ask, 'How will this affect our resources?'"

Priorities aside, Caverly and all park personnel are warm, welcoming hosts. Several years ago Caverly gave me a wonderful grand tour. Seasoned professional that he is, after more than 30 years of working in the park, he's still like a kid in a candy store whenever he has a chance to show off the park's beauties: moose wading in a stream, loons calling, island campsites amid vast lakes, the howls of coyotes heard from mountain ledges.

To all would-be visitors and campers at Baxter, Caverly says, "The first thing we ask is tell us what you enjoy. Fishing? Mountain climbing? Bird-watching? Flatland hiking? Technical climbing? Photography? Tell us what you like, and we'll try to marry your likes to what we have available."

It takes about 30 minutes to drive to Baxter State Park from Millinocket, the small mill town nearest the main entrance. There's not much to see in between, except the Big Moose Inn and the North Woods Trading Post, which Caverly calls "the last outpost of civilization." Here the electricity and telephone lines stop, and a sign notes that the paved public road soon ends.

"From here you have 8.3 miles to prepare yourself for the wilderness experience at Baxter State Park," Caverly says.

Contact Baxter State Park Headquarters, 64 Balsam Dr., Millinocket, ME 04462; 207-723-5140. Reservations for each year can be made after January 1, either by mail or in person, but not by phone.

CAMPSIDE COMFORTS In the 1950s Jim and Dora Keen owned a few cottages on a Pennsylvania lake. One day someone stopped by and asked permission to put up a tent, and that was the start of Keen Lake Camping & Cottage Resort, 300 sites surrounding a 90-acre lake, in addition to cottages and homes for rent. All but 45 sites have hookups; 75 are for tents only.

There's a game room, train rides, heated swimming pool, five playgrounds, nightly indoor movies on a

OFF THE BEATEN PATH

A booklet called *The National Parks: Lesser-Known Areas* is available for $1.50. Send request and payment to Superintendent of Documents, U.S. Government Printing Office, Washington, DC 20402. Ask for stock number 024-005-00911-6.

60-inch screen with SurroundSound, a snack bar, gift shop, security patrol, and full-time activities director. Theme days include a Mother's Day champagne breakfast, pirate weekend, and Halloween in August, complete with a parade and campsite trick or treating. For $2 per day, you can hook up to cable TV. Heck, we don't even have that at home.

Sound like too much? Keen Lake hasn't forgotten about campers like us, in search of solitude. We're directed to the back of the lake, about a mile away from the more central sites, to 25 wooded, more secluded sites. In contrast to the tiled bathhouses on the other side of the lake, this section boasts outhouses and a pump for water.

Maybe we should charge the RVers $2 for the privilege of watching us primitive types build a campfire.

But seriously, there's a lesson here. Maybe a relative (your kid?) drags you to a place like this. Maybe it's the only campground handy. Ask for a secluded site without the extras, and you may get one.

Contact Keen Lake Camping & Cottage Resort, R.R. 1, Box 1976, Waymart, PA 18472; 717-488-5522 or -6181.

BEYOND TENTS

For a change of pace, explore some additional options besides the family tent. Cabins, for instance, are particularly good in foul weather, offering more protection than a tent and giving kids more room to play.

I never slept in a lean-to until after I was married, during my first visit to Baxter State Park. Here was a whole new way to camp, with pleasures for adults and kids alike. The elevated wooden structure, open on one side, had the feel of a fort or treehouse. There was no tent to pitch — just unroll your sleeping pads and bags — and more room and protection from rain.

Many camping areas and trails offer lean-tos. Some are available for car campers, others are in the backcountry. Check trail guides and inquire at various park headquarters.

Ever hear of a yurt?

Sounds like a pack animal to me, but it's actually a circular domed tent that sits on top of a plywood floor, available in numerous parks, including state parks in Oregon.

The Oregon yurts are 16 feet in diameter with 10-foot ceilings, furnished with a bunk bed, fold-out couch, small table, electric space heater, and lights. Call 800-452-5687 for information.

Many campgrounds, inns, lodges, and federal and state parks offer cabins — some rustic, with no lights, water, or plumbing, others with most of the comforts of home.

We've had family reunions in the basic, though well-appointed cabins at Pipestem State Park in West Virginia. Even my mother, who is not a camper, enjoyed her stay.

We've also stayed in a primitive cabin at Baxter State Park. There was an outhouse and no water — my mother would never stay here. To us, it was wilderness luxury.

RESERVATIONS
Taking Chances

If I can avoid it, I don't like to make reservations. On overnight trips, I like to check the latest weather forecasts on Thursday and Friday nights, and make sure everyone is healthy and in the mood. Luckily, there are plenty of fine places to camp where reservations aren't needed, even on summer weekends.

On week-long vacations, when-ever possible, I like to have the freedom to go where I want, when I want. Also, on longer trips away from home, I'm less likely to be familiar with various campgrounds, so I like to inspect them in person.

With kids along, however, you want to get settled early; long, drawn-out searches can ruin a trip. To strike a balance between maintaining your freedom and ensuring a campsite, have some specific places in mind before you set out, and call ahead to determine whether you're likely to be safe without a reservation. Timing can be everything. Ask about peak visitation months. Certain places fill up only on weekends; be particularly aware of holidays.

RESERVATIONS IN NATIONAL PARKS

Campsites in many national parks are available on a first-come, first-served basis. If you aren't able to get a spot, the best thing to do is camp outside the park, then try again very early the next morning.

If you want to make a reservation in those national parks that allow them, there's no central number, and policies, sometimes phone numbers, change from year to year. For instance, in 1995 you could reserve a campsite no sooner than eight weeks in advance at cer-tain parks; in 1996 the timing changed to five months. The best advice I can give you is to call the specific park you're interested in as far ahead as possible. At Yosemite, for example, sites are usually spoken for within the first hour of the reservation period.

For more information, contact the National Park Service Office of Public Inquiries, Room 1013, U.S. Department of the Interior, 1849 C St., N.W., P.O. Box 37127, Washington, DC 20013-7127; 202-208-4747; http://www.nps.gov.

continued on page 178

RESERVATIONS

continued from page 177

Currently, reservations for Yellowstone can be made by calling 303-297-2757. A company called Destinet (800-365-2267) handles reservations for several parks, including Acadia, Assateague, Cape Hatteras, Death Valley, Grand Canyon, Great Smoky Mountains, Joshua Tree, Rocky Mountain, Sequoia-Kings Canyon, Shenandoah, Whiskeytown, and Yosemite. Outside the United States, call 619-452-8787.

Note that camping fees are separate from park entrance fees. If you plan to visit several national parks within a year, check into a Golden Eagle Passport for $25, which allows passengers in one vehicle entrance into national parks, monuments, historic sites, recreation areas, and national wildlife refuges for a one-year period.

Lifetime passes are also available for those ages 62 and older ($10, Golden Age Passport, good for everyone in the vehicle), and for those who are blind or permanently disabled (free, Golden Access Passport). The latter also provides a 50 percent discount on additional usage fees, such as camping.

Pending legislation may change fees for the Golden Eagle and Golden Age passports.

Once on the road, make a point to get to potential campgrounds as early as possible, especially on Fridays and Saturdays. Even if you're met with a "Full Camp" sign out front, check in at the office. These signs don't always represent the latest comings and goings. We checked in at an allegedly full campground in New Hampshire this summer, but had our choice of several sites.

Booking Ahead

Late one September night we watched a car in front of us get turned away from the North Rim of the Grand Canyon — we felt lucky to have called ahead. Sometimes you need a guaranteed place to pitch your tent. If you want to camp in places as popular as the canyon, don't leave home without one.

The same is true for many lesser-known spots as well; Baxter State Park is a prime example. Although it's remote, don't expect to sail in. Reservations there can be made each year beginning on January 1, by mail or in person, but not by phone.

Certain sites and times are so prized that each New Year's Day, about 250 people brave northern

Maine's frigid weather to try to be first with their requests. Early in the morning they crowd into a motel restaurant across from park headquarters, sip coffee, munch doughnuts, and swap Baxter Park tales as they wait their turn to talk with park personnel. They could mail in their requests, but worry they wouldn't get the reservation they want.

"Because we maintain capacities and control access," Caverly says, "you may not get in the first time you apply for reservations. But when you do get in, you'll have a better experience because of the policy."

Some campgrounds place two-night minimums on weekends and holidays. Cabins and yurts usually require reservations, as do lean-tos at Baxter.

Even at the busiest campgrounds, however, it always pays to call for an update on openings, even at the last minute. Inevitably, there are no-shows, and sometimes you get lucky.

But remember, this isn't a lottery. Usually a simple phone call from home will tell the story.

GEAR: FAMILY FRILLS

The just-mentioned camping trip at Sequoia occurred before Will was

---

AGES AND STAGES

CAR CAMPING

Children of any age make great car campers. This is the place where backpackers and other wilderness lovers are born.

INFANTS AND BABIES

Go for it! Your baby's likely to enjoy sleeping in a tent more than a cradle or crib; Mom and Dad are right there.

TODDLERS

This is probably the most difficult stage of camping with kids, but still fun. As at home, constant attention is necessary at any campsite.

PRESCHOOLERS

Preschoolers can get into the spirit. Parents must keep a watchful eye, but aren't nearly as exhausted as with toddlers. Nighttime fears often run rampant at this age (see Chapter 7).

6- TO 10-YEAR-OLDS

They can really camp, help with camp chores, and actually accomplish something. Some are ready for their own tent.

11 AND UP

By this age, kids either love or hate camping. If they love it, they may be experts. Newcomers learn quickly.

Be sure to include some light loads so small children can help pack and unpack the car. Boxes and plastic milk crates make excellent storage containers. Pack according to use: food that won't spoil in one container, utensils in another, dinnerware in another, small toys, and so forth.

born. We flew from Boston to California for a two-week vacation combining camping and motel stays. To simplify our luggage, we took only bare necessities — when camping, for instance, we ate freeze-dried dinners.

In Sequoia we camped beside a family of three who traveled in style. They had everything, even a portable heater. They took pity on us as we tried to dine by the light of our dim headlamps, and brought over an extra propane lantern. We liked its wonderful glow so much, we went home and bought one.

Now that Will has joined our expeditions, we've stopped traveling light. Since we're spending more time in camp, it makes sense to spoil ourselves.

We've got all the basics: sleeping bags, mattress pads, tents, cooking gear and stoves (both backpacking and a Coleman two-burner), flashlights. Now we're deciding which "luxury" items to purchase. Many can be small and inexpensive — a tablecloth is a homey touch on any picnic table; a citronella candle can be a lifesaver. Here's our want list —

things that any camping family might find useful and fun:

CAMP CHAIRS Picnic tables and logs will quickly leave you with a backache. Outdoor stores and department stores carry all sorts of fold-up, lightweight chairs, suitable for backyards, beaches, and camping. Get off the ground — if you're car camping, you have room for more than a cushioned backpacking lounger.

CAMP COFFEE No more coffee bags for us. If Will is going to rise with the birds, then Jim and I deserve a decent cup of coffee in the morning. It's easy and good with the Nissan vacuum bottle and coffee cone, which allows you to brew directly into the bottle. You supply coffee, filter, and hot water. (Get the same effect by borrowing the pot and filter holder from a drip coffeemaker at home, and adding hot water.)

COOKSTAND A foldable, chrome-plated steel wire stand for large camping stoves. This gets the stove off the picnic table and leaves more room for young campers to play or help with meal preparation.

ENAMELWARE These sets come complete with large dinner plates, bowls, cups, fry pan, and kettle. I've had it with our little metal bowls, hand-me-downs from my brothers' Scout days.

KITCHEN ESSENTIALS KIT If you're tired of using kitchen castoffs and tag sale finds, REI makes a dandy kitchen kit, complete with a pouch filled with utensils, including a set of measuring spoons, and containers for condiments. Why should I scramble for this stuff — or leave it behind — every time we go camping?

OUTBACK OVEN These turn camping stoves into ovens. One advertisement shows two children and says, "Let them eat cake." I agree . . . and also suggest pizza, muffins, and brownies.

POPCORN POPPER Comes with a long handle, good for over a stove or campfire. Will will learn that popcorn doesn't grow in microwave ovens. Meanwhile, our camping neighbors will be drooling.

SCREENHOUSE Some friends just bought one, and already they swear by it. Not only do they keep out the bugs, they're a big playpen for little wanderers.

SLEEPING PADS We've already got

? AGE-OLD QUESTIONS

BABIES

"My husband is planning a family camping weekend that includes me and our three-month-old baby. I'm still nursing the baby and he still wakes up several times each night. Frankly, I'm too exhausted to camp right now. Am I being a party pooper?"

Hardly. While there's no reason the three of you can't camp, assuming the weather isn't severe and you have the proper clothing and gear, moms deserve preferential treatment at this stage of the game. When you've settled into more of a routine and are getting enough sleep, perhaps you'll reconsider.

TODDLERS

"My two-year-old is a sleepwalker. I'm afraid she'll walk right out of our tent."

Highly unlikely, unless the rest of you sleep like zombies. Tent zippers make lots of noise. Position your sleepwalker away from the door, and make additional barricades with your gear.

PRESCHOOLERS

"Our four-year-old is terrified of bears. We camp in bear country, and after watching us hang our food, she stayed awake virtually the entire night. Now she refuses to camp. How can we get her out again?"

Start by taking her somewhere where she doesn't have to worry about bears. You need to be able to reassure her, but you can't give any 100 percent guarantees when you camp in bear country.

A chat with a friendly ranger might also help. But talk to the ranger yourself first, without your daughter, to make sure his pep talk will be reassuring. Also try some friendly bear books and movies, such as *Gentle Ben*.

Once you're ready to venture back into bear country, you can try explaining the concept of measured risks. Tell her, for instance, that roads can be dangerous, but when you follow safe driving and crossing rules, you're unlikely to get hurt.

continued on page 182

SCHOOL-AGE CHILDREN

"My 11-year-old wants a penknife. Is she old enough to have one?"

That's a call only you and your spouse can make, based on your child's maturity, your own instincts, and the safety instruction and supervision you can provide.

I got a Girl Scout knife at about that age and still have it. I never cut myself with it or injured anyone else, and it was definitely a treasure. But I liked to look at it more than use it. Many kids — especially, I must say, boys — want to tease and stab, try risky endeavors, play dangerous games. Also take into account whether younger siblings might get hold of, or in the way of, a knife.

"My eight-year-old son wants to take a friend along on one of our family camping trips. I don't know the boy well and am not sure whether this is a good idea."

Depends on the boy. Get to know him better, and have an extended conversation with his parents. Has he camped before? Invite your son's friend on some dayhikes and for an overnight stay at your house. Also consider asking his family or one of his parents to accompany him on a camping trip.

Aside from Girl Scout weekends, my first camping experience was with my friend Sarah and her family. I'm thankful they invited me.

You may be introducing your son's friend to something he'll love for years to come, and you're likely to keep your own son happy.

---

nice Therm-a-Rest inflatable mattresses. But I've just seen the king of camping mattresses: thick foam ones, at least 4 inches. I'm trying to decide between that and an air mattress, both of which promise a good night's sleep. They're useful at home, too, for overnight guests.

MIND YOUR MANNERS

Not all of our camping neighbors have been as kind as our neighbors in Sequoia. Worst were some college-age males we encountered in a private campground in New Hampshire, where we had lakefront sites.

The trouble started in the morning, not at night, as is more typically the case. We saw these guys throw their leftovers in the water, including milk and eggs. Moments later they began to chop down a tree.

I went straight to the manager. While it's often a good idea to try to solve problems camper-to-camper, in this case I felt the property damage should be reported. Fairly soon a police cruiser pulled in, and the vandalizing campers were fined. I was happy they got their due.

Noisy neighbors are the most common problem you're likely to encounter. Campgrounds generally have posted quiet hours; some are even patrolled.

Sometimes, however, there's no one on duty, and you have to ask other campers to keep their noise down. Many will oblige, assuming your request is reasonable. You can't expect other campers to tiptoe during your child's afternoon nap, or to stop speaking at 7:00 P.M. just because it's your baby's bedtime.

The key to successful car camping is finding great campsites, whether by word of mouth or plain checking out campgrounds for yourself and moving on down the road until you come upon one that feels just right.

If a fair request is ignored, however, your only recourse is often to grin and bear it. The more you plead with someone who's rude and insensitive, the louder they're likely to become.

At the same time, you've got to be aware of your own noise levels. You may be used to your children's shouts and hollers, but the elderly couple next door may not be.

For the sake of politeness and safety, keep a close eye on your kids

BEST-BET READING

FOR ADULTS

Check with state tourist bureaus for annual campground listings.

AAA CAMPBOOK GUIDES (*Automobile Association of America*). Regional campground listings.

CAMPER'S GUIDE TO U.S. NATIONAL PARKS, by Lillian Morava and Mickey Little (*Gulf*). A two-volume set of ideas.

✳ COMPLETE GUIDE TO AMERICA'S NATIONAL PARKS, by the National Park Foundation (*Fodor's*). Includes basic information on parks, monuments, and other sites, as well as information on weather and peak visitation times.

WOODALL'S ANNUAL CAMPGROUND DIREC-

continued on page 184

BEST-BET READING
continued from page 183

TORY (*Woodall Publications*). Includes maps, listings, and directions for campgrounds catering to both tents and RVs for the United States and Canada.

WOODALL'S PLAN-IT, PACK-IT, GO: GREAT PLACES TO TENT, FUN THINGS TO DO (*Woodall Publications*). An excellent annual directory geared for tent camping. Includes campground listings as well as articles on bicycling, hiking, canoeing, and other activities, for the United States and Canada.

FOR KIDS

CURIOUS GEORGE GOES CAMPING, adapted from the Curious George film series (*Houghton Mifflin*, ages 2–6). Curious George and the man with the yellow hat go camping, and George helps prevent a forest fire.

HARRY ON VACATION, by Dyan Sheldon (*Candlewick Press*, ages 8–12). A girl named Chicken goes camping with her family, accompanied by Harry, an alien who resembles a cat and creates lots of fun.

JUST ME AND MY DAD, by Mercer Mayer (*Golden Books*, ages 2–6). Little Critter takes his father camping.

LET'S GO CAMPING WITH MR. SILLYPANTS, by M. K. Brown (*Crown*, ages 3–7). Poor Mr. Sillypants gets lost *before* he gets started. Kids will love this guy.

A TASTE OF SMOKE, by Marion Dane Bauer (*Clarion*, ages 10 and up). Thirteen-year-old Caitlin goes camping with her older sister, only to discover the ghost of a boy who died in a fire 100 years ago. A well-written, intriguing mystery.

WHEN I GO CAMPING WITH GRANDMA, by Marion Dane Bauer (*BridgeWater Books*, ages 3–7). A girl and her grandmother share a wonderful time.

(see Chapter 7). Don't let them roam through other people's sites, and try to keep them reasonably quiet.

Be especially mindful at night and in the morning. Are your neighbors still trying to sleep? Is your crying child likely to awaken them? Since you're car camping, consider taking her inside your vehicle, where the noise will be muffled, or going for a ride, and lulling her to sleep.

In a nutshell, be thoughtful and hope your neighbors will return the favor.

In addition to being courteous,

show your family how to practice low-impact, no-trace camping. This means carting away everything you bring in, including things like orange peels, apple cores, and peanut shells. If you've had a campfire, check the ashes the next morning to make sure everything burned. If anything besides wood remains, dispose of it.

Most campgrounds have their own set of rules. Read them, explain them to your kids, and heed them.

BACKPACKING

"It's an Expedition. That's what an Expedition means. A long line of everybody."

A. A. Milne, *Winnie-the-Pooh*

The term "family backpacking" makes purists chuckle, or — worse yet — groan.

After all, real backpacking calls for strength, endurance, and mileage, not young dawdlers who can hardly manage a daypack, much less a full load of gear.

Many parents venturing forth want their children to at least be able to walk on their own, since lugging gear *and* a child turns parents into true beasts of burden. However, determined couples do take babies, toddlers, and preschoolers along.

Is your family ready to backpack? This is where we separate the dabblers from the diehards. Where does your family stand (or collapse) on the subject?

● "Never in a million years." Whether you're a kid or an adult,

BABY BACKPACKERS

Our son loved our trip last year, on the shores of Lake Minnewanka near Banff. There were rocks and streams and logs and a fire and deer, all wonderful things to a 14-month-old. Of course, there are rocks and garden hoses and sticks and fireplaces and bathtubs and cats in our backyard, so he probably would have enjoyed camping out there just as much as backpacking.

John Abraham — Calgary, Canada

backpacking isn't for everyone. Don't sweat it. Just because backpacking isn't your bag doesn't mean you have to forgo the pleasures of wilderness adventures with your children.

● "We'll wait until the kids are older, strong enough to carry some weight." Not a bad idea. For many children, a camping trip is plenty, and backpacking brings nothing but frustration. Hold off on backpacking for a while, but not too many years or your kids will be busy. Plan a short trip as soon as your little hikers can

Books like this one may help spark your child's interest, but getting out on the trail is the true test. It's usually met with great enthusiasm.

carry their sleeping bags and clothes. Meanwhile, continue to camp. Talk up the first backpack as a reward for "expert" hikers and campers, a rite of passage.

● "We'd like to try but don't want to kill ourselves." You don't have to. Family backpacking can mean anything from short and sweet to rough and rugged. Instead of walking 10 miles to a site, establish a base camp fairly close to the trailhead and take day trips from there. You'll get the feel of the wild without the struggle, and without the pressure of attaining a certain number of miles each day.

● "We've always backpacked and nothing will stop us now — certainly not a child." You're tough. And you're probably out on the trail now, not home reading this book.

Assuming you do forge ahead at one point or another, this chapter contains numerous strategies to make your backpacking trips easier and more enjoyable. A successful outing is an ideal chance to give children a big boost in self-confidence. There's something utterly satisfying about setting out with everything you need on your back, a feeling of self-reliance that can't be gotten elsewhere.

There are also countless lessons in cooperation. Where else will you and your offspring play, work, eat, and sleep together 24 hours a day? Not at home, certainly. Even on most other family vacations, other diversions beckon. With backpacking, there are no TVs, computers, hoops, malls, or museums. If you want real togetherness and are prepared for the trail, backpacking is the way to travel.

CHOOSE YOUR STYLE

Before you head for the hills, take note of a few caveats. Since backpacking is a combination of hiking and camping, be sure your family is experienced at both. Don't even think about backpacking until everyone has several dayhikes and car-camping trips under their belts.

Ideally, one or both parents should have backpacking experience before you take the kids out. If not, bring yourself up to speed by consulting a guidebook for adults and talking to experienced friends or acquaintances.

Consider bringing someone experienced with you. Adults without kids are ideal, since they can help haul. But families are fun, too, and kids enjoy having other kids along. An added bonus is that they often gripe less about perceived drudgeries — they'll sometimes stifle their whines with peers around.

Finally, provide appropriate challenges but don't ask too much of your kids. It's a fine balancing act to

push them beyond their expectations but not their abilities. This is true of practically everything, but essential for backpackers.

If you fear you're planning too ambitious an outing, picture your child perched atop his pack,

announcing he's going on strike —
and you're hours away from a campsite. Or picture yourself carrying
everyone's gear uphill. Remember
your own abilities as well.

It's supposed to be backpacking,
not backbreaking.

Yo-Yos, Base Camps, Loops, and Car Spotting

You don't need to be psychic to predict how a family will fare on a backpacking trip. Aside from wild cards
presented by weather, illness, and
injury, any experienced backpacker
can examine a route and itinerary,
then venture a sound guess how a particular family is likely to fare.

Consider several types of trips.
The simplest is called a yo-yo: You
hike to one spot, camp, then hike
back. You'll probably want to try a
short "yo-yo" on your initial family
backpacking trip.

A wonderful variation for families
of all ages is the base-camp approach,
especially if you want to hike more.
Walk to one campsite carefully chosen
for its proximity to interesting sites
within a half-day's jaunt. Set up camp,
then take dayhikes from there, elimi-
nating the hassle of lugging heavy
packs great distances and making and
breaking camp every day.

Design your own base-camp trip,
or join a group. For example, the
Sierra Club sometimes offers family
trips to the Big Pines Lakes area in
the John Muir Wilderness, a cluster of
lakes at 10,800 feet near Bishop, California. Packers carry all the gear into
camp while participants hike 6 miles
to the camping area. The rest of the
week remains for dayhikes, fishing,
swimming, and relaxing.

A third option is loop trips, in
which you end up where you started
without retracing your steps. Loops
come in all sizes, from dayhikes to
overnighters and more, and they're
usually less boring than yo-yos.

Another way to avoid retracing
your steps is to spot a car at the end of
the trail. Because the logistics make
planning a bit more complicated, car
spotting works especially well if you're
backpacking with another family or a
group — more cars and drivers. Make
sure the beginning and end of the trail
aren't too far apart by road, so your
family doesn't have to hang out for a
long time while you retrieve the car.
Your hike may be only a few miles
long, but — surprise — mountains or
hills in between may mean that the
drive is much longer.

Walk-In Campgrounds

Want the ease of a primitive campground combined with the "leave-the-
car-behind" aspect of backpacking?
Walk-in campgrounds are a wonderful
option for families, especially those
new to backpacking. You still have to
haul all your gear, but you've got a
good place to establish base camp.

There are a good many of these
campgrounds, for instance, in the
White Mountains of New Hampshire.
Franconia Brook Campsite is a

favorite spot for many families, requiring a 2.7-mile flat hike beside the Pemigewasset River, a refreshing wading and playing spot on a hot day.

The amenities are usually basic: a water source, fire rings, perhaps a tent platform, and an outhouse. Inquire about walk-in campgrounds in national and state parks you plan to visit. Many require reservations.

Altitude with Ease: High Huts

Want to backpack without carrying mountains of gear?

High huts are a good compromise between car camping and backpacking. You can't reach them by car, but they offer some of the amenities of a campground or lodge.

Mollie, Summer, and George Wuerthner at a hut in Willamette National Forest, Oregon. High huts outfitted with bunks and fully provisioned, offer families a superb way to pack into the mountains without carrying mountains of gear.

For example, the Appalachian Mountain Club operates nine mountain hostels in the White Mountains of New Hampshire, each offering bunkhouses, outhouses, breakfast, and dinner. Kids are warmly welcomed and usually find the bunkhouse exciting. There are even special preschool weekends, for families with children ages three to five.

What's more, these huts are spaced a day's hike apart, so even families with young children can spend a week in the high country with little difficulty.

Guests must bring their own sleeping bags, clothes, lunch, and snack food. However, packs are considerably lighter without tents, stoves, cooking utensils, and extra food. On the downside: While fairly reasonably priced, the costs do add up.

Similar facilities are located across the country, such as Yosemite National Park's five High Sierra Camps, and in the low country, such as Phantom Ranch at the bottom of the Grand Canyon.

Hut hopping is also quite popular in other countries, especially Europe. I once stayed at several Norwegian huts — reached only by ferry or foot — that were as immaculate as well-kept inns. In fact, they were so inn-like that some families carried suitcases!

All of these facilities are quite popular, so be sure to book reservations well in advance. For instance, the National Park Service has instituted a lottery system for the High Sierra Camps; applications must be made before the first of the year in which you hope to go.

DESIGNING FAMILY TRIPS

The success of any backpacking trip is determined long before the first hiker sets foot on the trail. The most essential stage occurs at home, during planning and packing.

Let me confess that I never went backpacking until I was in my 20s. My first big trip was a glorious 8 days and 50 miles along Vermont's Long Trail.

I'll always be grateful to our fearless leader, a man named Ralph Larrson, by then a veteran of many family and Scout outings. He gave our group of six all the lessons we needed.

Having already hiked the entire Long Trail, Ralph carefully mapped out our route, including each day's mileage and each night's stopping point. He chose sections offering a multitude of rewards — peaks, views, interesting terrain. As with any trail, some sections are boring, so always be choosy, especially with kids along.

Before setting off, we took several weekend warm-up trips and had additional meetings to discuss equipment and menus. Ralph nailed down every detail. His wife and daughter even met us at trail's end with an impromptu bathhouse made of sheets stretched across branches — and provided clean towels, soap, and gallon containers full of warm water. Once we washed away the trail dust, we headed to Ben & Jerry's Ice Cream Factory to celebrate.

We met Ralph when we joined a local outing club. Every backpacking family needs a Ralph. You may be able to find your own mentor through a scouting group or outing club, or after a lengthy discussion with an outfitter or ranger.

First Tries

Start with several simple overnight excursions.

Select a campsite close to a trailhead, not much more than a mile or two away on easy terrain.

The short distance means that if you're carrying a baby, at least you don't have far to go. Older toddlers can manage the hike while parents don't have to kill themselves hauling gear. Nor will the walk overwhelm older kids, who can always run off any leftover steam by helping set up camp, or hiking or playing afterward. Better they be rambunctious than exhausted.

You don't even need to carry all the gear in at once; you can make several trips. Also, should bad weather, illness, or injury strike, or if you've forgotten something absolutely essential, your car — and civilization — is within manageable reach.

We're planning just such a trip

this summer in New Hampshire, Will's first official backpack. Jim and I will don packs while the three of us hike a mile or so along a wide, flat path that parallels a brook. When we reach a series of large pools and wide ledges, we'll pick our tent site. I've camped there before and know Will will love it.

Meanwhile, in Utah, Ray and Laura Dahl are also planning several outings for their three children, ages one, two, and four. Ray and Laura are veteran hikers and backpackers — Ray is such an active outdoorsman

NEED A MAP?

Trails Illustrated publishes topographic recreation maps covering major national parks and other popular areas, such as sections of the American Discovery Trail, Cape Cod National Seashore, and many areas in Colorado and Utah. They're tearproof and waterproof. Call 800-962-1643.

that he works at REI part time, in addition to a full-time job, to help support his pursuits. Before becoming parents, the Dahls led groups of teens on wilderness trips.

They know they must start their children on small trips, so they'll hike about a mile to a lake in the Uintah Mountains, in the northeastern part of the state. "They're a relatively benign mountain range," Ray says. "But they're fairly high — 9,000- and 10,000-foot trailheads are not uncommon. Water, fishing, and beautiful scenery are abundant."

Laura will carry the youngest child and Ray will act as sherpa for the gear. First he'll take in the tent and food, and they'll pitch the tent and feed the kids. Then he'll return to the car for sleeping bags and the remaining gear. They've got a workable, fun plan.

There's no reason for backpacking to be brutal. Try an easy trip, and if that goes well, try another, similar jaunt. After that, stay out for more than one night, but don't step up the mileage much. Take it from there, working up to longer adventures, making sure everyone is having a good time.

Trails and Mileage

As with hiking, the first decision is where to go. Pick a backpacking trail just as you would a dayhiking trail, making sure the terrain is interesting and keeping in mind weather and seasonal considerations.

The big difference is distance. Carrying fully loaded packs, you and your family aren't going to travel as quickly or as far as you do on a dayhike.

For starters, cut your usual mileage by at least half. If you typically hike 8 miles on a dayhike, don't plan on more than 4 for your first day of backpacking.

Also scour trail guides and topographic maps for elevation changes — packs seem to weigh more going uphill. Your child may need to get used to the extra weight before being ready to scramble and climb.

Be sure to get your kids in on the planning. Have them help scan trail guides, or present them with several options, allowing them to make the final decision. This will not only build enthusiasm but may put a lid on later griping. After all, you can remind them, *you* picked this trail!

Whatever your plans, don't be embarrassed by low expectations. Even world-class mountaineers are in the same boat. For instance, Rick Wilcox of Eaton, New Hampshire, has climbed some of the highest mountains on earth, including Everest. However, family treks are hardly formidable expeditions. When he and his wife take their six- and eight-year-old backpacking, they plan an easy 2 or 3 miles. Maximum.

"When my kids didn't know anything about hiking," Wilcox says, "they were fine. But now that they've done enough that they know what's coming, I have more trouble getting them going. The first thing they say is, 'Oh no, it's going to be hard.' "

Wilcox makes sure that it isn't.

Yet another essential: Don't overestimate the progress you'll make on downhill sections. Going down a steep trail is just as hard as going up, especially with a heavy pack. Gravity pulls the pack down on top of you, and the descent adds pressure to the knees and legs. Easy does it — be sure to tell your kids that this is when it's easy to fall. Their joints and reflexes may not be as good as yours.

Campsites and Rest Stops

Pore over trail descriptions and topographic maps. Where you stop is just as important as where you go.

Let's say you're planning a fairly ambitious long weekend for your family: 3 days and 12 miles. Your days may not logically break into three 4-mile segments. Mileage is more than a question of math; it's usually a matter of topography.

On this hypothetical journey, perhaps you won't reach the trailhead until early afternoon. If there's a beautiful campsite

by a pond that's 3 miles away, it makes sense to stop here for the night. Even if you could go a bit farther, why miss an idyllic spot?

On the second day, let's say you'll encounter a particularly steep climb. Play it safe by taking long rests and taking advantage of a

Rest stop: when your burden becomes your backrest. Such brief breaks, punctuated by a snack and drink of water, can make all the difference to flagging kids.

Lunch with a view: overlooking the Big Pine lakes and Temple Crag in the John Muir Wilderness, Sierra Nevada, California. Plan to have lunch at such memorable spots rather than simply saying, "It's noon, time for lunch."

campsite just 3.5 miles away from the first one.

That leaves 5.5 miles for the last day, but since this section of trail happens to be flat, no problem.

Once you've decided on possible campsites, do some research. Are they likely to be crowded this time of year, this day of the week? If you plan to sleep in a shelter or lean-to, this information can be vital. Take a

tent as a back-up in case the shelter is full, or in case you don't get that far.

Lunch stops should also be planned. If you've got an interesting destination as a goal, it can keep everyone motivated in the morning, and provide a good rest spot once you're there, getting everyone ready for the rest of the day's journey.

As Ray Dahl advises, "Having a destination is a big part of a successful trip, even subdestinations."

Before becoming a father, he led a group of 12-year-old Scouts to tackle 52 miles in the Uintah Mountains.

Dahl says, "Planning lunch at a lake, river crossing, mountain pass, or some definitive point is much nicer than saying, 'It's noon, time for lunch.' "

Layover Days

The bigger the hike, the bigger the rests you'll need.

On long trips, plan on at least a day or two of rest, play, dayhikes, or swimming, when no one has to lug his pack. Give those aching shoulders a break.

Avoid scheduling two big mileage days back to back. Leave sufficient time and be flexible, allowing for possible changes in plan. Dahl learned these lessons the hard way.

During the previously mentioned Scout trip in the Uintah Mountains, Dahl admits that he broke all of his own planning rules. After a day of long and hard hiking, the group's next goal was to reach an 11,000-foot-high pass. The morning went smoothly, but the boys became unusually quiet during a steep section. One suddenly started crying, saying he missed his baby sister.

Dahl realized he was pushing too hard. Luckily, he spotted a small pond and spring, features not shown on his map. They stopped and camped for the night, finishing the climb the next day, refreshed.

Getting in Shape

Once the entire family agrees on a plan, make sure they're not only excited but prepared, both mentally and physically.

Get everyone psyched with a family meeting or two. Show pictures of what you'll see, if you have any. For younger kids, read a picture book about hiking or camping. Pitch the tent in the family room or backyard.

If older kids will be carrying real packs, make sure they try wearing them on neighborhood walks or hikes, at least partially loaded, to get used to the feel.

You shouldn't need to do much physical training for first trips. However, for longer trips, you may all need to get in shape, perhaps with dayhikes, short backpacks, and other activities, such as cycling. Schedule some short sessions to discuss gear, menus, and packing. Older kids should be aware of the amount of planning that goes into big trips.

GEAR

Now is the time to scrutinize the gear everyone in your family is using. If you plan on backpacking often, you'll want to invest in some quality gear, especially if it weighs less than what you've been using.

Sleeping bags are a perfect example. Those slumber-party kids' bags may be fine for car camping, but for backpacking, they're likely to be heavy (about 5 pounds), bulky, and

not particularly warm. Forgo ineffi-
ciency and ineffectiveness and buy
your child a synthetic mummy bag,
significantly lighter at close to 3
pounds, and costing $75 and up.

Graduating to a Real Pack

One fine day that magic moment is
likely to arrive: Your child demands
a genuine backpack. Rejoice — and
get thee to an outfitter's.

Some children, especially those
with older siblings, may make such a
request before they're physically
capable of carrying significant loads.
Don't let this deter you. Get a real
pack, even a used or inexpensive one
— just don't put much in it at first.

If your child doesn't express
interest in a real pack, but you're
sure she's more than physically ready
to carry more, offer to let her pick
one out, or go ahead and buy one as
a special gift. Present it as an honor,
not an obligation, and don't rush to
fill it with extra gear.

Keep in mind that youngsters
carrying real packs need real hiking
boots, not tennis shoes.

Internal vs. External Frames

By age 9 or 10, your child will probably be strong enough to carry a real
backpack on overnight excursions.
For backpackers of any age, the big
question is whether to go with an
internal or external frame.

By and large, external packs are
simpler and cheaper than their more
modern cousins. If you were a Boy
Scout, you probably used one.

Now, however, most adult backpackers use internal-frame packs; in
addition to looking and feeling good,
they're better for balance and fit more
easily into car trunks and duffel bags.

In addition to financial considerations, external frames are usually
more practical for kids. Some children's sleeping bags, for instance,
tend to be bulky and often won't fit
into an internal pack, but they can be

GEAR TALK

A PARENT'S BEST FRIEND

One of the most valuable pieces of gear a parent can have is a frame
extender, which attaches to the top of your pack and provides more room
for strapping on extra gear, such as sleeping bags.

Parents also need plenty of straps for attaching all of this extra gear.
Another invaluable tool is a compression sack, which squeezes bulky
loads into more manageable form. Also, don't forget pack covers —
featherlight protection to keep your gear dry, even more crucial, if possible, with kids along.

strapped to the outside of a frame pack.

Some children, like adults, find internal frames more comfortable, and so they're worth the extra price. However, when internal frames are filled with a heavy load, they may force a child to lean forward under the weight — something I experience with my own internal-frame pack.

✎ Buy a backpack that will grow with your child. Several manufacturers, including Kelty and REI, make adjustable, external-frame, "junior" models

Ben Wiltsie's external-frame pack is draped with gear, including a sleeping pad and climbing gear. Once your child is ready for a real pack, look for scaled-down versions of adult models.

that sell for less than $75. REI's Long Trail Jr. is a good choice, with a capacity of 1,885 cubic inches and a price tag of about $50.

For added capacity and an internal frame, two packs by Tough Traveler work well: the Camper, with a capacity of about 2,200 cubic inches, about $100, and the Ranger, with a capacity of 2,400–3,200 cubic inches, at $130. The Camper is intended for 5- to 11-year-olds, or anyone from 3'6" to 5'; the Ranger is for 9- to 14-year-olds, or anyone from 4'6" to 5'6".

WEIGH THOSE
CALORIES

The biggest mistake is bringing too much food. It's easy to imagine how good something will taste when you're standing in the grocery store, but when you're schlepping it up a mountain, you may come into camp too tired to even want to cook or eat. Make meals simple and light.

Dinner, for instance, is a one-pot pasta meal. For four people we use two boxes of Tuna Noodle Helper and one 6-ounce can of tuna. When we boil the noodles, we also add dehydrated veggies. We vary the pasta and meat, but the proportions remain the same.

I take the noodle packets and seasoning packets out of the box and put them in a large Ziploc bag along with the veggies and tuna. Thus, each dinner is in one pouch.

John Stoop — Portland, Oregon

Whatever your decision, look for the same features desired in adult packs: padded hip belts, padded shoulder straps, durability, easily accessible compartments, and, most of all, comfort.

PACKING

Planning a family backpacking trip gives new meaning to the phrase "weighing your options."

You'll need a lot of stuff. But not too much, or the trip will be ruined. At first, the task may appear impos-

sible. Don't be overwhelmed. That's the beauty of short starter trips: They allow you to field-test what you really need and how much you — and your child — can carry. After a few such trips, you'll develop your own personal list of "must-haves."

How Much Should Your Child Carry?

A rule of thumb is that adults should carry no more than $1/4$ to $1/3$ of their body weight. Kids should *never* carry more than $1/4$ of their body weight.

Now that you know the rule, forget it. A 32-pound two-year-old should never be expected to haul 8 pounds. And be thankful if your 50-pound six-year-old manages to walk to your campsite — don't hold out for him to carry 12 or 13 pounds.

Marit Sawyer, outreach coordinator for the National Outdoor Leadership School (NOLS), remembers how important she felt at age six to be carrying her clothes on a family trip in the Adirondacks. However, when she eventually got tired, her father hoisted her and her pack onto his shoulders — on top of his own pack. Thankfully, he ended this Herculean feat when they neared a busy trail junction.

"Marit," he said. "You probably want to get down now. You don't want anyone to think you couldn't make it."

The ruse worked.

Instead of getting hung up on age, weight, and pounds, remember that your child must learn to hike and haul at his or her own pace. Prepare yourself for a slow process that will take a number of years to complete.

The first step is having your child carry a fanny pack or daypack. The next step is putting a few things in the pack — a small toy, and a snack and drink — the last two essential in case your child gets separated from you, even for a short time.

Slowly build on this token load. Next add an entire lunch, not just a snack. Later add a change of clothes, perhaps. Keep in mind that your child is more likely to carry something in which he has a vested interest: candy, potato chips, toys, marshmallows, for instance. A young hiker is likely to suddenly develop muscles if he's carrying something he's sure he can't live without, like new binoculars or a Charlotte Hornets cap or jacket.

The ultimate goal is for young backpackers to carry *all* of their own personal gear: trail food, water, clothing, sleeping bag, and pad. Until they're preteens or teens, however,

don't bank on them sharing the weight of group gear such as meals, cooking utensils, or shelter. Until then, Mom and Dad will have to take up the slack — along with any adults you can convince to join you. This is where unmarried or childless friends or relatives come in handy!

Loading Your Child's Pack

Even with a pack that fits perfectly, a child may be miserable or off-bal-

TECHNIQUE TIP

WRAP IT UP

✏ When I took a group of teenage girls backpacking, I tried to teach them to compartmentalize everything in their packs into gallon-size Ziploc bags. They thought I was being compulsive until my stove leaked, but all my clothes and food stayed dry because of the bags. They stopped kidding me after that.

Laura Dahl — Kearns, Utah

Ten-year-old Ben Wiltsie carries his full share on a trek into a remote Wyoming canyon. Children should never be allowed to carry more than ¼ of their body weight.

Pack real backpacks just as you would your own. For external frames, place the heaviest items high and as close to the back as possible, to keep the weight over the hips and prevent shoulder strain. Sleeping bags usually go on the bottom — although this can be a problem for kids. If a low-riding bag makes walking awkward, put it on top, or have an adult carry it.

For the best balance with internal-frame packs, place heavy items in the middle, close to the back. Stash sleeping bags in the lower compartment made just for this purpose.

Pack your child's bag a day or two in advance and let him give it a test ride around the neighborhood. Watch how he copes. He may say the load is fine, but if he's tripping or stooping over, something's wrong. Once you know exactly how much your child can manage, you'll know what's left for the adults to carry.

If your child is old enough to pack his own bag, encourage the independence. However, inspect everyone's bag before you set off, checking for essential items and excess weight.

ance if it's improperly packed. Unfortunately, kids often end up carrying most of their pack's weight on their shoulders instead of their hips — yet another reason not to overload them.

With daypacks, put bigger, heavier objects near the child's center of gravity, in the small of the back — without having anything poke awkwardly at the back, of course. A hip belt also helps manage the load. If a pack doesn't have one, you can sew one on fairly easily.

MIND YOUR MANNERS

Backpacking etiquette is a combination of hiking and camping rules. Be especially mindful of blocking the trail, quite easy when everyone's wearing big packs and traveling more slowly. During rest stops, teach kids not to lay down their loads in the middle of the trail. At the same time, don't let them damage vegetation by leaving packs off the trail.

Even if you're trying to get away from it all, you may find yourself sharing a campsite or shelter with other people. Just because you reach a shelter first, for instance, doesn't mean you can claim it for yourself. They're usually meant for sharing, so make room with good humor. On the other hand, some areas can be reserved, so check the relevant rules.

The usual commonsense rules apply: Keep your kids out of the way of other campers, and don't rely on others to keep your kids safe. Don't expect everyone else to adjust to your family's schedule. And, for safety's sake, keep a close eye on your kids, both on the trail and at your campsite.

Show young backpackers how to leave trails and campsites just as you found them, or better than you found them. Carry out everything you bring in. Take along an empty garbage bag just for this purpose.

Most important, backpack-

ing should be fun. Remember, this isn't an exercise in lifting weight and racking up miles. Stop and smell the honeysuckle!

ON THE TRAIL

You're finally at the trailhead. We always start by taking a group photograph to capture the moment.

If you've done your homework — planned within everyone's ability and packed carefully — the hardest work is over.

Sibling companionship on the trail, John Muir Wilderness, Sierra Nevada, California. For some kids, inviting a non-family friend encourages a more positive attitude.

Packs always seem to weigh more the second day of a trip, even though they're actually lighter, so make the second day an easy, low-mileage one.

Shouldering the Load

If your child is carrying a real pack, you may need to teach him how to put it on and take it off with ease. You don't want any pulled muscles before everyone starts walking

You may even want to help kids on and off with their packs at first — hold it up and let them slip their arms through the straps. However, if your child is having real troubles this early in the game, chances are he's carrying too much.

Make sure your youngster's pack is properly adjusted. Follow the same steps as you would for adjusting your own pack. Tighten the hip belt first, letting it ride just above the hipbone. Next are the shoulder straps, which should be just below shoulder level. However, getting the hip belt and shoulder straps in exactly the right position is often a problem because of the way kids are built. As mentioned before, the biggest priority is having the weight centered low.

Make sure your child uses the load-adjuster straps and the sternum strap. All should be snug without being tight.

Pay special attention to the fit at the shoulders and hips, the areas most apt to get sore. Double-check that nothing is poking your child in the back, such as an awkwardly placed water bottle.

Kids usually have less natural padding than we adults, so they're likely to start hurting more quickly. You may want to add extra foam to your child's straps.

Moving Along

Backpacking with kids should never be a marathon. It's more of a slow-motion relay with plenty of fits and starts. (With luck, these fits are the stopping kind, not the fussing kind.)

Once you set off, take your first rest stop after 20 minutes or so, unless you hear complaints earlier. Have a snack and check for hot spots, from both footwear and backpacks. Adjust as needed — any problems will only get worse if not attended to. Take plenty of breaks, especially after extensive uphill or downhill sections.

Before going up, tighten the top tension strap and loosen the hip belt. This small change in the center of gravity may help with balance. On the way down, undo these changes to give shoulders a rest.

For a psychological boost, children carrying similar loads may occasionally want to switch packs. There may be no real physical advantage to the switch, but the change can be a mental diversion.

In addition to breaks, when the going gets tough, start singing and

playing guessing games.

Sometimes, however, especially with older kids, silence works best. If they're moving along slowly but steadily, let everyone simply dig in on their own terms.

The last mile of the day can be the longest, so when you're within a mile or so of the campsite, start guessing when you'll be there, or have a low-key race.

On any backpacking trip, be sure to allow more than enough traveling time to reach camp well before darkness falls, before hunger sets in. It's hard enough to check into a hotel room at a late hour, much less wrestle with packs, tent poles, and stakes when you're also chief cook and bottle washer. Have some snacks ready, and allow an hour or two to set up camp and fix dinner.

In Camp

Help your child experience the wonderful satisfaction of just being in camp, away from "civilization," and having gotten there on his own two feet. These are some of the finest moments any outdoorsman can expe-

EVENING ENTERTAINMENT

Most times the kids can keep themselves entertained, but having a book of short stories, a star chart, or things like that can be helpful for off-trail times.

Ray Dahl — Kearns, Utah

rience. Help him learn the joyful routine of turning a campsite into "home" for the night, setting up camp, and, at long last, cooking.

Everyone should pitch in, as in pitching the tent. If your child is completely exhausted, assign at least one token chore — gathering some water, perhaps. A fun chore, like making pudding, can help revive a tired young backpacker. Give young children a break, allowing them to rest or play within well-established boundaries (here's where some small toys come in handy — Matchbox cars, cards, Legos, a tiny sketchbook). Most routines are the same as on any camping trip; you just don't have as much gear (see Chapter 7).

Learn to lower your standards of cleanliness. Your pots and pans aren't going to sparkle, nor are your children. Kids probably won't mind; they're likely to love a fine dirt patina. Wash 'em up the best you can with spring water, then relax. The bathtub will be waiting when you get home.

Once darkness falls, even seasoned young car campers may become tentative. It's lonelier out there away from all the cars and people, so don't be surprised if a sudden case of the jitters strikes. Be reassuring, and help everyone learn to appreciate the solitude.

Your sleeping arrangements may also change. You may car-camp with one tent for the adults and another for the kids. In the backcountry your kids may want an adult beside them. Don't suggest any change in normal procedure, but make allowances if fears are voiced.

Time allotted to enjoy a great campsite is time very well spent. On longer treks, allow for a layover day or two when everyone settles down to some "domestic" time in camp and casual explorations.

Once a new day dawns, don't underestimate the time you'll need to eat breakfast, break camp, and hike the day's miles. If the morning is chilly or cold, the first order of business is a warm beverage to get everyone moving. A cold morning is difficult for anyone to face, especially a child.

Fix breakfast, get dressed, break camp. Setting a takeoff time will keep you on schedule. Assign tasks to older children; let younger children play or finish breakfast while you work.

Enjoy yourselves, but don't dally. Unless this is a layover day, you've got miles to walk before you sleep.

The Second Day

Just as packs weigh more going uphill, they seem to weigh more the second day of a trip. No matter that you've eaten some of your food and are actually carrying less — your

? AGE-OLD QUESTIONS

INFANTS AND BABIES

"We spent weeks preparing for our first family backpack. We packed everything we needed. The weather was perfect. Our 10-month-old was a jewel, all things considering. But her father and I thought the trip was too much hassle. We're not sure what to try next."

Backpacking with very small children can be a pain in the neck — and the shoulders, and the back. . . . For some people, the pleasures outweigh the pain. It's certainly not for everyone.

Give it another try. If you still don't have fun, wait until your child can at least walk a mile or two. In the meantime, search for car-camping spots with a wilderness feel. They do exist.

You can also investigate using pack animals, such as llamas, goats, or horses. If you feel like a mule, maybe you should take one along!

SCHOOL-AGE CHILDREN

"My seven-year-old daughter hates to backpack. She says it's too hard. Her five-year-old sister loves our trips. What's the problem?"

Perhaps one of two things. Maybe the trips you've taken *are* too hard for your daughter, even though she's older than her sister. Scale down your trips and see if her attitude improves.

If not, you may have to accept the fact that your daughter isn't a backpacker. Try other outdoor activities, and make alternate arrangements for her when the rest of you go backpacking. Don't give up hope; she may grow to like it later.

"Our eight-year-old insists on taking a Coke on our backpacking trips. His mother and I think the extra weight is heavy and inefficient. How can we convince him?"

continued on page 206

I'm with your boy. Sometimes a special treat is worth an extra pound or two, and at least a Coke will help keep him hydrated. Forget the argument unless he tries to take a six-pack.

"Our 10-year-old used to love to backpack, but now he doesn't think it's cool anymore, especially with Mom and Dad. How can we win him back?"

Take one of his friends along. If you don't want to take on the responsibility of another child alone, ask the child's parent or parents to come, too.

Your son's enthusiasm might also return if you let him design the trip.

PRETEEN GIRLS

"Our eleven-year-old daughter is beginning puberty. Will this have any effect on her backpacking ability?"

In the long run, she'll just get stronger. However, be sensitive to the fact that she may not feel like backpacking during menstruation if she has severe cramps. And even if your daughter hasn't had a period yet, take along some pads. Avoid the trauma of being unprepared should her first period begin out on the trail.

Backpacking — especially with babies — means being *fully* prepared. Gore-Tex rain gear for yourself as well as a child carrier rigged with protection from the elements are essential.

second day easy. Even if your child was a real trouper the first day, today she may have more get-up-and-stay than get-up-and-go.

Be prepared. Lighten her load, if necessary. Also be armed with an appealing plan, an enticement to keep going — a special swimming hole, a cave, the car ride home — whatever it takes.

muscles are probably starting to talk, maybe scream.

This is good reason to make the

INFANTS AND BABIES

Only diehard backpackers will enjoy the challenge of carrying a child and all the attending gear on top of standard backpacking equipment. Such a feat is definitely a challenge, but quite possible.

Infants and young babies must be carried in front carriers. Because of their lack of head and neck control, be careful of the effects of long distances and rough terrain. Be especially careful to protect all babies from sun, heat, and cold. Keep them hydrated and fed.

The going gets a fraction easier once your child graduates to a backpack-style carrier — although by this time your baby weighs more.

TODDLERS

If anything, toddlers are harder to take backpacking than babies. They weigh more. They're more willful. They can walk, but not far. However, once a child can go a mile or so on his own two legs, he may be ready for a short hike to camp.

PRESCHOOLERS

Don't count on them going farther than a few miles, or expect them to carry more than a token few pounds. However, they'll enjoy the adventure of an outing scaled to their abilities.

6- TO 8-YEAR-OLDS

Most can hike a little farther than younger children, and can carry a little more. However, stamina for both hauling and hiking can still be unpredictable.

8- TO 10-YEAR-OLDS

Some kids this age can hike a fair distance and haul their own sleeping bags and clothes. Some may be ready for a real backpack. Take it easy, though — many kids aren't.

10- TO 12-YEAR-OLDS

At this age many kids are ready for real backpacking trips. They can hike well and carry their own gear. They're ready for a real backpack. Don't expect them to carry items such as stoves and tents.

ADVANCED TRIPS

If your family loves to backpack, chances are you'll want to try some advanced trips — go farther, stay longer, and, perhaps, climb higher.

I know of several families who plan special trips as high school graduation gifts. Hike an entire trail, either all at once or in small sections, weekend after weekend, even year after year.

I once met a father and son at a New Hampshire shelter along the Appalachian Trail. The father was at least 60 years old or more; his son, an adult. They had been making their

Establishing a base camp from which to make day hikes to nearby attractions is a great way to explore the backcountry without pushing the kids or yourself to cover too much ground.

the rest step, a way to maintain a steady, efficient pace on steep trails. Master it *before* you really need it:

● Lift your right leg forward and up, but keep your weight on the left leg.

● Transfer your weight from the left to the right foot, locking your right knee and "resting" for a moment. The pause momentarily transfers weight from muscles to skeleton, something like the momentary rest the heart takes between beats. For an instant all motion stops: Your muscles can relax and you can breathe. The left leg bears no weight, but the toe of the boot can touch the ground for balance, if needed.

● Lift your left leg and repeat the process, this time locking your left knee and resting, with the right leg dangling behind.

This method is slow but sure, def-

way north in week-long or more intervals, for a good many years. The long-term challenge gave their backpacking trips, and, I suspect, their relationship, added purpose.

The Rest Step

✐ Once your kids become "serious" hikers, they're old enough to master some tricks of the trade. Foremost is

I'm the type of person who always needs a book on hand, even during backpacking trips. I've finally found the perfect-sized volumes: small, 95¢ paperbacks called "Penguin 60s," in honor of the publishing house's 60th anniversary. The series includes a glorious variety of titles, such as short stories by Leo Tolstoy, Garrison Keillor, Stephen King, and James Joyce. There are even some for kids, great for read-alouds: *Winnie-the-Pooh, Peter Pan,* and *Mother Goose.*

FOR ADULTS

✳ APPALACHIAN ADVENTURE (*Longstreet Press*). In 1995 a team of reporters, illustrators, and photographers from five newspapers hiked and recorded their impressions of the Appalachian Trail. Both older children and adults will enjoy this beautiful book, and learn why so many hikers are lured to the AT.

BACKPACKER'S HANDBOOK, by Chris Townsend (*Ragged Mountain*). What you need to pack and get on the trail.

HIKER'S COMPANION: 12,000 MILES OF TRAIL-TESTED WISDOM, by Cindy Ross and Todd Gladfelter (*Mountaineers*). Practical tips from a pair with plenty of experience.

✳ THE MODERN BACKPACKER'S HANDBOOK: AN ENVIRONMENTAL GUIDE, by Glenn Randall (*Lyons & Burford*). Not only the right way to backpack, but the low-impact way.

✳ NOLS WILDERNESS GUIDE, by Peter Simer and John Sullivan (*Simon & Schuster*). With this book, you can backpack like a pro.

✳ HIKING & BACKPACKING: A COMPLETE GUIDE, *Trailside* series, by Karen Berger (*W. W. Norton*). Berger's trail-tested, no-nonsense approach gives the background you need to take your family into the backcountry.

FOR KIDS

ARTHUR'S CAMP-OUT, by Lillian Hoban (*HarperTrophy*, grades 1–3). In this beginning reader, Arthur the monkey heads for the woods.

BONES ON BLACK SPRUCE MOUNTAIN, by David Budbill (*Puffin Books*, ages 10 and up). Two boys on a backpacking trip encounter a frightening secret.

THE LITTLE RED ANT AND THE GREAT BIG CRUMB: A MEXICAN FABLE, retold by Shirley Climo, illustrated by Francisco X. Mora (*Clarion Books*). This picture book is a pertinent tale about determination, perseverance, and strength — all the qualities a backpacker needs.

✳ THE LOST LAKE, by Allen Say (*Houghton Mifflin*, ages 4–8). A boy spends the summer with his divorced father and is bored until they go on a backpacking trip. Caldecott-winning artist Say's story and illustrations are both superb.

TAKE A HIKE! THE SIERRA CLUB KID'S GUIDE TO HIKING AND BACKPACKING, by Lynne Foster, illustrated by Martha Weston (*Sierra Club*, ages 9–12). Hand this one over and your kids may be telling *you* what to do.

FATHER AND DAUGHTERS

I started my daughters on overnight back-pack trips at 2 to 3 years old. By the time they were 10, all of them had been on several one-week hikes of 50 miles or more with full-frame packs carrying clothing, sleeping gear, some group equipment, and food. They were all capable of 1,000-foot vertical climbs in a day. I've found that girls can be easier to work with, and sometimes stronger, than boys.

Charles Vaughan — Woodlinville, Washington

initely good for the long haul. Adjust the timing to different inclines: the steeper the pitch, the longer the rest.

Experiment with counting aloud — step, rest, step, rest — to help your kids get the rhythm. Explain that the goal isn't to finish a steep section *first*, but to hike steadily, without having to gasp for breath or collapse.

Resupply

No matter how strong you are, there's a limit to what you can carry. At some point you'll need additional food and fuel. As all backpackers know, resupply stops are usually a much-needed break, a chance to freshen up and chow down.

Again, I think of Ralph, who so carefully planned my first back-packing trip. Midweek, his wife, Carole, met us at a spot where the Long Trail crosses a road. She offered

clean clothes, more toilet paper, and more food, including hamburgers and a Boston cream pie.

With kids along, make resupplying an extra-special event. You'll definitely need plenty of food and rest. If you're on a long trip, you may want to spend a night or two in a real bed. If one parent isn't on the trip, this can be a chance for a visit.

After the rest, all systems should be go. Should your child want to call it quits at this point instead of continuing, don't force the issue.

All-Terrain Challenges

Challenge yourselves, but carefully. Pushing the limit too far may lead to serious, even deadly trouble. Hike with experts, take some courses, read, hire a professional guide.

Be especially wary of water crossings, overly steep slopes, high altitudes, and snowfields. Don't cross the line separating hiking from serious mountaineering unless you know what you're doing.

Most of all, don't expect too much. A child who doesn't want to disappoint won't tell you he's hurting. You, not your child, have to judge the limits.

PART IV: SAFE, HEALTHY ADVENTURES

L O S T
A N D
F O U N D

"People want to know why I didn't stay where I was. Someone was sure to find me, they say. Well, I'd like to see anyone stay up there in that wind and sleet with the night coming on. You'd freeze stiff before morning. I was already getting stiff. I had to keep moving, just to warm up. I shouted once more, as loud as I could — then I stood and listened — nothing but that strange noise."

Donn Fendler, as told to Joseph B. Egan
Lost On a Mountain in Maine

It only takes a minute.

Look away — you're rummaging through your pack, perhaps changing another child's diaper — and your child is gone.

Usually they haven't wandered far, but don't count on it.

Children — and adults — get lost all the time. I seem to hear a story in the news at least every two

LITTLE GIRL LOST

I just returned from a canoeing trip in the Boundary Waters Canoe Area Wilderness in Minnesota, where an eight-year-old girl was lost in the woods for six hours. Her parents had entrusted her and her older brother with a hatchet to search for firewood. The children bickered, parted company, and she lost her way.

Once the search began, a Forest Service plane spotted her on some low cliffs, but couldn't land. Searchers then headed for the area by canoe; they had to swim and climb to rescue her.

The girl and her family made several mistakes, the first of which was allowing young children to wander alone in the woods, especially with a hatchet. It's extremely important for kids to be taught to stay put and hug a tree if they're lost, and they should also have whistles. Back in my husband's air force training days, pilots learned the following verse: "When in trouble/When in doubt/Run in circles/Scream and shout." It makes a lot of sense when you think about it.

Patricia J. Bell, author of
Roughing It Elegantly:
A Practical Guide to Canoe Camping
Eden Prairie, Minnesota

months; several come to mind. Not long ago three brothers in the greater Boston area spent a night lost after straying in the woods near their house. Some other kids were lost with their aunt after straying just a few yards off a trail and getting mired in a bog. A teenage girl got separated from her parents in Yosemite and was missing for several days.

Thankfully, all of these stories had happy endings. Even the good stories, however, can leave scars.

When Harvey Dulberg was 10 years old, he got lost for a night at summer camp with his counselor and fellow campers. To this day, Dr. Dulberg, now a sports psychologist in Boston, feels uneasy in the woods. Whenever he has to go someplace new, he often scouts his way ahead of time, consulting maps carefully, making sure he has a full tank of gas.

"Getting lost is not something that I feel comfortable with," he says. "I get pretty anxious."

While leading his charges on an overnight hike, Dulberg's counselor became confused by trail markings. The group spent an afternoon and night walking about 20 miles to a nearby town. Even though he had confidence in his counselor, Dulberg was frightened by the darkness and the noises of the night. They followed railroad tracks and had to cross a bridge over the Hudson River, which terrified Dulberg.

"It was traumatic," Dulberg says. "We came back and laughed about it, but kids are more cocky on the outside than they really feel."

Despite the lingering effects, Dulberg hasn't let the experience paralyze him. He sent his son to the same summer camp without hesitation.

"I wasn't worried. I told him,

'Have a good time,'" Dr. Dulberg says. "I didn't want to lay my fears on him."

STAYING ON TRACK

Despite the high number of people who get lost, such predicaments can almost always be avoided by following these rules:

- Always stay together. Don't let kids wander. If you're in a campsite, set specific boundaries. Older children can have some freedom, but

Mist veils the peaks: Big Pine Canyon, John Muir Wilderness, California. *Always keep young children on the trail and within sight. Particularly in the mountains, you never know when bad weather might roll in.*

should always use the buddy system. Everyone should know where they're off to and when they'll return. If older children hike or bike slightly ahead on a trail, instruct them to wait for the rest of the group at every trail junction.

- Know where you're going and stay on designated trails. *Carry a detailed map and compass even if you're*

familiar with an area.

- Set time limits. Be wary of approaching weather and darkness. Before you start out, decide what time you need to turn back to end the day at a reasonable hour. And if you say you're going to turn back at 2:00 P.M., no matter where you are, stick to your guns. It's easy to get sucked into the

When the weather begins to turn bad, err on the side of caution, getting your family to safety or pitching camp ahead of possible problems.

joy of the moment, only to be sorry a few hours later, when you're still not back at your car. Err on the side of caution; when in doubt, get your family to safety ahead of possible problems, such as nightfall or a thunderstorm. Don't push your family beyond their abilities — that's when problems are likely to occur.

● Equip your children with whistles,

WHICH WAY TO CAMP?

Renowned nature educator Joseph Cornell, founder of the Sharing Nature Foundation, says this is one of his favorite stories: "I took a group of children on a night hike to listen for owls, then asked everyone to point in the direction back to camp. Their answers covered the whole 360 degrees of the compass. They wanted to find their own way back because they were Scouts. It was a summer night in the Sierras, it was warm, and no one was waiting for us, so we just kept going. We finally stopped and slept together piled like a little pack of chickadees. In the daylight we found our way back. They learned a good lesson about paying attention and wayfinding."

and teach them to use them in emergencies. The international distress signal is three repeated signals of any kind; in this case, whistle blasts. Teach kids to remember the whistle and blow it three times, time after time, if they're lost or injured.

● Tell a friend or relative where you're going, what trails you'll take, and how long you expect to be gone. Always check in at trail registers, and heed park and ranger advice. If a trail is closed, don't use it.

Showing Kids the Way

The wonderful thing about safety is that it's absolute. Parents can lay down the law, stick by it no matter what, and feel good.

On other issues, the rules occasionally become muddy. Should I read him one more book? Can he have another cookie? At various times, every spouse throws his or her partner a questioning look, asking "What's our party line going to be on this one?"

Except when it comes to safety.

Will has to hold my hand near dangerous water, ledges, and vehicles, or I carry him, regardless of whether he's crying or kicking. He must stay close to his father or me on trails, or in the child carrier he goes.

On such serious matters, there are no second chances.

Even if your child has never been to the woods before, the concept of staying close to Mom and Dad is nothing new. Being lost is a universal

DELAYED, THEN SPRAYED

For five days we had been not exactly lost, but "delayed" in the Bandelier Wilderness of New Mexico with my two teenage daughters. For the last two days we had had little food and had been drinking muddy, hot, boiled Rio Grande water. After a rough ascent out of a canyon, we finally found our way back to a marked trail.

We all threw down our packs in relief. What did my 16-year-old daughter have to say? Not: "Wow, that was a close one!" Not: "Thank goodness we're back on the trail!" Not even: "I'm never hiking with you psycho, death-defying off-trail lunatics again!"

Nope. She stood up, stretched, looked up at the dusty trail, and piped in a true Valley Girl accent: "Does anyone have any deodorant?"

Ellen Lanterman — Pine, Colorado

fear. Precautions are part of daily life. Kids hear the drill over and over again, at home, at school, on television shows, and in books.

Nonetheless, kids need to be reminded, and the words bear repeating every time you start a new venture. The rules may be the same, but the terrain is new, and so are the temptations — a butterfly to follow, a cave to explore, a ledge to climb. The author of *Tom Brown's Field Guide to Nature and Survival for Children* has an excellent

A great time to test your and your kids' map reading skills is when fog or rain alters the appearance of the landscape, even along familiar, well-marked trails.

home? Which way are we going? Where have we been? Have we been here before? What do you recognize? Point out blazes, trail signs, and landmarks, such as a prominent mountain or tree.

Let your child lead or point out the way from time to time. As soon as kids are old enough, involve them in map reading and trailblazing, and teach them to use a compass. Young children can't read maps, but they can understand simple instructions about the lay of the land.

They can also comprehend simple maps you draw. Encourage them to draw their own maps. Not only is this a good safety lesson, it's a great way to keep them busy and interested in the day's journey. Don't worry about drawing to scale or using correct mapping signals; let kids have fun. The final product becomes a keepsake, a reminder of their trip.

Children of any age should always carry their own water and snack, whistle, plus a layer of warmer clothes, including a warm hat (*not* a

term for such precautions: He calls them "lostproofing."

Instill some healthy fear. In game-like fashion, show your child how easy it is to get lost. Blindfold him in his own bedroom, spin him in circles a few times, and ask him to point to the door. Point out that you can lose your way anywhere, even at home.

Take a short walk in some nearby woods. Wander off the trail a bit or go somewhere new, being careful not to get lost in the process. After a few moments, ask everyone to point to the trailhead. Usually, everyone points in different directions.

From toddlerhood on, make wayfinding and directions part of your conversations. Which way is

baseball cap). The warm clothes are essential because it's important to stay in one place when lost, which means it's easy to get cold.

Tom Brown recommends that each adult and child carry a more extensive survival pack that includes such things as waterproof matches, a compass, a pocketknife, water purification tablets, a small flashlight, and first aid supplies. Many of the items Brown recommends require maturity to use properly and safely; they're more appropriate for kids ages 10 and older.

LOST!
WHAT KIDS SHOULD DO
Stop.
Blow a whistle.
Stay put.

◆
L O S T P R O O F I N G   K I T

MPI Outdoor Safety Products offers the Kids Kit, designed to educate parents and children about what to do if they become separated. Call 800-3434-5827.

The first mistake lost children make is wandering away from their parents. The second — the one that can make a bad situation dangerous, even deadly — is that kids keep moving, usually in an attempt to get "unlost."

It's natural to want to move, to take action, in an emergency. Safety, one reasons, is just a short distance away.

That's exactly how Donn Fendler got into trouble in Baxter State Park in Maine. In 1939, the 12-year-old was nearing the top of Mount

TIPS FOR LOST KIDS
(AND ADULTS)

Here are several basic principles taught by the Hug-a-Tree and Survive program, founded in California after a nine-year-old boy got lost and died:

Hug a Tree. Once you know you are lost. One of the greatest fears a person of any age can have is of being alone. Hugging a tree or other stationary object and even talking to it calms the child down,

and prevents panic. By staying in one place, the child is found far more quickly, and can't be injured in a fall.

Always Carry a Trash Bag and Whistle. On a picnic, hike, or camping trip. By making a hole in the side of the bag for the face (to prevent suffocation) and putting it on over the head, it will keep the child dry and warm. The whistle can be heard farther away than the

continued on page 218

TIPS FOR LOST KIDS
continued from page 217

child's voice, and takes less energy to use. (Trash bags are handy emergency gear, but better to have warm clothes and rain gear with you.)

MY PARENTS WON'T BE ANGRY AT ME. Time and time again, children have avoided searchers because they were ashamed of getting lost, and afraid of punishment. Anyone can get lost, adult or child. If they know a happy reunion filled with love is waiting, they will be less frightened, less prone to panic, and work hard to be found.

MAKE YOURSELF BIG. From helicopters, people are hard to see when they are standing up, in a group of trees, or wearing dark and drab clothing. Find your tree to hug near a small clearing if possible. Wear a red or orange jacket when you go near the woods or desert. Lie down when the helicopter flies over. Make crosses or "SOS" using broken shrubbery or rocks, or by dragging your foot in the dirt.

THERE ARE NO ANIMALS OUT THERE THAT WANT TO HURT YOU IN THIS COUNTY. If you hear a noise at night, yell at it. If it is an animal, it will run away to protect itself. If it is a searcher, you will be found. Fears of the dark and of "lions and tigers and bears" are a big factor in panicking children into running. They need strong reassurance to stay put and be safe.

(These guidelines were originally written for children in San

Katahdin, the state's highest peak. Donn and his friend had hiked ahead of their group, which included his father and brothers. Heavy fog set in, obscuring visibility.

Instead of waiting for everyone else to arrive, Donn decided to retrace his steps. He was cold and kept moving, sure he could find his way to safety. He wandered off the trail and was lost for eight days. His disappearance prompted one of the largest search efforts in the history of the Maine woods. He was finally found at least 30 miles away from the summit of Katahdin, in rough, wild country.

Had Fendler simply waited for his father — or not hiked so far ahead in the first place — the ordeal could have been avoided. If he'd had a whistle, if he'd stayed put once he realized he was lost — if, if, if. At least he survived his ordeal.

In 1981, a nine-year-old boy named Jimmy Beveridge had a similar experience, but wasn't so lucky. Beveridge and his two brothers were camping with their family on Palomar

Diego County. Spurred on by a resurgence of mountain lions in the area, Hug-a-Tree recently changed the wording of this statement from "no animals out there that can hurt you" to "no animals out there that want to hurt you." If, for instance, you're hiking in bear country, parents should have further discussions with their children. Kids should be taught what to do if they encounter a bear.) YOU HAVE HUNDREDS OF FRIENDS LOOKING FOR YOU. We have had children in the local area of a search tell us, "My parents would never spend the money to search for me with all these people." Search personnel are mainly volunteers who work with other professionals and charge nothing and do it because they care. Many children who are lost don't realize that if they sit down and stay put, one of the many searchers will find them. Some are afraid of strangers or men in uniform and don't respond to yells, and have actually hidden from searchers they knew were looking for them.

More advice to parents from Hug-a-Tree: "Call the sheriff quickly if your child is lost. The search area expands so quickly due to the victim's possible movements that rapid response is critically important. A call to the sheriff which is canceled [because a child is located] gives the searchers practice and helps keep them alert. A slow response is dangerous, especially if bad weather wipes out the track, and exposure is a consideration."

Mountain, about 60 miles from San Diego. As their parents prepared lunch, the boys explored a nearby nature trail, then raced back to their site.

Jimmy never showed up. His family searched for an hour, then contacted a park ranger. Before long the local search-and-rescue team was on the scene. A huge search was mounted, but there was no sign of Jimmy.

That night the temperature dropped; fog and rain moved in. Helicopters couldn't fly, and the rain washed away Jimmy's scent. Searchers systematically searched for several days. Four days later Jimmy's body was found, dead from hypothermia, just 2 miles from the campground.

In an effort to prevent more tragedies like Jimmy's, several of the anguished searchers developed a program for children called "Hug-a-Tree and Survive" — a 40-minute presentation to be given by law enforcement personnel and search-and-rescue teams to schools, scouting groups, and other children's organizations.

The slide show portrays a mock search and rescue, and is designed to teach basic survival principles to children ages 5 to 12.

Hug-a-Tree is a nonprofit organization manned by volunteers, with chapters in Canada, Sweden, Australia, and every state except Hawaii. For more information, send a self-addressed, stamped, legal-size envelope to Hug-a-Tree National Office, 6465 Lance Way, San Diego, CA 92120.

What if your child gets lost where there aren't any trees to hug?

If you're exploring the tundra or some other treeless area, come up with a substitute slogan, such as: Hug a boulder. Also make sure to explain that if a child gets cold while waiting for help, it's a good idea to jump up and down, run in place — anything so long as he stays put.

With caution and luck, your child will never have to embrace these measures.

As Rick Wilcox notes: "It's probably easier to lose your way in Disney World than it is to get lost in the mountains."

But when a child does get lost in the mountains, Mickey, Minnie, and Donald aren't waiting to lead him back to Mom and Dad.

DID YOU KNOW

Backpackers now have the technology of the United States Department of Defense at their fingertips. The new global positioning system (GPS) uses 24 satellites to tell you where you are, accurate to about 50 feet. It can also calculate compass bearings to your destination, distances, and your rate of travel. Receivers that allow you to use GPS weigh in at 18 ounces. Prices range from $500 to $1,500. But before you throw away your compass, take heed: It's never wise to depend on a piece of equipment to do what you should be able to do yourself. The GPS is a helpful tool, but it's no substitute for knowing how to read a map and use a compass. After all, what if the batteries went dead?

SEARCH STRATEGIES FOR PARENTS

If your child is missing, you naturally panic.

Don't. That's how mistakes can be made. What your child needs most at this moment is a calm, clear-thinking parent.

❖

BEST-BET READING

FOR ADULTS

✳ BE EXPERT WITH MAP & COMPASS: THE COMPLETE ORIENTEERING HANDBOOK, by Bjorn Kellstrom (*U.S. Geological Survey and Orienteering Services, Macmillan*).

✳ INTO THE WILD, by Jon Krakauer (*Villard*). An account of a young man named Chris McCandless, who walked into the Alaskan bush, determined to live off the land. He never walked out, but might have, had he had a map.

MAP & COMPASS: THE BASIC ESSENTIALS, by Cliff Jacobson (*ICS*).

✳ THE OUTWARD BOUND MAP & COMPASS BOOK, by Glenn Randall (*Lyons & Burford*). STAYING FOUND: THE COMPLETE MAP & COMPASS HANDBOOK, by June Fleming (*The Mountaineers*).

FOR KIDS

✳ HATCHET, by Gary Paulsen (*Aladdin*, ages 11–13). In this Newbery award book, 13-year-old Brian is the sole survivor of a small plane crash. Armed with his clothes and a hatchet, he manages to survive.

✳ LOST ON A MOUNTAIN IN MAINE, by Donn Fendler, as told to Joseph B. Egan (*Beech Tree Books*, ages 9 and up). A riveting, firsthand account of Fendler's terrible adventure.

MAP & MAZE PUZZLES, Usborne Superpuzzles,

Advanced Level, by Sarah Dixon and Radhi Parekh (*EDC Publishing*). These puzzles involve a variety of maps, including a topographical map for hikers, a star chart, a flight chart, and a pyramid of hieroglyphics. They're difficult, too — adults will also be challenged.

MAPS: GETTING FROM HERE TO THERE, by Harvey Weiss (*Houghton Mifflin*, ages 10 and up). A fun, interesting, and extremely well-written discussion.

✳ THE SIERRA CLUB WAYFINDING BOOK, by Vicki McVey (*Sierra Club Books*, ages 10 and up). This, too, contains excellent explanations as well as activity suggestions. Pertinent sections on hiking and orienteering.

✳ TOM BROWN'S FIELD GUIDE TO NATURE AND SURVIVAL FOR CHILDREN, by Tom Brown (*Berkley Books*, ages 12 and up). Detailed, serious lessons that will help parents and children alike. I would want to have this book on hand if I became lost or stranded!

✳ WILLIE TAKES A HIKE, by Gloria Rand, illustrated by Ted Rand (*Harcourt*, ages 3–8). Willie the mouse takes a hike and gets lost, but does everything right: He hugs a tree and has emergency gear on hand to keep him safe until searchers arrive. An entertaining story with all the right details you want your child to learn — an excellent book.

The first thing to do is call and whistle for your child. Loudly. Enlist the help of others nearby.

Don't let other children wander

off on the hunt, or you'll end up with more than one missing person.

Do a quick search of the immediate area. Look for footprints and other signs of disturbance. If you don't get results, have one parent stay put with anyone else in the group, while the other starts a search of the surroundings, returning to the spot the child was last seen, or has likely gone to. Search in circles, spiraling outward.

If authorities, such as park rangers, are nearby, contact them. Give them every detail possible, including a description of your child and his clothing, time of the disappearance, and exact locations. Know what kind of shoe or boot your child is wearing.

If you're in the backcountry and several hours away from help, search the area thoroughly for no more than 30 minutes. After that, it's time for one parent to go for help. The other parent, however, should remain in the area — close, one hopes, to the missing child.

Be optimistic. Brown, a noted tracker who has found many lost children and adults, says most children are found the same day or within 48 hours. Many are found near water, probably because it's intriguing and soothing.

BACKCOUNTRY
9 1 1

"I'll go get some water to cook with. You can look around, George, but don't get into trouble."

Curious George Goes Camping
edited by Margret Rey and Alan J. Shalleck

I hope all of your outings are safe, that you never face any medical dilemmas. If you do, I wish I could provide all the answers you'll need. However, there isn't space, and this isn't the place to describe treatments for every hazard you're likely to encounter. Many excellent first aid books do just that. Instead, I'll concentrate on some major principles as well as medical information specifically related to children.

What Every Parent Needs
You can't depend on this or any book to save the day. When a child is hurt, you're not going to have time to flip through an index, then bring yourself up to speed on various treatments. You can't afford to be studying. It's

A first aid kit is only as good as the training you bring with it. Don't venture into the backcountry without taking a Red Cross or other first aid course.

the proper maturity. Never overestimate their abilities or rely on their judgment, however. This is one area where it's vital to micro-manage. Call the local chapter of the American Red Cross for information on first aid classes, or contact Red Cross National Headquarters, 431 18th St., N.W., Washington, DC 20006; 202-737-8300. (For information on wilderness medical training, see Sources & Resources.)

What Every Parent Fears

Many parents in the wild harbor nagging fears that disaster may strike. Drowning. Concussions. Bears. Broken arms and legs. Big, bad stuff.

More often than not, however, adversity runs on a smaller scale. Scrapes. Bruises. Sprained ankles. Bug bites. Sunburn.

No matter how big or small, the majority of outdoor problems are preventable. If you're smart and watch your family closely, calamity is unlikely. Hazards such as sunburn, hypothermia, heat exhaustion, and dehydration are easily avoided. Once you spot symptoms, cures are blessedly simple, provided the problem is caught early. If ignored or missed, however, the situation may become serious.

final exam time, and you must know what to do, whether to act quickly and immobilize your child. How can you be sure to pass the test?

By arming yourself with medical training and wilderness knowledge. Consider these standard equipment, as crucial as a pair of hiking boots or a canoe paddle. Basic courses are a good place to start, but if you want to take solo family trips deep into the backcountry, you need wilderness first aid training.

Before you can take care of your family, you must take care of yourself. If you're hypothermic or suffering from altitude sickness, you won't be able to bail out anyone else. Even if you're not hurt, but merely uncomfortable, your judgment may be impaired.

Enroll your children in first aid classes as well. Teach them how to be wise explorers, to take responsibility for themselves once they have

Do your job.
Don't be negligent.

First Aid Kits

Wilderness first aid isn't so much a question of knowing what to bring, but how to improvise.

"You don't need to have fancy gear with you," explains Rick Wilcox, head of the rescue service in New Hampshire's White Mountains. "You need to know how to use a branch or a foam pad to make a splint if you need one. So you don't need a massive first aid kit — just a normal kit appropriate for the length of your trip."

What's the first thing you need?

"With kids along, bring plenty of bandages," says Wilcox, father of two.

JUST FOR KIDS: BACKCOUNTRY FIRST AID PRODUCTS

✎ Buck Tilton, a father and founder of the Wilderness Medicine Institute, knows how to stock a backpack first aid kit with products made especially for kids:

SCRAPES AND CUTS Start with Johnson & Johnson's No More Germies antibacterial liquid soap and pre-moistened towelettes. There are plenty of bandages for kids, but Tilton conducted a test and concluded that flexible fabric adhesive strips are more comfortable and adhere better than cheaper plastic strips. The brand deemed most effective was Curad Acti-Flex.

COLORFUL SUNSCREEN Sawyer Products makes Summer Stuff, waterproof sunscreen in colors packaged with a crayon and educational coloring book (800-356-7811).

AFTER THE BURN Johnson & Johnson offers No More Burn, a mild, non-irritating spray for sunburn pain.

BUG STUFF Kids need insect repellent made with low concentrations of DEET and nonabsorbents. Look for DEET-Plus from Sawyer, Skedaddle from LittlePoint Corp. (800-243-2929), Sun & Bug Stuff from Reflect (800-942-7900), or Ultrathon from 3M (800-852-3934). Products containing no DEET and made from natural repellents include Buzz Away from Quantum (503-345-5556), Bygone Bugs from Kenyon (800-537-0024), and Natrapel from Tender Corp. (800-258-4696).

AFTER THE BITE Johnson & Johnson also makes No More Itchies, a mild hydrocortisone cream helpful for itchy insect bites and poison ivy.

"Most young kids are going to fall down on the trail. And they play in the dirt, so bring things to clean cuts."

Another vital item is any medication your child may take. For extended backcountry trips, ask your doctor to prescribe some antibiotics in case of an ear infection or other problem your child may encounter.

In addition to a regular first aid kit, I keep a small medical travel kit for Will that includes a thermometer, children's painkiller (both drops and tablet form), children's decongestant, ipecac, sunscreen, children's bug repellent, and bandages. It goes on all our trips, whether we're visiting grandparents or camping.

Remember, first aid kits aren't talismans, whose mere existence is supposed to provide protection. Once you buy a first aid kit or make your own, be sure you know how to use everything in it. Several companies manufacture first aid kits specifically for families (see Sources & Resources).

In case your memory needs refreshing in the field, it's a good idea to tuck in a small instruction sheet or booklet. An excellent choice is ✳ *Backcountry First Aid & Extended Care*, by Buck Tilton (ICS Books), a pocket-sized book designed to be carried in first aid kits and backpacks.

BIG THREATS TO LITTLE BODIES

Here's one of the most important things I can tell you. Some hazards are a greater threat to your children — because of their smaller size — than they are to you.

Because children have higher ratios of body surface area to overall size than adults, they warm up more quickly in the heat and lose heat more rapidly in cold weather. Heat exhaustion and hypothermia take over more quickly, as does dehydration. Equivalent amounts of a poison — from a spider, snake, or poisonous plant — are more toxic. Remind yourself of this often, especially whenever you see your child shiver or sweat.

TAKE YOUR KIDS SERIOUSLY

If your child has an unusually hard time during an outing, pay attention. Some friends of ours noticed that their seemingly healthy 15-year-old daughter became *extremely* winded during a hike. They were so concerned that they took her to a doctor, where she was found to have a congenital heart condition requiring surgery. Thankfully, her parents were on their toes, and didn't ignore her body's warning signals.

One of your most important jobs is to keep children at the right temperature: not too hot, not too cold. You can't be overvigilant. In addition to being more likely to be victims of heat exhaustion or hypothermia than adults, children are less attuned to their bodies' needs, and therefore less likely to detect early warning signs.

Hypothermia

As I write this, it's 65°F, pouring, and windy — a perfect day for hypo-thermia. The inability of the body to keep warm isn't just a winter problem. It's a year-round threat, just as likely to happen on a windy or rainy summer day as on a snowy day in January. Maybe more so, since you're less likely to have warm clothes on hand. And, as mentioned, children are particularly vulnerable. They don't admit they're cold for a variety of reasons. I remember having wrinkled skin and goose bumps but not wanting to get out of the pool because I was having

STAGES AND TREATMENT OF HYPOTHERMIA

MILD Skin feels chilly, numb, with goose bumps. Slight clumsiness, stiff fingers, shivering. Responses may be slow — for example, child may refuse to change into proper clothing.
MODERATE Child may stumble, seem lethargic. Talks less, becomes uncooperative, complains. May slur speech and seem confused. Behavior may be inappropriate.
TREATMENT Warm the child. Replace wet clothing with dry, add extra layers, apply heat, administer warm beverages. Be sure to insulate the head and neck, where heat loss is rapid. Simple foods, such as a candy bar, followed by a meal will help.
    If these measures don't help, put the child in a sleeping bag. Build a fire. Pitch a tent. Hot water bottles applied to the armpits, neck, and groin also help, but wrap the bottles in socks or a sweater to avoid burns.
SEVERE When body temperature drops below 90 degrees, shivering stops. A child won't be able to walk and will be incoherent and irrational. Exposed skin is very cold, often blue. As the condition worsens, the child becomes unconscious, pupils become dilated, and breathing and a pulse may be undetectable.
TREATMENT Requires prompt medical attention by professionals, preferably in a hospital. The act of transporting the patient can be dangerous — jarring and bouncing can trigger abnormal heart rhythms.

HYPOTHERMIA
TRAVAILS

Some years ago during a February troop outing, I discovered that one Scout was having trouble keeping warm. I gave him hot chocolate, soup, and warmer clothes, all to no avail. Rather than embarrass him, I claimed to be too sick to stay so we all went home.

Another time I took a group winter camping to a High Adventure base that used to be in northern Wisconsin. One young man showed up with no long underwear and only jeans and sweatshirts under a barely adequate parka. He got very cold before he would accept a pair of long underwear from me. I learned early on that an extra pair isn't too heavy to carry.

By the way, the first young man is now a very accomplished four-season outdoors person who also happens to have earned the Eagle Scout award.

John H. Leisgang — La Crosse, Wisconsin

too much fun. A 3-year-old can shiver so hard he's practically blue, without realizing he's cold. A 10-year-old may be chilled, too, but refuse a windbreaker because he perceives it to be "wimpy."

Meanwhile, you may be hiking along, working up a sweat, while your baby shivers inside his child carrier. Adults can ward off hypothermia by maintaining a brisk, steady pace — a virtually impossible feat for young children. As a result, they need more layers than adults.

Hypothermia is easy to prevent:
- Stay dry.
- Snacks and warm beverages are a quick way to fuel the furnace.
- Always have extra layers of clothing along, even on warm, sunny days (see Chapter 3). Rain and wind gear are a must, as are warm hats and mittens, since the body loses tremendous amounts of heat via extremities. Add layers during rest breaks, *before* you feel cold.
- Be boss. Your child may insist she's fine, but reserve the right to say, "Great, put this on anyway."

The tricky part is the fact that the earliest sign of trouble — general discomfort — may be missed. Many symptoms — stumbling, complaining, inappropriate behavior — are things parents see every day. You may wrongly conclude that your child is tired and grumpy. However, it's essential to combat hypothermia at the onset; once symptoms become more obvious, the problem is much more serious and difficult to treat.

The solution? Constantly monitor both your family's comfort as well as the weather. Such inspections should become second nature on outings; just as you periodically check a baby to see if she's hungry or wet, you must periodically check everyone for early symptoms of hypothermia (see page 227).

Heat Exhaustion

Will is a little furnace. His hair becomes bathed in sweat before I feel

Little bodies are more vulnerable to exposure to the elements, including powerful high-altitude sunlight; an annoying sunburn to an adult can become a serious threat to a toddler.

hot. Also, he's more likely to run around on a hot day, while I prefer to relax in the shade. Children are like this, so it's up to you to be their thermometers.

Heat exhaustion is the first sign of trouble: lightheadedness, sweating, thirst, nausea, headache, rapid pulse, and clammy skin. More serious is heat stroke, when body temperature gets so high that cells start to die. Victims have a fever, confusion, and dry (not clammy) skin; they can no longer sweat.

With common sense (rest often on hot days and drink plenty of fluids), trouble can be easily avoided. Be especially wary of babies and toddlers, who can get hot in child carriers, and can't tell you what the problem is.

Swim. Wade. Cool off by soaking hats and bandannas in streams.

A good rest usually cures heat exhaustion. For heat stroke, rapid cooling is key. Lie the victim down, remove his clothing, immerse or soak him in water. Give cool sips of water.

Dehydration

Blood — part of the gas that makes humans go — is 90 percent water. It needs to stay that way. Dehydration is a common problem with an extremely simple solution.

Drink.

Drink.

Drink.

Just as you must eat before

Keep your kids well hydrated. Sport drinks, which include electrolytes, are a good choice, and the screw-cap plastic bottles in which they're sold make great water bottles into the bargain.

they're not thirsty. No matter. Pretend to be pirates swigging down rum. Make a game of who can drink the most. Have drinking rounds: Mom, Dad, and each child take turns taking swigs. Bribe them by requiring them to drink *before* the snacks come out. Don't move until they drink.

Children love to have their own water bottles, one of the first items your child carries. Water bottles are inexpensive and come in all shapes and sizes. Instead of buying Nalgene bottles in outdoor stores, we recycle plastic drink bottles with screw-on tops.

Your child's water supply should be readily available — not buried inside a pack. Either sling it on a cord over the shoulder or attach it to the outside of a pack.

Some more tips on avoiding dehydration:

● Plain, cool water is best. The body absorbs cold fluids more quickly than warm ones.

● Sport drinks are another good choice. When given variety and

you're hungry when exercising, you need to *drink before you're thirsty*. This isn't just a dog-day rule — it's deceptively easy to become dehydrated on a winter day, for instance, or on a windy day.

Just as kids tend to tire and become hungry more quickly than adults do, they can become dehydrated with surprising speed. There are physiological reasons: Children sweat less than adults do and therefore get hotter. This is true for all preteens, but especially for children under age four. Be especially careful with babies: Be sure to supplement formula and breast milk feedings with water.

Don't listen if children claim

choices, kids are more likely to drink. If they prefer fruit juice, dilute it with water.

● Children who are getting enough to drink usually urinate at least once every two to three hours. Urine should be clear; a problem is signaled by urine that's darker than usual, or seems to contain crystals. (For diaper wearers, make sure you're not detecting the gel-like crystals from saturated disposable diapers.)

The warning signs of dehydration include pale skin, sweating, cracked lips, tearless crying, weakness, dizziness, headache, nausea, and irritability. A reliable test for severe dehydration is the "tent test": You pinch the victim's skin and the skin retains a tent shape. Hydrated skin collapses back to its normal shape.

Treatment is the same as prevention: Drink. For severe cases, hospitalization is needed.

Safe Drinking Water

While you're nagging your family to drink plenty of fluids, be sure to teach them an important corollary: Untreated water isn't safe. That

Store juice bottles in side pockets or in the top of the pack so that they're easy to reach at a moments' notice. Frequent drink breaks keep energy and spirits high.

proverbial line from *The Rime of the Ancient Mariner* — Water, water, everywhere/Nor any drop to drink — may help them with the conundrum.

Kids see a stream and naturally want to drink. Just the other day while playing with a cup in a puddle,

Will raised the cup to his lips. "No!" we shouted, and explained the problem. Keep a close eye on children of any age, because water looks tempting, even if the dangers have been thoroughly discussed. A child is likely to take a sip, then decide it's okay because he doesn't immediately feel sick.

Contamination can come from a litany of sources, many man-made, plenty not. Feces from any mammal are a big contaminant, especially near water, and a major culprit in the East is the beaver, now in the midst of a population boom. Even in the most pristine backwoods setting, you need to be especially wary of a parasite called *Giardia lamblia*, more commonly referred to as *Giardia*. Trust me, neither you nor your children want to risk getting giardiasis, the intestinal disease that results from drinking *Giardia*-infested water.

The bottom line on safety: Some water is safe, some isn't, and it's extraordinarily difficult to tell the difference with any certainty. Playing

---

BEE STINGS AND BABIES

"People who know they're allergic to bee stings carry bee sting kits. What about babies and young children who have never been stung — their parents don't know whether they're allergic."

The human body must be exposed to a protein, in this case bee venom, before it can develop a fatal hypersensitivity to it. So a first-time sting will not cause a fatal reaction. Often the second, third, fourth, etc., stings are not fatal.

However, earlier stings in people, young or old, who are susceptible to fatal anaphylactic reactions can produce a greater-than-normal response, such as unusual swelling and redness. Therefore, some — but not all — severely allergic people know they're allergic because they've had a bad, but not fatal, reaction. For these people, there is a chance that only a bee sting kit of injectable epinephrine can save their lives in the event of future stings. Unfortunately, an individual's reactions to a bee sting cannot be predicted accurately based on prior experience.

I suggest that parents who take their kids far from a doctor carry a kid-sized bee sting kit, or at least talk to their doctor about it. We carry one for our son. A prescription is required. Better safe than sorry.

Buck Tilton, director,
Wilderness Medicine Institute

it safe is admittedly a bit of a hassle, but why take risks? Carry water from home or from some other trustworthy source; treat any other water you drink with filtration devices, by boiling, or with chemicals such as iodine or Potable Aqua. Chemicals, however, are unsafe for pregnant women, nursing mothers, babies, or anyone with an untreated thyroid problem.

COMMON WOES
Bugs, Bites, and Stings

Aside from bad weather, biting bugs are the number one annoyance you're likely to encounter outdoors. Though usually harmless, they can transmit disease or cause severe allergic reactions, or simply make you miserable.

Know what you're likely to encounter — and when — in any area you explore. Bugs are out there all the time, so you can't avoid them, but you can think about time and place. At home in the summer, we avoid evening walks in the woods, for instance, because mosquitoes attack like kamikaze squadrons.

Dress your family to avoid distress. Bright, dark, and flowered clothing attracts insects. Head nets are effective war gear, especially for babies. Long sleeves and pants are a help if it's not too hot.

Keep a close eye on babies and toddlers, easy targets who can't defend themselves. Have one person be on "bug patrol" and walk slightly behind a child in a carrier, swatting away any pests.

If a welt develops on your child's skin, it's helpful if Mom or Dad knows which beast did the biting. The symptoms of severe allergic reactions include acute swelling, difficulty breathing, fever, and nausea. Seek immediate medical help.

Repellents

Some people swear by various folk remedies, such as eating garlic or rubbing orange peels on skin. If any of these work for you, hats off. But if you're going to be in bug country, I'd advise taking along genuine repellent.

Be careful, though. Children under age two should not be exposed to DEET, the most effective chemical bug repellent. High concentrations can dissolve fishing line and other materials, so you don't want this stuff anywhere near your baby. In fact, a Duke University review includes

DID YOU KNOW

Do you worry more about snakebites or bee stings? Turns out stingers are the real zingers. Only a handful of people, if any, die from snakebites each year, while about 40 to 50 typically die from allergic reactions to bee stings.

DEET in a list of chemicals that may contribute to Gulf War syndrome.

If not DEET, then what? The most effective natural ingredient is citronella; the most effective brand, Naturapel. It works so well that it should also be your first line of defense for older children, as well as yourself. Many people also tout the effectiveness of Avon's Skin-So-Soft bath oil, but it contains only 0.05 percent citronella, as opposed to Naturapel's 10 percent. Natural formulas are safe, but don't repel as well as brands containing DEET. The only drawback is that citronella occasionally causes a skin rash.

Another option in avoiding DEET is a repellent containing the active ingredient termethrian, which is designed to be applied to clothing, not to skin (in fact, the chemical is not absorbed by the skin). These sprays come in aerosol cans and are most effective when applied to clothing and then left sealed in a bag for an hour or so, to soak up fumes. This approach is considered safe for children of all ages.

For those over age two, you can use formulas containing no higher than 10 percent concentrations of DEET, but only when absolutely necessary. Skedaddle lotion is the best, containing 6.2 percent DEET, with an effective time-release formula. Do not apply these repellents near the mouth, eyes, and any cuts, or on the hands of children who may rub their eyes or suck their fingers.

Conduct your own field tests close to home before big trips to find which repellents work best for members of your family — body chemistry and reactions vary from person to person.

Scratching bites may cause infection. Hydrocortisone creams can soothe the discomfort. Wash any open sores and cover with a bandage.

Bees

Try to keep your family away from their territory: fields of wildflowers, clover, and garbage. Stepping on a nest is a frightening, painful experience, and multiple stings can be life-threatening.

Carry a bee-sting kit if anyone is allergic. All adults in the party should know about a child's allergy, and how to administer the kit.

Ice or cool compresses may reduce pain and swelling. A small black dot at the center of a sting indicates that the stinger is still present. A venom sac may also be attached. Remove it quickly; in a matter of minutes. Time is essential, and being too gentle can waste precious time.

Spiders and Ticks

Most spider bites are harmless, but consult an expert and beware if you'll be exploring areas inhabited by female black widows, brown recluse spiders, or other dangerous species.

When in tick territory, inspect your children and yourself several times a day and at bedtime. Repellents can help. Also avoid tall, grassy areas.

The ones to worry about are deer ticks, which can carry Lyme disease. They're tiny, about the size of a speck of dirt or a pinhead. Lyme disease can be hard to diagnose. One symptom is a rash that looks like a bull's eye — a red, circular patch around a pale center. Not everyone afflicted, however, gets the rash. Other symptoms resemble flu: aches, headache, fever.

If left untreated, Lyme disease can become very dangerous and can cause recurring illness. It's vital to treat Lyme disease in its early stages, so if any question exists, consult your doctor.

Where we live, dog and wood ticks are abundant. We sometimes come inside carrying several. These ticks are easy to spot and we almost always catch and kill them before they dig in.

Wood and deer ticks can carry Rocky Mountain spotted fever, although it's relatively rare. Contrary to its name, the disease occurs more frequently in the East than in the Rockies.

If a tick becomes embedded, pull it off gently with tweezers, being careful not to leave the head behind, then clean the bite with soap and water. Do not use remedies such as alcohol, nail polish, or a hot matchhead, which can cause a tick

Top: The dog tick (actual size at right) can carry very rare Rocky Mountain spotted fever.
Bottom: The tiny deer tick is the greater potential threat to hikers because it carries Lyme disease, which is becoming more and more common. In both instances, prevention is the best defense.

to dig deeper.

Chances are you'll be okay; it takes several hours for ticks to transmit disease. However, if a rash, fever, or flu-like symptoms appear after a tick bite, consult a physician. Tick-borne diseases are treated with antibiotics.

Sunburn

Skin is your child's (and anyone's) largest organ. Protecting it with suntan lotion is one of the easiest and most important safeguards you can provide outdoors. Many scientists believe that the most dangerous sunburns of all are those gotten before age 18, even though damage, including skin cancer, may not show up for decades.

Tans may look like a healthy glow, but they're evidence of skin damage. There's no such thing as a safe tan. They do help prevent further burns, but the sun's effects continue to be harmful. The bottom line: Always use suntan lotion and wear protective clothing, such as hats with brims and sunglasses. But take note: Once cotton is wet (with either water or sweat) it no longer protects against UV rays.

Toddler's tender skin is especially vulnerable to burning. Look for sunscreens made for children and apply them often and liberally. And encourage everyone to sport brimmed hats.

guideline is to choose a sunscreen and test it on a small portion of your child's skin. If there's no negative reaction, keep using it."

Some children are sensitive to an ingredient called PABA (para-aminobenzoic acid), but PABA-free sunscreens are widely available.

The higher the SPF (sun protection factor), the better. SPFs of 30 or more are best. At the very least, use 15; 30 for fair children. Reapply every two to four hours, more often in intense sun. Use waterproof sunscreen as needed. Avoid scented lotions, which may attract bugs. Don't forget to cover the feet, backs of legs, ears, nose, the back of the neck, and hands. Don't apply sunscreen, however, on the hands of babies who suck their thumbs or fingers.

If your child gets a sunburn, lotions and cool baths back at home or in camp can help. Add baking soda to bathwater but don't use soap.

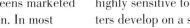

Even on cloudy days, over 70 percent of the sun's rays still penetrate. I got one of my worst burns on a cloudy day. Be especially wary near water and above treeline. Rays become 4 percent more intense with every 1,000 feet of elevation gain. SUNSCREENS I asked Buck Tilton, founder of the Wilderness Medicine Institute, about sunscreens marketed specifically for children. In most cases, he said, the ingredients are exactly the same as sunscreens for adults, only the labels are different. "SPF 25," he says, "will work exactly the same whether the package says for kids or not. The most important

Sunburns can cause fevers in children. Acetaminophen will help both fever and pain. Call a doctor, however, if your child develops a sudden fever greater than 102°F, if your child's eyes become highly sensitive to sunlight, or if blisters develop on a sunburned area.

OTHER DANGERS
Poisonous Plants
The Peterson Field Guide to Venomous Animals and Poisonous Plants

lists more than 250 species of plants in the contiguous 48 states and says hundreds more could have been listed, "especially those known to cause livestock poisoning."

How serious are poisonings likely to be?

It's difficult to make generalizations, because severity depends on what is ingested, how much, and the size of the child. In 1992, however, the American Association of Poison Control Centers reported more than 106,000 incidents involving plants. Of these, 81 percent involved children under six; 8 percent resulted in hospital treatment, and there were no deaths (although this may be misleading, because AAPCC data do not always reflect final outcomes).

While plants are unlikely to kill, your child could become sick or require hospitalization. With supervision and guidance, children can avoid any problems altogether.

Undeniably, many plants, especially berries, look appetizing to young children. The safest rule is to tell them not to eat *anything* wild without your permission.

While babies are known for putting anything and everything into

their mouths, they are usually in child carriers, seats, or tents, giving them few opportunities for unsupervised snacking. As much as Will loved to chew when a baby, we never had any problems with him mouthing anything he shouldn't.

Toddlers have more access, but you need to watch them constantly anyway, so you can usually prevent ingestion. If your toddler should start to graze, give him a stern no. If he disobeys, restrict access — put him in a child carrier.

At some point your child will be mature enough to easily identify a blueberry, for instance — but there's an in-between age when he might eat some other berry instead. Now that Will's approaching three, he's becoming a real berry lover, so this is the summer we're teaching him always to ask first.

You don't have to go to the woods to find poisonous plants; many are common in homes and gardens. If you suspect your child has ingested any, do not induce vomiting. Give activated charcoal and water; it will absorb the toxins. Then go to the nearest hospital. (Note: inducing vomiting is no longer recommended by physicians.)

POISON IVY, OAK, AND SUMAC The rash, the itching, the oozing — here's yet another good reason why your child should stay on the trail. For extra protection, long pants and sleeves can help.

Some people are allergic to poison ivy, some aren't. I am, Jim isn't; the verdict is still out on Will. I'm sure we'll know within the next year or so. The woods and roadways near our house are full of poison ivy.

Teach your family to recognize and avoid poison ivy, oak, and sumac. Allergic reactions develop within 12 to 48 hours of exposure. An oily resin called urushiol is the culprit; it is only released when the plant is bruised or damaged. It enters the skin rapidly, so the resin must be removed within 10 minutes to avoid a reaction.

If you know your child has come in contact with these plants, remove and wash his clothing. Wash the affected skin immediately and thoroughly — but gently — with cold water and mild soap. A special liquid soap called Tecnu, found in outdoor stores, is effective. However, a hot shower with a harsh soap and brisk rubbing can spread the problem.

Once a rash appears, calamine lotion, hydrocortisone cream, and other anti-itching lotions may help. If a rash is severe or involves the eyes, face, or genitalia, call a doctor, who may prescribe an antihistamine or steroid. Ask your family doctor for a prescription for extended back-country trips. Note that lotions containing Benadryl (diphenhydramine) cause a rash in many people.

Snakebites

Bites are more serious for children than for adults; because children are smaller, the venom is more potent in their systems. A bite that could kill a child may only cause illness in an adult.

Arm yourselves with knowledge and caution, and it's unlikely that you or your children will be bitten by a poisonous snake. In the United States mainland, you need worry about only four types. First is the coral snake; the other three are cousins: rattlesnakes, cottonmouths (also called water moccasins), and copperheads.

All are relatively easy to recognize. Teach your kids to do so, and to be careful. They should never touch a poisonous snake, tease it, or get closer for a better look.

It's essential to make children understand that snakes strike only when they're antagonized: if they feel threatened, or if they're touched or stepped on. Once you've backed out of a snake's "territory," they will not chase you.

Teach children to back up, stepping slowly, if they see a snake. If bitten, they must get out of the snake's striking range — the length of the snake. Second bites occur most frequently in youngsters who are so frightened they can't move.

If you're in an area where venomous snakes pose a threat, the National Outdoor Leadership School (NOLS) recommends:

- Watch where you step.
- Never reach into concealed areas (be careful when climbing and reaching up, for instance).
- Shake out sleeping bags, boots, and clothing before use.

- Never handle snakes, even if you think they're dead.

Keep a close eye on your family in snake country, especially if you're off the trail, during bathroom breaks, for instance. You may also want the added protection of long pants or gaiters.

TREATING SNAKEBITES Forget about most of the treatments you learned about as a kid. Any procedure involving cutting and sucking, as well as tourniquets, can do more harm than good. Cutting the skin can damage tissue and result in infection, for example, and is no longer recommended.

SNAKE IDENTIFICATION

The Great Explorations set of toy "Amazingly Real Snakes" contains seven plastic, yet authentic-looking snakes, including a lance-headed rattlesnake and an Arizona coral snake. They're smaller than life-size. While kids try to scare everyone by hiding them in tents and backpacks, they may learn to recognize these two dangerous varieties.

A coyote in Yosemite Park, California. Siting wild animals is one of the thrills of outdoor adventures, but you must teach children to keep their distance.

will still be necessary, but the extractor can be an important first step.

Avoid hysteria — this will help prevent venom from spreading. Hysteria may also bring on symptoms, such as nausea, that make it difficult to tell whether a bite is poisonous. Have the victim lie down and drink as much water as possible while waiting for help. Immobilize the extremity by making a splint, as if for a fracture.

Instead, the goal of treatment is to keep the patient quiet, while getting medical attention as quickly as possible.

One suction device — the Sawyer extractor — has been shown to be effective *if used within three minutes of a bite*. This high-pressure manual suction device, which costs about $12, does not require an incision. Additional medical treatment

It's important to know exactly what type of snake did the biting. Not all snakes are poisonous, and not all snakebite victims receive a significant amount of venom, if any. Therefore, try to find the snake to identify it.

BEWARE OF ALL ANIMALS

A visitor to Glacier National Park in Montana is said to have lost his car keys while attempting to lure a ground squirrel by dangling the keys out in front of the critter. The squirrel grabbed the keys and ran down a hole with them. The keys were never retrieved, a ranger cited the man for harassment of wildlife, and a locksmith was called to make new keys.

Wild Animals

No matter how cute or apparently tame wild animals may seem, they aren't Rovers and Fluffys. They're wild, which means unpredictable.

At Baxter State Park in Maine, director Irvin C. "Buzz" Caverly says "Don't feed the animals" is one of his most important pieces of advice for parents. Not only is feeding wild animals potentially harmful for people; it can also hurt the animals, making them dependent on humans for food.

Caverly cites a recent problem in which parents urged their son to feed a deer, and the deer became aggressive. Luckily, the boy wasn't hurt, but he could have easily been. "Stay your distance," he warns.

Teach your children to be respectful of wild animals without making them frightened:

● Explain that unless animals are sick (as with rabies), they don't usually attack unless provoked.

● Don't encourage children to get close to wild animals for any reason, whether to feed them, get a photo, or simply get an up-close look.

● In any area you explore, identify animals you need to watch out for, especially grizzly bears, and take necessary safety precautions, such as wearing bear bells and hanging food.

Water Safety

Water is the best outdoor treat of all, whether you're wading, swimming, or lounging beside a stream. But it's also one of the most dangerous, especially with kids. A large percentage of drowning victims are children, especially toddlers, who are inquisitive but don't know how to swim, and teenage boys, who may know how to swim but take risks and think themselves invincible.

Just last week I read about a family relaxing beside a river. They warned their son not to wade too far from shore, but he did, and got in trouble. The current was so strong that both parents drowned trying to save him. A passing canoeist managed to rescue the child.

A month or so ago, a four-year-old in a neighboring town was walking with his father and baby sister. When his father turned for an instant to attend to the younger child, the boy slipped and was swept away by a fast-moving creek.

These tragedies could have been avoided. Most drownings occur 10 to 30 feet from safety, frequently by victims who couldn't swim and had no intention of venturing into deep water.

Any water can be dangerous; all children see is a big, wet playground. Babies can drown in puddles. Many creeks and rivers have hidden dangers, tricky spots with fast-moving currents. Anyone can slip on rocks, hit his head, get tangled in weeds. A flailing, panicked child can be surprisingly strong and difficult to rescue.

Enjoy the water safely:

● Parents should know how to swim;

children should have swimming lessons as early as possible. While lessons are available for babies and toddlers, the American Academy of Pediatrics doesn't recommend them before the age of three.

- Children should always be supervised around water, even a shallow pond or creek.
- No rough horseplay.
- Assume diving is unsafe in most areas.
- Water shoes improve grip and prevent cuts.

🛈

DID YOU KNOW

Drowning is the second leading cause of unintentional, injury-related deaths in the United States among children ages 14 and under (the first is motor-vehicle-related injuries). Every year more than 1,000 children drown, and 4,000 more are hospitalized in near-drownings, according to the National Safe Kids Campaign. For tips on how to prevent injuries to your children, send a self-addressed, stamped, business-size envelope to Family Safety Check, The National Safe Kids Campaign, Suite 1000, Dept. P, 1301 Pennsylvania Ave., N.W., Washington, DC 20005.

- Personal flotation devices (PFDs) should *always* be worn when boating.

Lightning

I love thunderstorms and think they're exciting, but I like to watch them from my living room, not from a mountaintop. On average, about 100 to 200 persons in the United States are killed by lightning each year, and several hundred injured.

Lightning discharges heat and expands air, causing shock waves we call thunder. This means that if you hear rumbles, lightning is in the area, even if you haven't seen it. If you're in or near water, this is your signal to move to dry land. Once you see a flash, count the seconds until you hear thunder. You can tell how far away the lightning was: Each second represents 1,000 feet — which means count five seconds for every mile.

Lightning strikes the nearest object, which means that mountaintops, ridges, lone trees, and the highest tree in a forest are vulnerable. Avoid these places during storms, and avoid creeks and other bodies of water, anything metal (such as tent poles), caves, and overhangs. If you're in a canoe or swimming, go to shore. Stay away from bikes. Tents offer little protection; metal poles and wet cloth are conductors. If possible, head for your car; the grounded rubber wheels make it one of the safest harbors of all. Get in and close the windows; stay out of flatbed trucks or open convertibles.

Out in the open and far from medical help, you must take lightning's threat seriously. If you have the option of returning to your car at the trailhead, do so.

Don't look for a clearing in an attempt to avoid the tallest tree, because then you become the tallest object. You're likely to be safe in a low area of forest underneath a thick growth of saplings or small trees. Interestingly, however, ash and beech trees are least likely to be hit, while poplar, silver fir, pine, and oak are more likely targets.

If you're caught in a storm, the safest positions are often counterintuitive. Sit on something dry and non-conducting, such as a mattress pad or pack; don't sit directly on the ground. Instead of huddling together with your children, spread out from each other, several yards away, to lessen the chance of everyone being hit.

If anyone is struck, administer CPR, artificial respiration, and treat-ment for burns and shock as needed. Additional injuries, such as fractures, can occur when victims are thrown off their feet. As soon as backcountry treatment has been administered, it's essential to seek additional medical attention for the victim, since additional reactions may occur, especially in the first 24 hours.

Altitude and Kids

While studies have been done on children's tolerance to altitude, the problem has not been widely researched. Some believe that altitude may affect children age eight and younger more severely, but the consensus seems to be that there is little or no difference in its effects on children and adults.

While reassuring, the conclusion

✔

When the weather is lousy, the smartest thing to do is to go home. Don't consider your trip a failure, or fret that your family isn't hardy enough. Just blame Mother Nature.

Plan another trip and hope she'll be in a better mood.

is of little practical value, since adult responses vary so widely. One person may get sick at 9,000 feet while another may have no problems. What's more, the same individual can respond differently on different days, and no one is sure why.

At any rate, altitude problems are fairly easy to spot and easy to treat, provided they're caught early. The key to avoiding problems is acclimatizing gradually. If you're traveling from the East Coast to the Rockies, spend a few days adjusting, taking it easy in higher-altitude towns.

Once you hit the trails, be prepared to move more slowly. Above 10,000 feet, restrict over-night elevation gains to no more than 1,000 feet a day. Layover days are another big help, as is drinking plenty of fluids. It's also helpful to sleep at as low an altitude as possible.

Stop climbing if anyone in your family seems generally tired or has a headache, a loss of appetite, or insomnia. Kids experience these problems all the time — so the cause may or may not be due to altitude. However, such symptoms mean your child isn't having a great time, so it's time to descend anyway, and not take chances.

If you forge ahead, the headache may become severe, and your child may become nauseated and clumsy. Respiration and heart rates increase. At this point acute mountain sickness can become an acute altitude emergency, which can be life-threatening.

Don't fool around. Go down.

EMERGENCIES

What do you need to take care of your family in case of a wilderness emergency?

Parents often ask this question of Rick Wilcox, who replies: "People worry about what to put in first aid kits, whether to bring a cellular phone, and all this other kind of stuff," he says. "They'd be a lot smarter to bring a second adult along than all the safety precautions in the world. It gives you so much more flexibility."

With two adults, for instance, one can stay with an injured child while the other goes for help. The higher the adult-to-child ratio, the better off you are.

Knowledge, a hefty dose of common sense, and strength and endurance are the most vital pieces of equipment adults can carry. If an accident occurs and you're several hours, even days, from help, it's often up to you to be doctor, at least temporarily. You may have to make quick, yet crucial, decisions. You may need to go for help, or help carry your child to help. You would need to know the best place to go — which isn't always the trailhead — and how to get there quickly and efficiently.

Backcountry Rescues

Even with training, you can never be completely prepared for every mishap, especially in the wilderness. You'll also need some luck.

Take the case of an 11-year-old Canadian girl who was hiking with her family in Tuckerman Ravine during the early summer of 1995. "Tuck's," as it's called, is a beautiful glacial bowl on Mount Washington, New Hampshire — an intriguing, challenging destination for families and anyone else. Snow often remains there well into the summer, forming a snow bridge.

All was going well for the Canadian visitors until, suddenly, a rock tumbled from above, knocking the girl about 30 feet off the trail. When her family reached her, she was bleeding severely and her leg was badly fractured. The injury was life-threatening.

Fortunately, the area is extremely popular, help was on hand, and an amazing rescue team fell into place. Two hikers rushed to an Appalachian Mountain Club shelter, less than a half mile away. The caretaker was a Wilderness Emergency Medical Technician (WEMT), who organized rescue equipment while her assistant radioed for help.

Also in the area were a physician, several EMTs, a student nurse, and an experienced member of a local search-and-rescue team. Eventually, a human chain of about 50 volunteers formed to carry the girl on a litter down the steep, stony trail.

Even with all this assistance, the nearly half-mile journey took about four hours. There, a helicopter took the girl to a children's hospital, where she spent a week in intensive care, then began a slow recovery.

TEACHING CHILDREN FIRST AID

It is important to teach children that they are capable of accomplishing first aid during a survival experience. They must realize they are not helpless and even though there are no first aid supplies available, there are still things that can be done for an injury. . . . First aid makes children . . . aware of dangerous situations and carelessness.

Tom Brown
Tom Brown's Field Guide to Nature and Survival for Children

Nick Wiltsie regroups after a bad stubbed toe on a Sierra Nevada, California, backpacking trip. Many injuries occur in camp when your guard is down — or your shoes are off.

"I don't think people realize how long it takes to put together a rescue team and go into the mountains," Wilcox says. "It's not a matter of just jumping into cars like you see on TV. I would say that to get to someone an hour from the road takes three hours from when we get the call."

Once help arrives and initial treatment begins, carrying a patient on a litter — even a child — is heavy, slow work on challenging terrain.

I don't mean to paralyze you by this discussion — it's simply meant to inform, especially if you take children into the backcountry.

The risks may be too high, for instance, if your child has a serious condition. The son of a friend of mine used to have a severe heart rhythm problem. Until it was corrected by surgery, she never took him deep into the woods, far from prompt medical attention. She took these precautions despite her own extensive medical background — she is a cardiac intensive care nurse and an EMT.

Most children can travel deep into the wilderness with no problems. However, if you believe your child's health may pose a problem, consult your family doctor. You and your child may still be able to have wonderful outdoor experiences, although you may need to stick close to trailheads and roads.

Before beginning any outing, make sure you know whom to contact — and where — should an emergency arise. The drill is the backcountry equivalent of taking mental note of exits on planes or in theaters. Where is the nearest ranger headquarters, for instance? Might there be a backcountry hut in the area equipped with an emergency radio? Where is the nearest pay phone, and do you have change? If you're not sure of these details, find someone who can answer your questions.

Know *exactly* whom to call, advises Buck Tilton, head of the Wilderness Medicine Institute in Pitkin, Colorado. You can always dial 911, but if backcountry assistance is needed, a search-and-rescue team must be alerted. In New Hampshire, for instance, such teams fall under the administration of the state's Division of Fish & Wildlife, while in Colorado, Tilton says, the county sheriff's department must be called. Carry names, phone numbers, and change with you.

INJURIES

During Rick Wilcox's years with the White Mountain search-and-rescue team, he's seen an array of injuries, from sprains to deaths.

What, I asked him, is the biggest mistake that parents make when bringing their children into the wilderness?

His answer was immediate: "Overestimating the physical and mental capabilities of their children."

Makes sense.

That's when everyone becomes tired, frustrated, angry, and careless. They fumble; they stumble. They push too hard, or end up on a trail after dark.

Then it's time for Wilcox and other volunteers to come pick up the pieces.

Remember the low-impact, no-trace rule. Be as kind to your family's bodies as you are to the trail. You don't want a cast or crutches to be a souvenir of your trip.

Trail Treatment

As soon as your child is injured, you're faced with important decisions.

How serious is it?

Can we treat this ourselves?

If additional medical treatment is needed, can we get the child there on our own steam, without additional help?

Stay calm; you've got a job to do. And no matter how serious, reassure your child, while being as honest as possible ("Yes, darling, I think your leg may be broken, but we're going to get help and you're going to be fine.")

You're ahead of the game if you can treat an injury yourself, or get the child to a doctor without using a rescue team. Otherwise, be prepared to wait, often for a considerable period.

But here's the Catch-22. At times, as with spinal cord injuries, it's crucial *not* to move a patient, or you'll worsen the injury. You may be the only one available to make such a judgment.

If an injury is serious, one adult should stay with the child while the other goes for help — which is why you always want to have at least two adults along. Can you imagine being face-to-face with a seriously injured child and having to decide whether to stay or leave the child alone and go for help? Either option would be excruciating.

Once you decide to go for help, think carefully about the best place to go. In the case of the injured girl in Tuckerman Ravine, there was no need to return to a trailhead, several hours away. Anyone familiar with the area would know that the AMC Hermit Lake Shelter, less than half a mile from the accident, would be equipped with a caretaker and radio.

A final detail: Whenever you split your party up, whether for injury or any other reason, be sure each group has sufficient supplies,

TRUST YOUR INSTINCTS, TRUST YOURSELF

If you sense any type of danger, get yourself out of trouble as quickly as possible, advises *Trailside* host and mountaineer Peter Whittaker. Don't wait for someone else to take care of you or your family.

Whittaker climbed Mount Rainier at age 12 and four years later began guiding professionally. When he was 19, he, his father, and some climbers they were leading were caught in an avalanche on Washington State's premier peak.

"It was early spring," Whittaker recalls. "We didn't have radios and I was feeling uncomfortable. My father and I were each leading a rope. We went out on a very steep slope, and I remember telling him, 'Take it easy. We don't have radios.'

"He was ahead. When he had nearly reached the top, he turned around and yelled, 'Pete, this isn't looking good.' Then he took four more steps, and the whole slope just released. We slid about 800 feet.

"Fortunately, we had the worst injuries of anyone. He dislocated a shoulder; I broke my ankle. But it could have been a very, very bad accident.

"After that, I realized that even though my father was a world-class mountaineer, you can't trust anyone. You have to really listen to your own instincts and be conservative."

including food, clothing, and water. Your separation may be longer than planned.

When a Parent Is Injured

In this case, the drill is largely the same as when a child is injured. You can treat the injury yourself, or go for help. Again, the more adults along, the better. If there are three adults and an injury is serious, one adult and the children stay with the injured party, while the third adult gets help.

With only two adults, things can get tricky. One adult is injured, one must go for help, but what about the kids? Ask yourself: Can they stay behind, perhaps helping, or will they be traumatized? Might they get into trouble if left unsupervised? If, on the other hand, they, too, leave to get help, will they slow down response time?

Finally, in some cases, older, mature children can be sent for help while the healthy parent attends to the injured spouse.

With so many variables, there are no magic formulas, just judgment calls. You need to think clearly, assess the probable results of various re-sponses, and minimize any losses, such as additional injuries to your children.

ILLNESS

Is that runny nose just a cold? Are those aches and pains a 24-hour bug, a bacterial infection requiring antibiotics, dehydration, or a passing virus? It's often difficult to gauge the severity of our *own* illnesses, much less our children's.

Will has been blessed with extremely good health. On several occasions, however, I've been convinced he was coming down with something and forced to decide whether to forge ahead with plans or cancel. If he doesn't have a fever or nausea, we usually proceed as planned. Sometimes all symptoms miraculously disappear in an hour or two.

TAKE A THERMOMETER?

On many excursions, especially day trips or short weekend trips, you can get by without a thermometer. You can usually feel a child's head and have a good sense of whether she has a slight fever or a raging one. For short periods, exact numbers don't matter as long as you can gauge severity. Do take children's pain relievers, and administer them as needed. If a child's fever seems unusually high, or if symptoms are severe, seek medical attention immediately.

No matter where you are — on the trail, at home, or in a Holiday Inn — sometimes the only solution is to wait and see. At home I have the luxury of being able to call Will's pediatrician's office, describe the problem, and let a professional decide whether an office visit is warranted. My own medical books are close at hand; several hospitals are in the area.

Not so in the woods.

There, it pays to play it safe. How far are you from medical attention? If you're a good distance away and your child seems sick, it's time to get closer. Children can become acutely ill with frightening speed; happily, they often recover just as quickly.

When symptoms appear, either head home — you can always schedule another trip — or come up with a plan: If there's no improvement by such and such a time, we'll pack up.

Be extra cautious with babies, especially young ones, particularly if you're a first-time parent. I panicked the first time Will had an intestinal virus, when he was about a year old. Sure he was dehydrated, I was ready to rush to the emergency room. I glared at Jim for not jumping into the car; he gently suggested a call to the doctor's office might be a good first

DIAL-A-"RESCUE"

In 1993 a woman used her cellular phone to call 911 from the top of Half Dome in Yosemite National Park. She reportedly said, "Well, I'm at the top and I'm really tired." The answering ranger asked if she felt sick. "No," she said, "I'm just really tired and want my friends to drive to the base and pick me up." The ranger explained that she would have to hike down the trail she had ascended. The visitor replied, "But you don't understand, I'm really tired."

What happened next? "It turned out we got really lucky," the ranger said. "Her phone battery died."

A year later, a woman embarked on a solo hike to the summit of Yosemite's El Capitan. When she became lost and saw a storm brewing, she called 911 from her cellular phone and asked to be rescued. A helicopter found her barely off the trail and less than half a mile from the top. When the helicopter lifted off and the woman realized how close she was to the summit, she asked the crew to set her down on top. When they declined, she threatened to sue them for kidnapping.

step. It was, and a nurse told me to put Will to bed. Had the incident occurred in the backcountry, Will would've been all right, but I would've been sorely in need of a sedative.

What if you're about to begin a wilderness trip when your child becomes ill? Again, play it safe. Consult your family doctor or pediatrician. If you're several hours or days away from home, but not yet on the trail, you may need to hole up in a motel. You may have been planning this trip for months, but none of you will enjoy it if your child is ill.

Perhaps your child is prone to ear infections or some other illness. Let your family doctor know when you're going on a trip, so a long-distance emergency call won't come as a surprise. If you won't have access to a phone, your doctor may be willing to prescribe antibiotics for you to take on the trail in case of illness. Let your physician know if you won't have access to refrigeration; powdered antibiotics can be prescribed instead of liquids.

PHONE HOME?

People venturing into the outdoors are increasingly relying on cellular phones to get out of jams.

Don't.

For every instance of how a phone has helped, there are likely to be 10 cases in which they've failed or been misused.

You can't depend on it, and you're likely to lull yourself into a false sense of security. Your batteries may die; you may be out of satellite range. Abuse is rampant — people carelessly call for help as though dialing for a pizza delivery.

Even if you are able to dial 911

❖

BEST-BET READING

FOR ADULTS

✳ BACKCOUNTRY FIRST AID & EXTENDED CARE, by Buck Tilton (*ICS*). This pocket-sized book was designed to be carried in first aid kits or backpacks. Tilton is the founder of the Wilderness Medicine Institute.

✳ MEDICINE FOR MOUNTAINEERING & OTHER WILDERNESS ACTIVITIES, by James A. Wilkerson (*The Mountaineers*).

✳ MEDICINE FOR THE BACKCOUNTRY, by Buck Tilton and Frank Hubbell (*ICS*).

✳ NOLS WILDERNESS FIRST AID, by Tod Schimelpfenig and Linda Lindsey (*National Outdoor Leadership School*).

SIMON & SCHUSTER POCKET GUIDE TO WILDERNESS MEDICINE, by Paul G. Gill, Jr. (*Simon & Schuster*).

continued on page 252

FOR KIDS

✳ FIRST AID FOR YOUTHS, by Buck Tilton and Steve Griffin (*ICS*, ages 8 and up). An excellent book explaining what to do in a variety of emergencies, including drowning, head injuries, and burns. Each skill is introduced by a real-life emergency scenario.

✳ IMPROVE YOUR SURVIVAL SKILLS, Usborne Superskills, by Lucy Smith (*EDC Publishing*, ages 8 and up). Lots of illustrations and an abundance of dos and don'ts, presented in a no-nonsense, intriguing manner.

THE SAFETY BOOK FOR ACTIVE KIDS, by Linda Schwartz (*Learning Works*, ages 4–8). A fun, easy format is designed to help young children be prepared to face a variety of hazards and emergencies.

✳ TALES OF REAL SURVIVAL, Usborne Reader's Library, by Paul Dowswell (*EDC Publishing*, ages 10 and up). A fascinating book: Jim and I both fought over this one. Great stories from the present and past. WHAT WOULD YOU DO? A KID'S GUIDE TO TRICKY AND STICKY SITUATIONS, by Linda Schwartz (*Learning Works*, ages 8–12). Kids are asked to imagine themselves in numerous scenarios, then given explanations of the best solutions. Includes an extensive list of first aid dilemmas. The question-and-answer format makes this book a good car activity.

with a cell phone, your problem may not be solved. Wilcox says people who do so in the White Mountains reach the city of Concord, several hours away. The folks in trouble often can't provide the correct access code for a return call, so no one closer can call them back.

"We've had people waiting for the phone to ring," Wilcox says, "but the rescue squad doesn't know where they are. It's a stalemate. We have to hope they'll call back and say, 'Why isn't anyone here?' We've had some really crazy situations."

Your fingers can't do the walking in the wilderness.

ADVENTURES NEVER END

"Hey, I have long legs now!"

Will, age 2
after climbing over a small log on a New Hampshire trail

I worry that families may expect this book to contain handy solutions for every situation they encounter during their outdoor adventures.

How, I wonder, can *anyone* profess to be an expert on children, beings who are as unpredictable as the weather? A spider that fascinates one girl will terrify another; a lullaby may soothe a baby one minute but not the next.

Like parents the world over, I'm constantly playing the daily child-rearing lottery, trying to come up with winning combinations, often second-guessing myself. Sometimes right answers seem nothing more than lucky hunches.

However, when it comes to hiking, camping, and backpacking, there are certain unbreakable rules. Once you know them, you tend to take them for granted, to assume that everyone knows them.

Not everyone does, I was reminded during a recent hike on Mount Monadnock, New Hampshire. In the space of a half-hour, I witnessed a veritable parade of family hiking "don'ts." Sadly — and sometimes tragically — there are parents out there who don't understand even the most basic safety principles.

As I climbed a fairly steep, rock-strewn trail, a young man came barreling down, carrying a screaming toddler. Instead of using a child carrier, he held the boy, who bounced in his arms like a bowling ball. No wonder he was crying.

I was among several mothers who saw the pair zoom by. We held our collective breaths, praying the man wouldn't trip and send the child airborne. After they were out of sight, we all exchanged disapproving looks. "If my husband ever did that," one woman said. "I'd kill him."

Then, as if on cue, another family appeared, descending carefully, with a baby beaming in a child carrier. Yes, we reminded ourselves, young children can have a fine time on this mountain.

About 10 minutes later another family caught my eye: parents watching their five-year-old son lap up water off the trail, right where everyone was walking. The trickle wasn't even a stream, just runoff from a morning rain shower.

Normally I try to keep my mouth shut, but in this case I couldn't. "He really shouldn't be drinking that," I said, trying my best to sound offhand.

"Why?" the woman said. She didn't have a clue that the water could be full of bacteria or parasites, that her son could catch, among other diseases, giardiasis.

Along with obvious don'ts, like drinking unfiltered water or not using a child carrier on an extended hike, parents who take their children into the wilderness encounter all sorts of gray areas. Near the summit, for example, I spotted a man carrying an infant in a front pack. The baby was warmly dressed; the parents obviously knew what they were doing.

But . . .

Mount Monadnock's summit is a giant pile of boulders, requiring balance and caution. It's not a good place for babies still in front packs, since front packs aren't as safe as child carriers — in a fall, a parent is likely to crush the baby. What's more, on this day the wind howled and it was cold. I've climbed Mount Monadnock every month of the year, and this was by far the windiest summer day I've ever encountered. In my mind, this wasn't a wise place to bring an infant.

More than likely, these parents were careful and their child was fine — but why take unnecessary risks? When people take repeated chances in the wilderness, bad luck seems to have a way of catching up.

Thankfully, no matter what

you're doing, where you're going, or how old your children are, there are guidelines everyone agrees on, basic tenets of family adventuring:

- Don't plan too much, more than your family can easily handle. Outings should be fun, not a struggle.
- Don't expect too much of children. They're kids, not miniature adults. They're built differently, they work differently, they think differently.
- Always keep kids warm, dry, and protected from the elements, especially the sun, bugs, and other outdoor hazards.
- Give children plenty to eat and drink.
- Schedule plenty of breaks.
- Families on bikes must wear helmets; families in canoes must wear personal flotation devices (PFDs).
- Have fun. If you aren't, regroup or go home.

Like mountains, the task of parenting is filled with peaks and valleys. There are times that feel like an endless uphill trudge — Will whines, I reply sharply, we both feel glum. Happily, such moments are always tempered, such as when Will unexpectedly gives me the rare treat of a smooch on the lips, or shouts with glee as he explores a trail.

Just last week Will unknowingly gave me something to think about, good advice for all parents, since children grow up all too quickly. We were staying at a friend's summer cottage, and Will was having a hard time settling down for the night.

"We've got a big day planned," I pleaded with him, "so you need to go to sleep now so we can have fun tomorrow."

"But Mommy," he said, his face full of energy, "we can have fun *now*."

Will is right — make the best of every moment with your kids. There are day-to-day joys and struggles, year-by-year milestones. Through them all, it may help to think of your child as a client, and you as wilderness guide. Your family's safety and comfort must come before anything else. Do your job well, and the payoff is enormous — fun, memorable trips, and activities your family can continue to share for the rest of your lives.

Whether you're on the trail or at home, children are constantly learning; their abilities always changing. Each stage brings new challenges. Kids need to poke and dawdle before they're ready to really hike. Try to relish each delay; each development phase has its charms. A year from now, you're likely to be feeling nostalgic.

As I've written this book, I've had the pleasure of comparing notes with families across the country. It's heartening to realize that as we take our children to the wilderness, we may find the solitude we seek, but we're never alone in the endeavor.

One recent summer's night, for instance, a blue moon cast its rays on many. Here in Groton, Jim, Will, and I were at home, happy after a dayhike, sitting on the front porch watching fireflies, dreaming of adventures to come. The moon rose in the distance, shining over our field full of tiny flashes.

In Utah, Ray Dahl, father of three, was backpacking with a group of teenagers in the Uintah Mountains, the trails still steeped in snow. At dawn he peered out from his bivi sack, to be greeted by the sight of the moon dropping behind a ridge as the sun began to light the eastern sky.

Meanwhile, in Washington state, Charles Vaughan and his oldest daughter, 15, had just attempted to climb Mount Rainier. The Vaughans didn't make the tricky climb, but vowed to try again. After their exhausting day, they camped on the mountainside for the night, where Vaughan proclaimed the attempt a success. He said: "It was a gift to watch the sun rise at 12,000 feet on a wild glacier with my daughter."

The next time you gaze at the moon or the stars, think of the thousands of other families whose flashlights and headlamps twinkle as they settle down in their tents. There's hardly a cozier glow.

But enough, already.

The sun is shining and Will is waiting.

The woods and mountains are calling — *now*.

It's time to put a sign on my office door.

Gone Exploring.

SOURCES & RESOURCES

ORGANIZATIONS

ADVENTURE CYCLING ASSOCIATION
P.O. Box 8308
Missoula, MT 59807
406-721-1776
A tour organizer, information clearinghouse, and a source of maps for self-guided tours. Publishes the invaluable The Cyclists' Yellow Pages — *a virtual bible of the sport.*

AMERICAN CANOE ASSOCIATION (ACA)
7432 Alban Station Road
Suite B-226
Springfield, Virginia 22150
703-451-0141
http://www.aca-paddler.org

AMERICAN HIKING SOCIETY (AHS)
1422 Fenwick Lane
Silver Spring, MD 20910
301-565-6704
Fax: 301-565-6714
http://www.orca.org/ahs/
National society with more than 200 affiliated clubs, all dedicated to protecting and expanding public and private trails. Sponsors National Trails Day in June with many family activities, including family hikes, trail cleanups, equipment demonstrations, and bicycle rides. AHS is the creator of the American Discovery Trail, America's first coast-to-coast hiking trail.

APPALACHIAN MOUNTAIN CLUB (AMC)
5 Joy Street
Boston, MA 02108
617-523-0636
Fax: 617-523-0722
In addition to adult programs and publications, the club sponsors many geared specifically to families. AMC huts are an excellent way to introduce children to backpacking.

HUG-A-TREE AND SURVIVE
6465 Lance Way
San Diego, CA 92120
619-286-7536
A volunteer group dedicated to teaching families how to prevent children from getting lost in the woods and safe procedures should they become lost. There are chapters in every state except Hawaii, and also in Canada, Sweden, and Australia.

INTERNATIONAL MOUNTAIN BIKING ASSOCIATION (IMBA)
P.O. Box 7578
Boulder, CO 80306-7578
303-545-9011
Fax: 303-545-9026
http://www.outdoorlink.com/IMB
A non-profit organization dedicated to promoting mountain biking that is environmentally safe and socially responsible. Members can travel with their bikes without additional charge on several airlines (America West, Continental, Northwest, TWA, and Western Pacific).

LEAGUE OF AMERICAN BICYCLISTS
190 West Ostend Street
Suite 120
Baltimore, MD 21230
410-539-3399
The League serves primarily non-racing cyclists: commuters, tourers, recreational riders; promotes government support of cycling as a transportation alternative; and publishes a magazine eight times a year.

NATIONAL ASSOCIATION OF CANOE LIVERIES AND OUTFITTERS (NACLO)
U.S. 27 & Hornbeck Road
Box 248
Butler, KY 41006
606-472-2205
Renters and outfitters.

NATIONAL AUDUBON SOCIETY
950 Third Avenue
New York, NY 10022
212-979-3000
The Audubon Society and its local chapters offer a variety of family programs. Call for your nearest chapter's offerings.

NATIONAL BICYCLE DEALERS ASSOCIATION
2240 University Drive, #130
Newport Beach, CA 92660
714-722-6909
A good source for recommendations of local bike shops.

NATIONAL PARKS AND CONSERVATION ASSOCIATION (NPCA)
1776 Massachusetts Avenue, N.W.
Washington, DC 20036
800-951-1070
http://www.npca.org
NPCA is dedicated to protecting and preserving national parks. Sponsors annual March for Parks on Earth Day, a good conservation activity for families.

THE NATURE CONSERVANCY
1815 North Lynn Street
Arlington, VA 22209
703-841-5300
Oversees more than 1,000 wild preserves and safeguards millions of acres, many of which are perfect for family exploring. Ask for your local chapter information.

RAILS-TO-TRAILS CONSERVANCY
1400 16th Street N.W., Suite 300
Washington, DC 20036
A group working to convert thousands of miles of abandoned railroad tracks in the United States to bike trails. Also publishes guidebooks to these trails.

SERVAS
11 John Street, Suite 407
New York, NY 10038-4009
212-267-0252
An international cooperative system of hosts and travelers; apply to be both, either sharing your home with others or staying in host homes.

SHARING NATURE FOUNDATION
14618 Tyler Foote Road
Nevada City, CA 95959
916-292-3893
Founded by Joseph Cornell, an organization focusing on nature awareness, especially in children. Sponsors workshops for families, outdoor educators, and youth group leaders.

SIERRA CLUB
730 Polk Street
San Francisco, CA 94109
415-923-5630
http://www.sierraclub.org
This well-known environmental group has many programs, trips, and publications for families. Be sure to inquire about high mountain huts.

TOUR ORGANIZERS
These companies and organizations offer family trips:

APPALACHIAN MOUNTAIN CLUB (AMC)
5 Joy Street
Boston, MA 02108
617-523-0636
Fax: 617-523-0722
Many family trips and programs.

BACKROADS
1516 5th Street
Berkeley, CA 94710
800-462-2848
http://www.backroads.com
Considered one of the foremost active travel tour operators in North America.

HOSTELLING INTERNATIONAL— AMERICAN YOUTH HOSTELS
733 15th Street, N.W., #840
Washington, DC 20005
202-783-6161
Fax: 202-783-6171
American and European group programs for all ages.

ROADS LESS TRAVELED
P.O. Box 8187
Longmont, CO 80501
800-488-8483
Cycling tours for families; children must be at least 10 years old.

SIERRA CLUB
730 Polk Street
San Francisco, CA 94109
415-923-5630
http://www.sierraclub.org
Many family trips and programs.

OUTDOOR ADVENTURE SCHOOLS
Here are several standouts:

BILL DVORAK'S KAYAK AND RAFTING EXPEDITIONS
17921 U.S. Highway 285
Nathrop, CO 81236
719-539-6851
All canoeing instruction involves some whitewater; children must be at least 10 years old.

NANTAHALA OUTDOOR CENTER
U.S. 19 West, Box 41
Bryson City, NC 28713
704-488-2175
Offers general canoeing instruction for ages 16-up. Private lessons available for families with younger children; a variety of kayaking lessons geared to ages 10-18.

NATIONAL OUTDOOR
LEADERSHIP SCHOOL (NOLS)

Department R
288 Main Street
Lander, WY 82520
307-332-6973
http://www.nols.edu
Offers adult courses in hiking, mountaineering, and canoeing; some for college credit. Teenagers 16 and older can participate in some, and a month-long backpacking course is offered for 14- and 15-year-olds.

OUTWARD BOUND

Route 90
R2, Box 280
Garrison, NY 10524
800-243-8520
The school has a solid reputation for safe and professional wilderness courses. All participants must be at least 14 years old; several family and parent-child programs are offered.

FIRST AID TRAINING
AMERICAN RED CROSS
NATIONAL HEADQUARTERS

431 18th Street, N.W.
Washington, DC 20006
202-737-8300
Call for information on first aid and CPR classes offered by local chapters.

STONEHEARTH OPEN
LEARNING OPPORTUNITIES
(SOLO)

P.O. Box 3150
Conway, NH 03818
603-447-6711
Minimum age is 18.

WILDERNESS
MEDICAL ASSOCIATES

189 Dudley Road
Bryant Pond, ME 04219
800-742-2931
Offers a variety of courses; minimum age is 16.

WILDERNESS
MEDICINE INSTITUTE

P.O. Box 9
Pitkin, CO 81241-0009
970-641-3572

In addition to varied course offerings, the Institute is a source for backcountry first aid supplies and a variety of books on the subject, including several by executive director and founder Buck Tilton.

FIRST AID KITS
FOR FAMILIES
AND CHILDREN
ADVENTURE MEDICAL KITS

P.O. Box 43309
Oakland, CA 94624
800-324-3517

ATWATER CAREY, LTD.

339 East Rainbow Boulevard
Salida, CO 81201
800-359-1646

CHINOOK MEDICAL GEAR, INC.

P.O. Box 3300
Eagle, CO 81631
800-766-1365
Fax: 970-328-4404

OUTDOOR RESEARCH (OR)

2203 First Avenue South
Seattle, WA 98134
800-421-2421
Fax: 800-421-2419
http://www.orgear.com

SAWYER PRODUCTS

P.O. Box 188
Safety Harbor, FL 34695
800-356-7811
Fax: 800-497-6489

MAGAZINES

Few outdoor magazines focus specifically on families, although most have occasional articles on family participation.

BACKPACKER

Rodale Press
33 Minor Street
Emmaus, PA 18098
610-967-5171
http://www.bpbasecamp.com
The annual equipment guide is a must for hikers, campers, and backpackers.

BICYCLING

Rodale Press
33 Minor Street
Emmaus, PA 18098
610-967-5171
The nation's leading magazine on cycling, covering all aspects of the sport, but with a principal focus on road riding and touring. Online version available on America Online.

CANOE & KAYAK

Canoe America Associates
P.O. Box 3146
Kirkland, WA 98083
206-827-6363
Publishers David and Judy Harrison are accomplished family paddlers and the authors of numerous guides. The magazine's annual "Beginner's Guide" is helpful.

FAMILY FUN

244 Main Street
Northampton, MA 01060
800-289-4849
Unlike many parenting magazines that focus on child-rearing issues, Family Fun emphasizes activities the entire family can enjoy. Annual "Summer Vacation" issue is an especially good resource.

MOUNTAIN BIKE

Rodale Press
33 Minor Street
Emmaus, PA 18098
610-967-5171
An off-road off-shoot of Bicycling, this is the circulation leader of mountain bike magazines.

OUTSIDE

Outside Plaza
400 Market Street
Santa Fe, NM 87501
505-989-7100
http://outside.starwave.com
Broad coverage of outdoor activities. Has published summer "Family Vacations" special issue.

RODALE'S GUIDE TO FAMILY CAMPING
Rodale Press
33 Minor Street
Emmaus, PA 18098
610-967-5171
A good resource published biannually in the summer.

TANDEM MAGAZINE
P.O. Box 2939
Eugene, OR 97402
541-485-5262
http://tandemmag.com
A quarterly devoted to adult tandem cycling. The editor is a father and has published issues devoted to family cycling.

MAGAZINES FOR CHILDREN
There's a gap waiting to be filled here — none is devoted to outdoor activities, such as hiking or biking. However, the National Wildlife Federation publishes two excellent children's nature magazines: *Your Big Backyard* (ages 3–6, $14) and *Ranger Rick* (ages 7–12, $15). A subscription to *Ranger Rick* also includes a "Nature Club" membership (membership card, window decal, pledge, and nature journal). For subscriptions, contact:
National Wildlife Federation
P.O. Box 777
Mt. Morris, IL 61054-8276
800-588-1650
http://www.nwf.org/nwf

THE INTERNET
Like a trail, the 'Net can lead you in many directions, but "conditions" are always changing, which means addresses may have changed since publication time. The Internet is an invaluable resource for such things as trail and park information, weather conditions, magazine articles, and information from gear manufacturers. You can order gear, talk with outfitters, or ask other outdoor enthusiasts to suggest outings your family might enjoy.

Major online providers such as America Online (AOL) and Compuserve have areas devoted to both outdoor recreation and family issues; for example, Parent Soup can be found on AOL; Compuserve has a camping forum.

Whether you're a hiking, biking, or canoeing family, a good place to start is with GORP, the Great Outdoor Recreations Pages *(http://www.gorp.com)*, full of information on gear, books, attractions, feature articles, and links to other web sites of interest. Also check out the Backcountry Home Page *(http://io. datasys.swri.edu/overview.html)*, with information on hiking clubs, trip reports, gear reviews, weather information, state maps, photos, and hiking wisdom.

An excellent site, especially for families, is Family Planet, featuring 365 Outdoor Activities *(http://family.starwave.com/funstuff/outdoor/index.html)*.

Here's a sampling of additional sites likely to interest families:

Let *http://trailside.com* be your up-to-date source of outdoor recreation information on the internet. Daily updates, user feedback, active message boards, and hot links to the best websites offer broad and in-depth information for the adventurous. A great place to "put-in."

The official National Park Service web address is: *http://www.nps.gov* Many individual federal and state parks have their own addresses, some official, some offered by individuals or companies. For example:
• Mount Rainier National Park: *http://www.halcyon.com/rdpayne/ mrnpa.html*
• Rocky Mountain National Park: *http://estes.on-line.com/ rmnp*
• Southwestern parks: *http://www. infomagic.com/parks /index.html* Contains information

on parks such as the Grand Canyon, Arches, Mesa Verde, and Canyonlands.
• Yosemite National Park: *http://www.nps.gov/yose/*
• Grand Canyon:*http://star. ucc.nau.edu/~grandcanyon/*

In addition to web sites, check out mailing lists and newsgroups. Mailing lists are particularly helpful; they were a big help to me while researching this book. They allow you to get in touch with other families interested in the outdoors and obtain outing suggestions from those familiar with specific areas, campgrounds, and trails.

To subscribe to a general mailing list for outdoor enthusiasts (especially hikers and backpackers, but also others, such as paddlers and rock climbers), send a message to listserv@ ulkyvm.louisvile.edu with "subscribe outdoor-L fname lname" in the body of the message area (fname lname means your first name and last name).

To subscribe to a mailing list for backpackers, send an e-mail message with the command "subscribe backpack-L" in the body of the message area to list-server@switchback.com.

Newsgroups of potential interest include *rec.backcountry; rec.outdoors.camping; alt.rec. camping;* and *rec.outdoors. national-parks.*

CD-ROMS FOR ADULTS
The best adult outdoor title I've come across is a hike planner called ✳ GeoTrek's *TrailMaster* (Win.), a wonderful example of what the medium has to offer outdoor enthusiasts. *TrailMaster* contains photographs, hiking information, trail descriptions, and topographical maps of more than 1,000 New England trails, 1,000 peaks, and nearly 600 lakes and ponds. Families can select a trail according to area, difficulty, or distance; print a

customized map; and keep a log of hikes.
GeoTrek Corp
100 New State Highway
Suite 285
Raynham, MA 02767
508-285-2890
http://www.gtrek.com
Southwestern Trails, Volumes 1, 2, and 3, ages 8-up, Win./Mac. Narrated photographic tours of a number of Southwestern U.S. parks and tourist sites, including the Grand Canyon. Infomagic, 800-800-6613.

CD-ROMS FOR CHILDREN
(see also Chapter 5, "Nature Discovery," p. 92)

Junior Nature Guides: Insects, ages 8-up, Win./Mac. Illustrations, video, and sound, plus an activity book. ICE, 416-868-3294.

Microscope Nature Explorer, ages 8-up, Mac. "Collect" specimens from different habitats and examine them under the virtual microscope. Orange Cherry, 914-764-4104.

The Multimedia Bird Book, The Multimedia Bug Book, ages 8-up, Win./Mac. An animated game of collecting and identifying specimens along with a field guide. Workman/Swifte, 302-234-1750.

✶ *One Small Square: Seashore*, ages 8-up, Win./Mac. Another superb title in the *One Small Square* series, this one focusing on the seashore and offering a fully-rotational 3-D scene to explore. Virgin Sound and Vision, 800-814-3530.

Snoopy's Campfire Stories, ages 4-8, Win./Mac. Scenes, stories, letter writing, and games — such as fishing and bug collecting, with Charlie Brown and friends. Not a nature focus —

but kids will enjoy Snoopy and his gang at their campsite. Virgin Sound and Vision, 800-814-3530.

VIDEOS
Our own *Trailside* series of videos that aired on public television are the best inspiration we can offer, including tips and techniques from experts. Several programs focus specifically on families, such as *Family Backcountry Basics, Family Hiking Journal, Paddle Rafting in West Virginia, Dog Sledding in Minnesota, Family Camping in Virginia*, and *Family Mountain Biking in South Dakota*. All are $19.95. Call for a catalog or order by calling 800-TRAILSIDE (872-4574). Check the web site at *http://www.trailside.com*

BOOKS
In addition to "Best-Bet Reading" lists featured in each chapter, here are several more books of interest:

Adventuring with Children, Nan Jeffrey with Kevin Jeffrey, Avalon House Publishing. A guide to outdoor activities with a focus on international travel.

Family Adventure Guide series, various authors, Globe Pequot Press. A collection of state guides suggesting "great things to see and do for the entire family," including outdoor and indoor activities.

✶ *Fodor's Great American Sports and Adventure Vacations*, Fodors. Organized by sport and activity, this book lists great destinations as well as outfitters, tour guides, and schools.

Super Family Vacations: Resort and Adventure Guide, Martha Shirk and Nancy Klepper, HarperPerennial. A where-to guide including lists of "adven-

ture trips" and "nature places," as well as many resorts.

✶ *Travel with Children*, Maureen Wheeler, Lonely Planet. If you're going abroad, get this book. It is written by the co-founder of the excellent Lonely Planet travel guides, who is a mother of two.

MAIL-ORDER SOURCES OF BOOKS
Here are companies and publishers who offer a large selection of books and guides focusing on outdoor activities.

ADVENTUROUS TRAVELER BOOKSTORE
P.O. Box 1468
Williston, VT 05495
800-282-3963
Fax: 800-677-1821
http://www.adventuroustraveler.com
Large supplier of worldwide adventure travel books and maps. Doesn't specifically carry books for children, but carries guides for adventuring with children.

BACKCOUNTRY BOOKSTORE
P.O. Box 6235
Lynnwood, WA 90836-0235
206-290-7652

BICYCLE BOOKS
1282 Seventh Avenue
San Francisco, CA 94122
800-468-8233

THE CLUBHOUSE BOOKSTORE CATALOG
The Mountaineers
300 Third Avenue, West
Seattle, WA 98119
800-284-8554
http://www.cyberspace.com/mtneers
Adventure narratives, how-to, and where-to guides published by The Mountaineers; club members receive a 20% discount.

DAWN PUBLICATIONS
14618 Tyler Foote Road
Nevada City, CA 95959
800-545-7475
Publisher of books, videos and tapes by Joseph Cornell (Sharing Nature with Children) and others, many involved in the Sharing Nature Foundation. Many are for children. Call for a catalog.

THE GLOBE PEQUOT PRESS
P.O. Box 833
Old Saybrook, CT 06475-0833
800-243-0495
Fax: 860-395-0312
http://www.globe-pequot.com
Numerous how-to and where-to guides for families; also distributes Appalachian Mountain Club books and Woodalls camping guides.

ICS BOOKS, INC.
1370 E. 86th Place
Merrillville, IN 46410
800-541-7323
Fax: 800-336-8334
http://www.onlinesports.com/ics

MAIL-ORDER TOYS
ANIMAL TOWN
P.O. Box 485
Healdsburg, CA 95448
800-445-8642
Fax: 707-837-9737
Catalog offering exceptional selection designed to encourage cooperation, many with a focus on nature and the outdoors.

TOY MANUFACTURERS
Here are several manufacturers mentioned in the text. Check nearby toystores or call companies directly to find a local dealer.

EDUCATIONAL INSIGHTS
16941 Keegan Avenue
Carson, CA 90746
800-933-3277
Fax: 310-605-5048
A large selection for all ages and interests: nature kits, binoculars, telescopes, and other exploring gear — you name it.

FAMILY PASTIMES
RR 4
Perth, Ontario
Canada K7H 3C6
613-267-4819
Fax: 613-264-0696
Games encouraging cooperation, including Mountaineering, Beautiful Place *(an ecology game),* and Explorers.

F. X. SCHMID JIGSAW PUZZLES
P.O. Box 74
Salem, NH 03079
800-886-1236
Many focus on nature, including a 550-piece National Parks puzzle.

KLUTZ PRESS
2121 Staunton Court
Palo Alto, CA 94306
415-857-0888
Fax: 800-524-4075
Games and activity kits galore.

UNIVERSITY GAMES
1633 Adrian Road
Burlingame, CA 94919
800-347-4818
Fax: 415-692-2770
Take A Hike!, Sierra Club Games; *sponsors annual National Young Game Inventors Contest.*

WILD PLANET TOYS
123 Townsend Street
Suite 665
San Francisco, CA 94609
415-247-6570
Fax: 415-247-6574
I.N. Gear (Investigate Nature) *collection.*

MAIL-ORDER SOURCES OF CLOTHING AND EQUIPMENT FOR CHILDREN (AND ADULTS)
AFTER THE STORK
P.O. Box 44321
Rio Rancho, NM 87174
800-441-4775
Fax: 505-767-7101
Offers "SunSkins" protective clothing.

BIKE NASHBAR
4111 Simon Road
Youngstown, OH 44512
800-627-4227
Fax: 800-456-1223
http://www.nashbar.com
Cycling clothing, helmets, and trailers.

THE BOUNDARY WATERS CATALOG
Piragis Northwoods Company
105 North Central Avenue
Ely, MN 55731
800-223-6565
Fax: 218-365-6220
http://www.piragis.com
Canoeing and camping equipment.

CAMPMOR
P.O. Box 700-BA96
Saddle River, NJ 07458-0700
800-CAMPMOR (226-7667)
Fax: 800-230-2153
http://www.campmor.com

L. L. BEAN
Casco Street
Freeport, ME 04033
800-221-4221
Fax: 207-552-3080
http://www.llbean.com

REI
1700 45th Street East
Sumner, WA 98390
900-426-4840
Fax: 206-891-2523
http://www.rei.com

SUPPLIERS OF EQUIPMENT FOR CHILDREN (AND ADULTS)
Here are some of the better-known companies offering children's gear. Most will send you catalogs and a list of dealers; some sell directly from the factory.

ADAMS CYCLE WORKS
P.O. Box 392
Alexandria Bay, NY 13607
800-265-9815
Adams Trail-A-Bike; also makes

a bike backrest that can be used for toddlers and children with physical disabilities.

BURLEY DESIGN COOPERATIVE
4080 Stewart Road
Eugene, OR 97402
541-687-1644
Fax: 541-687-0436
Bike trailers and trailer bikes

CANONDALE
P.O. Box 122
Georgetown, CT 06829-0122
203-544-9800
Bike trailers

**CARIBOU
MOUNTAINEERING, INC.**
P.O. Box 396
Chico, CA 95927
800-824-4153
Sleeping bags

CASCADE DESIGNS, INC.
4000 First Avenue South
Seattle, WA 98134
800-531-9531
Sleeping bags

CHERRY TREE
166 Valley Street
Providence, RI 02909
800-869-7742
Hats, clothing

EAGLE CREEK, INC.
1740 La Costa Meadows Drive
San Marcos, CA 92069
800-874-9925
Backpacks

**EASTERN MOUNTAIN
SPORTS (EMS)**
1 Vose Farm Road
Peterborough, NH 03458
603-924-6154
Packs, footwear, clothing, sleeping bags; no catalog or factory sales

**JACK WOLFSKIN/JOHNSON
WORLDWIDE ASSOCIATES**
1326 Willow Road
Sturtevant, WI 53177
800-572-8822
Sleeping bags

KELTY
1224 Fern Ridge Parkway
St. Louis, MO 63141
800-423-2320
Child carriers and backpacks

L. L. BEAN
Casco Street
Freeport, ME 04033
800-221-4221
Fax: 207-552-3080
http://www.llbean.com
Clothing, boots, backpacks, other gear

MERRELL FOOTWEAR
P.O. Box 4249
Burlington, VT 05406
800-869-3348
Boots

PATAGONIA
P.O. Box 8900
Bozeman, MT 59715
800-336-9090
Fax: 702-747-6159
http://www.pagagonia.com
Ask for their catalog of children's clothing.

RAD RAT RADZ
P.O. Box 895
Durango, CO 81301
800-595-1116
Cycling clothing and gear for children

RAICHLE OF SWITZERLAND
Geneva Road
Brewster, NY 10509
800-431-2204
http://www.outdoorlink.com/
raichle
Boots

REI
1700 45th Street East
Sumner, WA 98390
900-426-4840
Fax: 206-891-2523
(credit card orders only)
http://www.rei.com
Clothing, boots, backpacks, other gear

RHODE GEAR
Bell Sports
160 Knowles Drive
Los Gatos, CA 95030
800-776-5677
Bike trailers and child seats

RIDGE OUTDOOR
205 Suburban Road #6
San Luis Obispo, CA 93401
805-541-3900
Boots

TECNICA
19 Technology Drive
West Lebanon, NH 03784
800-258-3897
Boots

TOUGH TRAVELER
1012 State Street
Schenectady, NY 12307
800-GO-TOUGH (468-6844)
Fax: 518-377-5434
Child carriers, sleeping bags, backpacks

VASQUE
314 Main Street
Red Wing, MN 55066
Boots

PHOTO CREDITS

DUGALD BREMNER: 51
JOE AND MONICA COOK: 214
JOHN GOODMAN: 11, 17, 28, 32, 37, 53, 68, 69, 70, 71, 73 (bottom), 75, 79, 83, 84, 88, 90, 92, 93, 94 (bottom), 96, 97, 102, 105 (bottom), 114, 142, 150, 154 (bottom), 186, 215, 236 (bottom), 253
FRANK LOGUE: 206
BECKY LUIGART-STAYNER: 33, 54, 55, 143, 185, 211, 220, 223, 224
SID NISBET: 216
RICHARD HAMILTON SMITH: 202
SCOTT SPIKER: 4, 15, 21, 23, 25, 27, 107, 119, 121, 126, 135, 144, 208, 230
TERRY WILD STUDIO: 105 (top)
GORDON WILTSIE: 13, 14, 16, 35, 39, 44, 56, 60, 61, 73 (top), 76, 85, 87, 89, 94 (top), 98, 100, 111, 113, 124, 128, 132, 134, 139, 147, 149, 151, 155, 157, 164, 168, 172, 183, 193, 194, 197, 200, 201, 204, 213, 229, 231, 236 (top), 240, 243, 246
GEORGE WUERTHNER: 19, 31, 40, 66, 80, 146, 154 (top), 189

ACKNOWLEDGMENTS

Endless thanks to John Barstow for his editorial expertise, encouragement, unfailing good humor, and for being my compass every step of the way. Every writer should be so lucky.

Thanks also to the many families, friends, and experts who so generously shared their experiences and knowedge. I couldn't have written this book without you. Special thanks to Mary, Tom, Katie and Jeffrey Beal, Patricia J. Bell, Karen Berger, Joanna Biscegli and the Vermont Family Outing Club, Debbie Bockus, Robert Buchsbaum, Buzz Caverly of Baxter State Park, Ed Charles and Dr. Elizabeth Snuggs, Joseph Cornell and the Sharing Nature Foundation, Paul Couvrette of Hug-a-Tree and Survive, Ray and Laura Dahl, Dr. Harvey Dulberg, Austin Edgington and University Games, Lindsay Flora and New Media, the Funch family, Jean Craighead George, Helen Gingras, Samara Gooch and Wild Planet Toys, Kate Gregory, the staff of the Groton Public Library, Jeff and Dorothy Hanson, Mike Jacobs, Marty Joyce, Rob Kleine, Ellen Lanterman, Peter Lourie, Mike McCoy, Mike and Leigh Marion, John and Allison Meader, Jay Nelson, Charley Renn, Paul Rezendes, Cindy Ross, Rebecca Rupp, the Seigel-Boettner family, John Stoops, Lonna Thiem and Village Books, Buck Tilton and the Wilderness Medicine Institute, Charles Vaughan, Kit Ward, Peter Whittaker, Rick Wilcox, Alex and Jerelyn Wilson, Heidi Wilson and Educational Insights, Gordon Wiltsie, and Jane Yolen.

I N D E X